Weight Training
FOR
DUMMIES®
3RD EDITION

by Liz Neporent, Suzanne Schlosberg,
Shirley J. Archer

WILEY

Wiley Publishing, Inc.

Weight Training For Dummies,® 3rd Edition

Published by
Wiley Publishing, Inc.
111 River St.
Hoboken, NJ 07030-5774
www.wiley.com

Copyright © 2006 by Wiley Publishing, Inc., Indianapolis, Indiana

Published by Wiley Publishing, Inc., Indianapolis, Indiana

Published simultaneously in Canada

For general information on our other products and services, please contact our Customer Care Department within the U.S. at 800-762-2974, outside the U.S. at 317-572-3993, or fax 317-572-4002.

For technical support, please visit www.wiley.com/techsupport.

Wiley also publishes its books in a variety of electronic formats. Some content that appears in print may not be available in electronic books.

Library of Congress Control Number: 2005937354

ISBN 978-0-471-76845-6

Manufactured in the United States of America

10 9 8 7 6 5

3O/RV/QT/QY/IN

About the Authors

Liz Neporent: Liz's first set of weights (actually, her brother's) were made of blue plastic and filled with sand; when they started leaking sand all over the house, her mother relegated all weight lifting activities to the basement. Since that time, Liz has graduated into a well-known corporate fitness consultant, designing and managing fitness centers worldwide. Along the way, Liz also was a personal trainer, received a master's degree in exercise physiology, and got certified by the American College of Sports Medicine, National Strength and Conditioning Association, American Council of Exercise, and the National Academy of Sports Medicine. She is coauthor and author of several books, including *Fitness For Dummies* and *Fitness Walking For Dummies* and writes frequently for the *New York Times*, *Family Circle*, *Shape*, and others. She currently hosts a daily internet show on eyada.com.

Suzanne Schlosberg: Suzanne's writing career began her freshman year in college when she was assigned to cover a pre-season NBA game and found herself in a locker room interviewing a dozen, tall, muscular, naked Boston Celtics. She decided she liked this writing stuff. Suzanne went on to become a newspaper reporter and magazine writer. Now a contributing editor to *Shape and Health* magazine, Suzanne is the coauthor, with Liz Neporent, of *Fitness For Dummies* and the author of *The Ultimate Workout Log*. She is also an instructor in the UCLA Extension Certificate in Journalism program. Always happy when she has a barbell in hand, Suzanne has lifted weights in Zimbabwe, Morocco, Iceland, and Micronesia, among other locales. She is the women's record holder in the Great American Sack Race, a quadrennial event held in Yerington, Nevada, in which competitors must run 5 miles while carrying a 50-pound sack of chicken feed.

Shirley Archer: Shirley is a former New York City attorney who traded the fast life for the fit life. A survivor of Chronic Fatigue Syndrome from stress and overworking, her recovery helped her to become a champion of fitness for health and to live fully in body, mind and spirit. She's now a health educator and fitness specialist at the Health Improvement Program at Stanford University School of Medicine in Palo Alto, the author of ten fitness and wellness books, an international trainer of fitness instructors, and a frequently quoted media spokesperson worldwide. Her master's degree is in East Asian Studies from Harvard University, and she has special expertise in mind-body exercise. She's a mind-body spokesperson for IDEA, author of a monthly mind-body news column, and a spokesperson for the American Council on Exercise. She's certified by the American College of Sports Medicine, American Council on Exercise, and National Strength and Conditioning Association, among others. She's also a certified Pilates teacher and yoga instructor. She's created a number of corporate fitness programs, including *Walking for Workplace Wellness*, *Fitness 9 to 5*, and *Stretching and Relaxation Tips for Workday Survival*. Shirley believes that healthy bodies come in all shapes and sizes, and that you can live a longer, happier, and better life by choosing fitness every day.

Authors Acknowledgments

The authors wish to thank Richard Miller and The Gym Source of New York City for providing exercise equipment for many of our photos. We're also grateful to Zoran Popovic, Arthur Belebeau and Daniel Kron for their wonderful and speedy photography, and to Chris Gristanti, who generously donated several photos. Trotter Fitness Equipment provided additional photographs. Many thanks to all the models who appeared in this book. Your time, patience, and of course, images are much appreciated. The models are Georgia Archer, Shirley Archer, Patty Buttenheim, Aja Certain, Terry Certain, Katherine Cole, James Gaspard, Debbie-Deb Hanoka, James Jankiewicz, Spike Jozzino, Erica Kraus, Subhash Mandal, Amy Ngai, Alicia Racela, Fred Reid, Doris Shafran, Jay Shafran, Bob Weiter, Carrie Wujeik, and Norman Zinker. Thanks also to Reebok for providing clothing and shoes. Some additional clothing was provided by Marirose Charbonneau, M.Rose Sportswear, Everlast, Nike, and Brooks.

Acknowledgments from Liz

Much gratitude goes to my family, especially my husband Jay Shafran, who is supportive beyond belief. Thanks to Suzanne Schlosberg, the best writing partner ever. Ever! I would also like to acknowledge the following people who are forced to put up with me in some way: John Buzzerio, Nancy Ngai, Linda Strohmeyer, Patricia Buttenheim, Jimmy Buff, Jimmy Rotolo, Stephen Harris, James Jankiewicz, Bob Welter, Subhash Mandal, Holly Byrne, Grace De Simine, and Zoomer.

Acknowledgments from Suzanne

It would be impossible to find a better writing partner than Liz Neporent. She knows so much, works so hard, and accepts the fact that I will never, ever like her dog. I also want to thank my agent, Felicia Eth, for being on the ball. Alec Boga did a stellar job as my supervisor, and Nancy Gottesman was always there to entertain and distract me. As always, I'm grateful to my family for their support.

Acknowledgments from Shirley

It's my great pleasure to be in the writing company of such greats as Liz Neporent and Suzanne Schlosberg. Writing can often be tough since many hours are spent alone at the task. The following people made those hours much brighter: Natalie Harris and Kathleen Cox, Wiley editors; Carrie Burchfield, copyeditor extraordinaire; Georgia Archer, Anthony Dominici and Oliver Bialowons. Lastly, to my parents — Mitsuko Sugimura Iwama and Stephen M. Archer — thank you for all that you have given me.

Publisher's Acknowledgments

We're proud of this book; please send us your comments through our Dummies online registration form located at www.dummies.com/register/.

Some of the people who helped bring this book to market include the following:

Acquisitions, Editorial, and Media Development

Project Editor: Natalie Faye Harris

(Previous Editions: Leah P. Cameron, Colleen Williams Esterline)

Acquisitions Editor: Kathy Cox

(Previous Editions: Stacy S. Collins)

Copy Editor: Carrie A. Burchfield

(Previous Editions: Michael Simsic, Colleen Williams Esterline)

Editorial Program Coordinator: Hanna K. Scott

Technical Editors: Gina Allchin, Marlisa Brown, John Buzzerio, Holly Byrne, Grace De Simone, Brooke Spindler

Editorial Manager: Christine Beck

Editorial Assistants: Erin Calligan, Nadine Bell, David Lutton

Cover Photos: © Marc Romanelli/Getty

Interior Photos: Arthur Belebeau, Chris Gristanti, Daniel Kron, Zoran Popovic, Trotter Fitness Equipment

Cartoons: Rich Tennant (www.the5thwave.com)

Composition Services

Project Coordinator: Jennifer Theriot

Layout and Graphics: Carl Byers, Andrea Dahl

Proofreaders: Laura Albert, Aptara

Indexer: Aptara

Publishing and Editorial for Consumer Dummies

Diane Graves Steele, Vice President and Publisher, Consumer Dummies

Joyce Pepple, Acquisitions Director, Consumer Dummies

Kristin A. Cocks, Product Development Director, Consumer Dummies

Michael Spring, Vice President and Publisher, Travel

Kelly Regan, Editorial Director, Travel

Publishing for Technology Dummies

Andy Cummings, Vice President and Publisher, Dummies Technology/General User

Composition Services

Gerry Fahey, Vice President of Production Services

Debbie Stailey, Director of Composition Services

Contents at a Glance

Table of Contents

Introduction

*W*hen the first edition of *Weight Training For Dummies* was published, lifting weights was on the verge of becoming a mainstream phenomenon. Women, Baby Boomers, seniors — all these groups were starting to get the message: Hoisting hunks of iron benefits everyone, not just bodybuilders with shoulders wider than the wingspan of a DC-10.

Now, four years later, weight training has become even more popular. Some 87 percent of all health clubs now offer personal training, compared to 66 percent in 1996. In the same period, four million women have started using weight machines. Health club memberships have more than doubled for people over age 55. One gym in Palm Springs, California, has even stopped playing rap music because of complaints from the gym's increasingly gray-haired membership.

However, just because weight training has become more popular doesn't mean it has become any less intimidating for novices. It's only natural for a beginner to be baffled by the equipment and the lingo. You may look at a barbell and wonder how you're going to lift the thing while remaining on good terms with your lower back muscles. You may stare at a weight machine and wonder which end the homemade pasta comes out of. You may wonder what it means when a trainer says, "Do three sets of eight reps on the lat pulldown and then super set with the seated row."

In this book, we give you the knowledge and confidence to start a weight-training program, either at home or at the gym. We describe exercises suitable for rookies and veterans alike. We've added new information regarding how to train over a lifetime and feel comfortable around weight training equipment. Training tips for youth, teens, prenatal and postpartum moms, and older adults are included. Additional information for people who are larger sized is presented. And, the latest trends in fitness, core training, yoga, and Pilates are all demystified. You'll find this edition packed with workouts for every circumstance; whether you are on vacation or only have ten minutes to spare, you can fit a weight training workout into your day. New equipment that enhances balance and stability training is introduced and an entire chapter is devoted to stability ball exercises.

In *Weight Training For Dummies,* we tell you about safe weight lifting techniques, steer you toward equipment bargains, entertain you with stories about fellow lifters, and inspire you to keep pumping iron when you'd rather pump a keg and fire up the backyard grill. In fact, we take care of just about everything except lifting the weights. We saved that job for you.

About This Book

We all have different reasons for wanting to lift weights. Undoubtedly, many of these reasons have to do with looking better. Sculpted arms and toned abs have become somewhat of a fashion statement among certain age groups. But many of us can think of more compelling and, ultimately, more satisfying reasons to lift weights. Here's a reminder of how much weight training can benefit you:

- **Keep your bones healthy.** The average woman loses about 1 percent of her bone mass each year after age 35. Men are susceptible to brittle bones, too. Lifting weights can drastically slow the rate of bone loss and may even reverse the process. With strong bones, you won't become hunched over as you age, and you'll lower your risk of life-threatening fractures. No matter your age, it's never too late to start strengthening your bones.

- **Help control your weight.** When you lose weight through dieting alone or together with some aerobic exercise (such as walking or bicycling), you lose muscle along with fat. This can be a problem: When you lose muscle, your metabolism slows down, so you're more likely to regain the weight. By adding weight training to the mix, you can maintain (or increase) your muscle and thereby maintain (or even boost) your metabolism. Although weight training is no magic bullet for weight loss, many obesity experts consider it to be an essential part of any weight-control program.

- **Increase your strength.** Lifting the front end of a fire truck may not be among your goals in life, but a certain amount of muscle strength does come in handy. Weight training makes it easier to haul your stacks of newspaper to the recycling bin and carry and put away your groceries. It can also keep you out of nursing care homes in your older age and help you maintain your independence. Studies show that even 90-year-olds can gain significant strength from lifting weights and regain the ability to walk and dress themselves.

- **Boost your energy.** Forget about hokey dietary supplements. One of the best energy boosters around comes not in a bottle but on a weight rack. When you lift weights, you have more pep in your step. You can bound to the bus stop, sail through your company's annual charity walk-a-thon, and make it to the end of the day without feeling exhausted.

- **Improve your heart health.** For years we've known that aerobic exercise such as walking, jogging, and cycling can lower your risk of heart disease and high blood pressure. But new research suggests that weight training may offer these benefits as well. Specifically, studies show that lifting weights can lower your risk of having a heart attack or stroke by lowering your LDL ("bad") cholesterol and reducing blood pressure.

✔ **Improve your quality of life.** Any activity that accomplishes all the above has to make you a happier, more productive, and more self-confident person. (Research suggests that weight training can even relieve clinical depression.) Of course, hoisting hunks of steel is no instant cure-all, but you'd be surprised how much satisfaction a pair of 10-pound dumbbells can bring into your life, which also improves the lives of everyone else around you.

To gain these and other benefits of weight training, you can use this book in several ways:

✔ If you're a novice, we suggest you start by reading Parts I and II. These parts get you comfortable with the equipment, the lingo, the safety basics, and the etiquette. Then skip to Part IV, which explains how to design a weight routine that meets your needs. (You may want to refer back to this part every now and then.) Then go back to Part III, which shows you the exercises. In your spare time, like when you're not busy lifting weights, hit Part V.

✔ If you already know an E-Z Curl bar from a horseshoe grip, and know that in the weight training world, a circuit has nothing to do with electrical currents, you can go straight to Part III and find numerous exercises for each body part. You may also want to focus on Part IV, which describes how to combine these exercises into a variety of routines that fit your schedule and your equipment preferences.

✔ No matter what your level of knowledge about weight training, you can always use this book as a reference. Flip to the index and look up any specific topic, such as personal training, hamstring stretches, fitness magazines, or high-protein diet.

Foolish Assumptions

While each of us owns a body, we do not necessarily understand how best to train it. To write this book and make it truly friendly to anyone new to weight training, we assume that you are completely unfamiliar with weight training. Some of the information presented, therefore, may be review for people with more experience.

We also assume that you have been exposed to a number of popular myths about weight training — the "urban legends" of the weight room. We do our best to correct these myths and explain why they are not true.

How This Book Is Organized

Weight Training For Dummies is divided into five parts. In general, you can read each part or any chapter within it without having to read what came before. When you come to a section that does require prior knowledge, we refer you to the chapter that provides the background. Here's a rundown of each part.

Part 1: Before You Pick Up a Weight

Lifting isn't one of those activities like, say, checkers, that you can competently engage in after a one-minute explanation. Before you hop aboard the Leg Press, you need to know a bit of weight training jargon and understand key safety precautions. This part explains terms such as power cage, spotter, and plate-loaded weight machine — terms that you can use to impress guests at your next cocktail party. This part also shows you how to test your own strength and chart your progress in a weight-training diary.

Part 11: Weighing In with Weight Training Wisdom

In this part, we offer insight into the less technical aspects of weight lifting. We clue you in to equipment bargains, help you size up health clubs, and warn you about high-pressure salespeople. We tell you which video instructors to invite into your living room, which group strength training classes to avoid, and how to recognize a quality trainer. We also fill you in on the finer points of weight training etiquette, like what to do when a gym member is hogging the Butt Blaster.

Part 111: Tackling the Exercises

We suspect this part is what prompted you to buy the book. Here we demonstrate a wide variety of exercises for all your major muscle groups. Each chapter includes a muscle diagram (so that you can locate your "quads" and your "delts") and an ever-so-brief physiology discussion. We demonstrate exercises for novices and veterans, home lifters and gym members. We also explain how to modify many of the exercises if you have trouble with your back, your knees, or other joints.

Part IV: Setting Up Your Workout Programs

You can't combine any dozen exercises and call them a workout any more than you can throw various foods and spices in a pot and call it a stew. To get good results and avoid injury, you need to carefully select your exercises. In this part, we explain the essential elements of any weight routine. We explain how to custom design a program so that it suits your goals and your schedule. We also explain how to balance your weight workouts with the other important components of fitness. We introduce you to other disciplines that can complement your strength workouts, show you several exercises to improve your balance and lower back strength, and also help you tailor your exercise program for special situations, such as prenatal and postnatal considerations, training tips for kids and teens, and more.

Part V: The Part of Tens

This part is a hodgepodge of important weight training subjects. We recommend ways to educate yourself about dieting and taking supplements while weight training, and give you tips on using latex rubber and exercise balls to complement and add fun to your weight-training regimen.

Icons Used in This Book

The icons are the small drawings in the margins of this book. They're designed to draw your attention to specific topics, and they serve as guides to the kind of information being provided.

When you see the Tip icon, you know that we're pointing out an especially helpful weight training hint or giving you a heads-up on an effective strategy.

The Warning icon cautions you of potential dangers to beware while weight training, including the hucksters lurking at the depths of the fitness industry, hawking useless gadgets like electronic muscle stimulators. We also use this icon to signal mistakes that can cause injury, such as bending your knees too far or lifting too much weight.

The Myth Buster icon rescues you from misleading notions, fighting for truth, justice, and a good weight training workout. For example, this icon may point out that high-protein diets are not the key to weight loss and that abdominal training will not eliminate your love handles.

This icon reminds you about good technique so that you don't become the victim of an 11-80 (that's police code for "Accident – Major Injuries"). It points out when to keep your shoulders relaxed, your abdominal muscles tight, and your knees bent.

This icon suggests that you skip or modify the exercise if you've ever injured the joint indicated, such as the knee or lower back. Even if you've never suffered an injury, pay special attention to the joints in question and make sure that you don't feel any discomfort.

Where to Go from Here

Shirley recommends that you start with the first chapter. Even if you are not an absolute beginner, it provides a handy overview of the entire book so that you will know exactly where to zero in to fill in your information gaps. In addition, numerous studies show that one of the best ways to stay motivated to train is to remind yourself of the many benefits that you will gain and the negative consequences that you might experience if you don't make the effort.

All of us need a motivational boost from time to time, even those of us who have been training for years. Read up on the many ways that your life is improved by weight training. You will get excited and want to keep going with your weight training plans. Good luck on your journey. Come back here for support any time.

Part I
Before You Pick Up a Weight

In this part . . .

Part I takes the intimidation out of weight lifting. First, you discover all the benefits of incorporating a weight training program into your life regardless of your age, level of ability, or individual goals. If you want to become an Olympic champion or simply have more energy to get through each and every day, weight training benefits you. You get an overview of key weight training terms and important training concepts that are validated by research. After you understand training concepts, you realize how to assess your current level of muscle power on a variety of equipment, how to set goals successfully, and how to track your progress. And for the few, the proud, and the ambitious, you can check out the physical requirements for entrance into several fire and military academies.

To get you well on your way to lifting your first weight, you get a description of the major weight training tools: dumbbells, barbells, weight machines, rubber tubing, and a few other mysterious contraptions you're likely to come across at a health club or a home equipment store. Finally, and most importantly, you get a crash course in safety so you can begin to enjoy a lifetime of weight training without hurting your back, crushing your fingers in a weight machine, or whacking a fellow lifter in the ribs with a barbell.

Chapter 1

Weight Training for Life

*B*eginning a weight training program is one of the best decisions to make for your health, well-being, physical, and mental performance. Weight training on a regular basis improves your strength, endurance, confidence, appearance, health, longevity, and quality of daily living. Consistent weight training helps reduce your stress, manage your weight, strengthen your bones, lower your risk of injury, and gives you a competitive edge in all aspects of life.

In this chapter, you find out why weight training benefits all bodies at every age and fitness level; why it's important to assess your fitness and set goals; what tools to use; why safety measures are essential for a lifetime of enjoyable training; how to decide which exercises, routines, and training settings are right for you; and how to achieve total wellness beyond simply lifting weights. If you want to find out more, each section tells you which chapters provide the necessary details.

Weight Training for All Bodies

Modern living provides every convenience except one: a lot of natural physical activity. From young to old, we ride in cars, use remote controls, step into elevators, play on the computer, and shop on the Internet. Many activities that required us to get up out of the chair and use our muscles no longer exist. The result: We need to add weight training to our lives to stimulate our bodies and our brains to keep us healthy and strong.

People of all ages — kids, teens, young adults, pregnant women, older adults, and people with special needs — benefit from weight training (see Chapter 22). The risks of doing nothing are greater than the risks of injury from exercise — even for the frail and elderly. Whether you're a beginner who wants to get started safely or you're already fit and want to improve your performance, weight training improves your current condition (whatever that is) and helps you achieve your goals of feeling stronger and better about yourself.

Strong muscles help us move better and avoid pain and injury at all stages of life. Weight training provides the following benefits:

- Increased strength and endurance
- Improved sleep
- Reduced stress
- Enhanced feelings of confidence and well-being
- Reduced risk of falls
- Strengthened bones
- Boosted metabolism for more energy burn around the clock
- Full, independent living

Because weight training strengthens your muscles and improves your muscular endurance, you'll naturally have more energy to be more active throughout the day. When you're physically tired, you're able to fall asleep more easily and enjoy a deeper, better quality of sleep. As you're more refreshed and energetic, you feel better and accomplish more, which improves your mood and confidence level. In this manner, your consistent training stimulates an upward cycle of well-being.

Don't wait. Absorb everything you need to know from this book to get going with a program that is perfect for you. Keep taking the steps you need to achieve stronger, more toned muscles for a fuller, more enjoyable and active life.

Fitness Testing and Goal Setting for Success

When it comes to weight training, one size doesn't fit all. In order to create a program that best meets your needs, you need to know what your conditioning level is, what you want to achieve with your training, and how to set goals and monitor your progress for success (see Chapter 2).

Fifty percent of all people who begin a new training program quit in the first six to eight weeks. Most people say that the reason for quitting is that they don't have enough time. A research study of prison inmates, who had all the time in the world for their exercise program, showed the same dropout rate. Leading behavioral scientists conclude that the real reason people don't stick to new exercise programs isn't lack of time — it's hard to change your habits for something new.

To keep this from happening to you, strategies to avoid dropping off the weight lifting wagon are discussed further in Chapter 2.

Safety First to Enjoy Training

Before beginning any exercise program, ensure that you're both ready and able. Get clearance from a healthcare professional if necessary. Study and apply the safety tips discussed in Chapter 5 to avoid common mistakes that cause injuries.

Take time to discover the correct use of equipment (Chapter 4) and to perform exercises by using good form and technique (see Part III, "Tackling the Exercises"). Regular weight training improves muscle balance, posture, movement efficiency, stability, and body awareness. All these qualities reduce the likelihood of injury, as well as the onset of typical aches and pains such as those associated with the lower back, knees, shoulders, or hips.

Choosing Your Training Equipment

In fitness magazines, health clubs, and videos or DVDs, you often hear weight equipment referred to as *resistance equipment*. We hate to clutter your brain with jargon right off the bat, but resistance is a word you need to know. Resistance is an opposing force, like a weight or gravity; in order for your muscles to get stronger, you must work against resistance. Resistance equipment is actually a more accurate term than *weight equipment* because you can build muscle without using weights at all. Rubber exercise bands (covered in Chapter 24), for example, don't weigh more than a couple of ounces, but they provide enough resistance to strengthen your muscles. Throughout this book, we use the terms *resistance training, weight training, strength training,* and *weight lifting* interchangeably.

Keep in mind that understanding how to train your muscles is like studying a new skill. You aren't born with this knowledge, in spite of the fact that you were born with a body. Many people have the misconception that because they live in a body, they know how to train it. You'll benefit significantly by taking the time to study and acquire the skills from qualified professionals. Finding out how to use equipment properly is an early step in this process. In this book, we do our best to break this information down in a way that is complete and easy to follow. Take your time. Be patient with yourself. Soon, you'll be lifting like a pro. Chapter 4 outlines all the information that you need to know to demystify the weight room. Refer back to Chapter 4 as often as you need. Give yourself time to experience the equipment and absorb the information.

Resistance training equipment falls into many common categories:

- **Free weights:** Free weights include dumbbells, barbells, bars, and weight plates. These come in a variety of shapes, sizes, materials, and weights (see Chapter 4 for more information).

- **Machines:** Weight machines generally include a seat, a cable or pulley, a variety of weight plates for adjustable resistance, and movable bars. Similar to free weights, machines vary widely in design (see Chapter 4). Newer machines come equipped with computerized programming features and may even talk back at you while you're training.

- **Resistance bands and tubing:** Rubber bands and tubes provide opportunities for strength training any time and any place. Bands are flat and wide. Tubes are round and were initially used by doctors in surgery. Cheap, lightweight, and portable bands and tubes are the training tool of choice for frequent travelers. Latex-free versions are available for people with allergies (bands and tubes are discussed in Chapter 24).

While not strictly in the category of resistance training equipment, the following tools provide means to enhance your weight training programs.

- **Balls and foam rollers:** Add balls and foam rollers into many exercises to provide an unstable surface on which to work. Incorporating this element of instability increases the difficulty of the exercise by requiring the use of deeper abdominal and back muscles (see Chapter 25).

- **Body weight:** Your body may not feel like a training tool, but use your own body weight to provide effective resistance in a number of exercises such as the squat and lunge (see Chapter 16), and the push-up (see Chapter 14).

- **Yoga and Pilates:** Yoga and Pilates aren't styles of weight training; however, many yoga and Pilates moves involve challenges that strengthen muscles. The particular advantage of many of these exercises is that they also involve flexibility and encourage the development of strength, balance, and coordination through movement patterns (see Chapter 23 for more information on yoga and Pilates).

Selecting the Right Exercises, Routines, and Training Settings for You

Deciding whether to train at home or at the gym, to take a group exercise class or to hire a personal trainer, or to practice with a DVD or by yourself are tough questions to evaluate. Chapter 6 provides clear guidelines on how to determine whether training at home is right for you and how to set up a home gym. If you decide that working with a DVD at home is best, Chapter 6 also gives you a lot of practical advice for how to follow along.

Chapter 7 helps you select a gym that meets your needs and sets forth everything you need to know on how to fit in and follow the rules of gym etiquette. If you're thinking that a personal trainer may be your best option, check out Chapter 7 — it shows you how to pick a trainer to meet your needs. Chapter 7 also tells you how to select a group fitness instructor who makes you feel comfortable.

Getting started with your weight training program means selecting the right exercises and routines that meet your goals and fit your personality and lifestyle. The perfect program is the one that fits you. Part III describes all the exercises that you need. Part IV offers a variety of workout programs that feature the exercises.

Weight training today is for all bodies, not only the bodybuilders of previous eras. Whether you're a mom supervising your kid's fitness program or an older adult with special needs, find a program that suits you. There's no reason not to get started right away and to enjoy the many benefits weight training gives you.

Living a Healthy Lifestyle

Weight training is an important key to living a full and healthy life from childhood to older age. All things being equal, we lose muscle mass as we age due to the gradual loss of efficiency in the process of cellular reproduction (the same reason your hair turns gray). Unless you add stimulation to your muscles such as weight training to maintain or to build muscle mass, you'll lose your current muscle mass. Weight training, alone, can't provide everything you need to get and stay strong and fit. You need good nutrition, adequate sleep, stress management, and a strong network of good relationships with friends and family for social support.

Pumping up your heart and lungs

Aerobic exercise or cardio training is necessary to keep your heart and lungs healthy and to reduce the risk of diseases such as heart disease, hypertension, and diabetes, as you age. The best form of cardio exercise for most people is walking — it's cheap and easy, and walking requires little planning and offers a low risk of injury.

 Make time for cardio activity on most days of the week — anywhere from 4 days of the week to every day — for at least 30 minutes. Your efforts count even if you only walk ten minutes at a time, three times a day. To find out more about increasing your cardio activity through walking, read *Fitness Walking For Dummies* (Wiley).

Improving your flexibility

Stretching is one of the most enjoyable, feel-good exercises that improves your ease of movement and reduces your risk of injury. Stretching to improve flexibility is best at the end of your workout when your muscles are warm. See Chapter 8 for up-to-date information on the whys and how-tos of stretching.

Balancing options and training your brain

Twenty five percent of Americans who fall and break a hip after the age of 50 die within the first year after their accident. Balance training, while not sexy, can save your life. Like most aspects of fitness, if you don't practice balance, you lose your ability to maintain your balance and this loss increases the chance of falling. Certain sports, such as skiing, skating, and surfing, also require good balance for effective performance.

Adding a few extra balance challenges to your weight training routine is easy and makes all the difference that you need to move with greater confidence and skill. Coordinated moves that require concentration and challenge both the mind and body are also good for maintaining a healthy body and mind. Yoga and Pilates offer many valuable exercises that train these aspects of fitness. Read Chapter 23 to discover the latest important information about balance and coordination.

Chapter 2

Workout Lingo and Proven Training Concepts

*W*eight training is a lot like baking: part science, part art. Certain immutable rules govern baking. For instance, you can't bake oatmeal cookies without flour. However, you can add to your oatmeal cookies any ingredients — raisins, cinnamon, chocolate chips, coconut, or nutmeg. The cookie recipe you choose on a given day depends on a lot of factors, including your taste and nutritional preferences, the ingredients you have in the house, and how much time you have.

The same principles apply to weight training routines. You have your basic rules — you can't develop a well-toned body without chest exercises, for example. But you can pick from a whole variety of chest exercises. You can do them sitting, standing, or lying down. You can use dumbbells, barbells, machines, or no equipment at all. You can do one chest exercise or six.

In this chapter, you discover important workout lingo and proven training concepts — the ingredients essential to all training routines. You also understand the importance of rest and recovery and the significance of focusing your mind to achieve your best training results. Finally, you gain an understanding of the big picture of training and the meaning of training for a lifetime of health and fitness.

Defining Key Weight Training Jargon

Weight training has its fair share of gobbledygook. You don't need to be fluent in the language spoken at bodybuilding competitions and physiology conferences; but to design an effective workout, you do need to know the basics to better understand your trainer or training materials. In this section, key strength training terminology and training principles are defined.

- **Strength:** Muscular strength is the maximum amount of weight that you can lift one time — also called your *one-rep max*. For example, if you can squeeze out only one shoulder press with 45 pounds, that's your one-rep max for that exercise.

- **Endurance:** Muscular endurance refers to how many times you can lift a sub-maximal weight over a period of time. Muscular strength and endurance are related, but aren't the same. Muscular endurance is handy for everyday tasks like carrying a heavy box from your house to the car. Don't confuse muscular endurance with *cardiovascular endurance,* which is the stamina of your heart and lungs. Muscular endurance affects only the muscle in question and lasts only a minute or two; you improve the staying power of one muscle rather than the stamina of your entire body.

- **Specificity:** Your muscles develop specifically in response to how you train them. For example, if you want to get stronger hips and legs, you should do squats, not push-ups. Similarly, if you want to become a better runner, ultimately you need to practice running. Weight training can complement your running program, but can't replace the hours you need to spend at the track.

- **Overload:** To increase your strength or endurance, you need to train by pushing your muscles to do more than what they're used to. You can overload your muscles by lifting a challenging weight load, doing a lot of reps and sets, or increasing how many times per week that you train.

- **Repetition:** This term, often shortened to *rep,* refers to a single rendition of an exercise. For example, pressing two dumbbells straight above your head and then lowering them back down to your shoulders constitutes one complete repetition of the dumbbell shoulder press, as shown in Chapter 13.

- **ROM and movement speed:** Perform most of your exercises through the fullest range of motion (ROM) possible of your working joints to stimulate the muscles most effectively. Movement speed should be slow and controlled. Anyone who lifts weight for general fitness should perform four-second repetitions — two seconds to lift the weight, stop the motion, and two seconds to lower it. Stop for a moment at the mid-point of a rep to avoid using momentum, instead of your muscles, to power you through. Don't pause for more than a split second at the end of a repetition — otherwise, it becomes a rest. Each rep should flow seamlessly into the next. Athletes and those who're lifting for extreme strength or bulk may do slower or faster reps depending on their goals.

✔ **Failure:** To achieve overload, you need to take your muscles to failure. That is the level of fatigue where you can't do one more repetition with good form. For instance, when you can't complete the full ROM or lift your fist all the way up one more time when performing biceps curls, you can't do one more rep. Time to end your set.

✔ **Recovery:** When your muscles reach failure at the end of a set, you need to recover or rest before you can challenge that muscle to work again. This is also referred to as the rest period. Similarly, after you've worked a muscle group in your workout, you need to allow it to recover for at least 48 hours before you train it again. You'll understand more about why rest and recovery is so important later in this chapter.

✔ **Set:** A set is a group of consecutive reps that you perform without resting. When you've done 12 repetitions of the dumbbell shoulder press to failure and then put the weights down, you've completed one set. If you rest for a minute and then perform 12 more repetitions, you've done two sets.

✔ **Routine:** This term encompasses virtually every aspect of what you do in one weight lifting session, including the type of equipment you use; the number of exercises, sets, and repetitions you perform; the order in which you do your exercises; and how much rest you take between sets. By varying the elements of your routine — say, decreasing the number of reps or adding new exercises — you can significantly change the results you get from weight training because of the principle of specificity. Your routine (also referred to as your program or your workout) can change from one exercise session to the next, or it can stay the same over a period of weeks or months.

✔ **Progression:** Overloading your muscles by lifting a weight to muscular failure stimulates your muscles to get stronger. This is the principle of specificity in action. To continue to overload your muscles and keep making progress, you need to find new ways to challenge your muscles. This is why you need to change up your program or routine. In general, wait six to eight weeks to see visible results from your training when you're new. Internal changes start to occur immediately in response to your first training session.

See the Cheat Sheet in the front of this book for a list of terms commonly used in weight training to describe your body's muscles.

Understanding Rep(etition)s

The number of repetitions, or reps, you perform matters a lot. In general, if your goal is to build the largest, strongest muscles that your genetic makeup allows, perform relatively few repetitions, about four to six (perhaps even as few as one to two). Remember, this refers to lifting a heavy enough weight so that by the end of the last repetition, you can't do another one with good form. If you're seeking a more moderate increase in strength and size — for example, if your goal is to improve your health or shape your muscles — aim for 8 to 12 repetitions to failure.

The American College of Sports Medicine (ACSM) recommends repetitions for different people.

✔ **High intensity:** Perform 6 to 12 reps. Higher-intensity training poses a greater risk of injury. This approach to training is suitable for athletes and experienced exercisers.

✔ **Moderate intensity:** Perform 8 to 12 repetitions because this is the ideal number to strike a balance between building muscular strength and endurance and has a lower risk of injury.

✔ **Low intensity:** For older adults, the ACSM recommends doing between 10 to 15 repetitions, an even lower intensity.

Why does performing 6 reps result in more strength than doing 15 reps? Because the number of reps you perform links to the amount of weight you lift. So when you perform 6 reps, you use a much heavier weight than when you perform 15 reps of the same exercise. Always use a weight that's heavy enough to make that last repetition a real challenge, if not an outright struggle.

Weight training isn't an exact science so don't take these rep numbers too literally. It's not as if performing six repetitions transforms you into Xena: Warrior Princess, whereas performing ten reps makes you look like Angelina Jolie. Everyone's body responds a bit differently to weight training. Genetic factors play a significant role in determining the ultimate size that your muscles can develop.

Bodybuilders (who aim for massive size) and powerlifters (who aim to lift the heaviest weight possible) often train by hoisting so much poundage that they can perform only one or two reps. You may not desire to lift hundreds of pounds of weight over your head, so your goals are best served by doing between 6 and 15 repetitions. Doing more than 15 reps is generally not effective for building strength, but can improve muscular endurance.

To focus on increasing muscular endurance, you want to do at least 12 reps or more, but only two to three sets. To increase muscle size, you want to do between 6 to 12 reps, but more sets — anywhere from three to six. To increase muscular strength, you want to do fewer reps, no more than six, and anywhere from two to six sets each.

Getting Acquainted with Sets

Beginners should start with one set for each of the major muscle groups listed under "Previewing Weight Routine Essentials: Working all of your major muscle groups." That's roughly 11 sets per workout. The ACSM recommends one-set training because most of your gains occur from that first set. You'll, of course, gain more strength and faster results with more sets, but your program takes more time. After a month or two, you may want to increase the number of sets. But then again, you may not. If your goal is to gain moderate amounts of strength and maintain your health, one set may be as much as you ever need to do.

If you want to continue to increase your strength over time, studies show that trained individuals require multiple-set training of at least three or more. A trained person is someone who's been lifting consistently for at least three months. In addition to increasing the number of sets, you should also vary your training volume and intensity over time with periodized training as explained later in this chapter. Increases in training should be gradual to avoid injury from overtraining.

However, if your goal is to become as strong as you can or reshape an area of your body, you need to perform more than three sets per muscle group. Some serious weight lifters perform as many as 20. (However, they don't do 20 sets of the same exercise; they may do 5 sets each of 4 different exercises that work the same muscle.) See Chapter 21 for more guidelines on how many sets to perform if you're an experienced lifter.

The principle of specificity of training determines how much rest you should take in between sets. Beginners should take all the rest they need because you're just becoming acquainted with your body and want to avoid injury. New exercisers may take up to twice as long to rest as those who're more experienced. The National Strength and Conditioning Association recommends that your rest period be based on your training goal. If your goal is to increase endurance and you're lifting 12 or more reps, your rest period should be up to 30 seconds. If your goal is to increase size, and you're lifting between 6 to 12 reps, you should rest between 30 to 90 seconds. If your goal is to increase strength and you're lifting fewer than six reps, you should rest between two to five minutes. People who train for pure strength are going for all-out lifts — a very intense approach. Circuit training, which emphasizes muscular endurance or what is sometimes described as cardio-resistance (see Chapter 18), involves taking little or no rest between sets.

Previewing Weight Routine Essentials

If an orchestra were to play Vivaldi's *Four Seasons* minus the string section, the piece would lack a certain vitality and depth. Likewise, if you leave out a key element of your weight workout, you may end up with disappointing results. So follow the guidelines in this section.

Working all of your major muscle groups

Be sure that your routines include at least one exercise for each of the following muscle groups. (In Part III, we show you precisely where each muscle is located.)

- Butt or buttocks (glutes)
- Front thighs (quadriceps)
- Rear thighs (hamstrings)
- Calves
- Chest (pecs)
- Back
- Abdominals (abs)
- Shoulders (delts)
- Front of upper arm (biceps)
- Rear of upper arm (triceps)

In Part III, you have exercises for additional muscle groups, such as the wrist and shin muscles and inner and outer thighs. But for general fitness, the preceding muscles should be your highest priorities. If you neglect any of these muscle groups, you'll have a gap in your strength, and you may set yourself up for injury.

If you avoid training any particular muscle group, you also may end up with a body that looks out of proportion. You don't need to hit all your muscle groups on the same day — just make sure that you work each group twice a week. In Chapter 21, you find out several ways you can split up your workouts.

Doing exercises in the right order

In general, work your large muscles before your small muscles. This practice ensures that your larger muscles — such as your butt, back, and chest — are challenged sufficiently. Suppose that you're performing the dumbbell chest press, shown in Chapter 12. This exercise primarily works your chest muscles, but your pecs do require assistance from your shoulders and triceps. If you were to work these smaller muscles first, they'd be too tired to help the chest.

On occasion, however, you may specifically want to target a smaller muscle group, like your shoulders, because they're lagging behind in development compared to other parts of your body. If that's the case, you may want to design a program where you do shoulder exercises first one or two days a week for several weeks to build them up. In general, follow the rule of training larger to smaller.

In order to perform your exercises in the right order, you need to understand which exercises work which muscle groups. Many people do their routines in the wrong sequence because they don't realize the purpose of a particular exercise (the purpose isn't always obvious). When you pull a bar down to your chest, as in the lat pulldown (see Chapter 11), you may think that you're doing an arm exercise when, in fact, the exercise primarily strengthens your back. So, make a point to understand which muscles are involved in each move that you do. In addition, studies show that concentrating on the specific muscle that you're working and visualizing it becoming stronger increases the effectiveness of your training. You definitely want to make sure that you're focusing on the right muscles to get the best results.

When choosing the sequence of a workout, imagine your body splitting into three zones: upper, middle, and lower. Within each zone, do your exercises in the following order. Feel free to mix exercises from the upper and lower body. It's a good idea to train your middle body or core stabilizer muscles last as they stabilize your body during all the preceding exercises and help to prevent injury.

Upper body

1. Chest and back (It doesn't matter which comes first.)

2. Shoulders

3. Biceps and triceps (It doesn't matter which comes first.)

4. Wrists

Middle body

You can perform your abdominal and lower back muscle exercises in any order you want.

Lower body

1. Butt

2. Thighs

3. Calves and shins (It doesn't matter which comes first although we prefer to work our calves before our shins.)

Appreciating the Value of Rest and Recovery

When it comes to training, like many other aspects of life, more isn't necessarily better. Moderation and balance, as well as gradual progression, are critical to getting the best possible results and avoiding injury. When you train, you stress or overload your muscles. Microscopic tears occur in the muscle fibers. When you rest, your body repairs these tears and your muscles become stronger. Rest and good nutrition, therefore, are just as important to your training as your workouts.

Resting a trained muscle at least one day

Always let a muscle rest at least one day between workouts. This doesn't preclude you from lifting weights two days in a row; you could work your chest and back one day and then your legs the next. But if you're doing a full-body routine, don't lift weights more than three times a week and don't cram your three workouts into one weekend.

Avoiding overtraining

As unbelievable as it may sound to a beginner, many exercisers become overly enthusiastic after they start getting results and think that if a little is good, even more has to be great. Researchers have dedicated a lot of time to studying this topic and the ACSM even has a comment paper on the subject entitled, "Overtraining with Resistance Exercise."

Overtraining typically occurs in the following scenarios:

- Training too many times per week
- Doing too many exercises per session
- Lifting excessive numbers of sets
- Lifting too heavy a weight over too long a period of time

Avoid overtraining by following a periodized training program. See the last section of this chapter for more information.

Signs and symptoms of overtraining include, but aren't limited to, the following:

- Loss of strength
- Chronic fatigue

- Poor sleep or eating habits
- Reduced appetite
- Excess muscle soreness
- Mood changes
- Loss of interest in training
- Increased frequency of illness combined with slow rate of healing

Be sure to avoid overtraining through the following strategies:

- Use periodized training.
- Avoid monotonous training that lacks variety.
- Don't perform every single set of every exercise of every session to absolute failure without variation.
- Avoid overusing certain muscles or joints.
- Balance your weight training with your other sports activities or cardio-training.

Weight training provides so many benefits to your life. While the risk of overtraining isn't high, it's important to mention so you can appreciate the importance of variety in your program, of incorporating rest, and of ultimately listening to your body.

Getting enough sleep

Regular training improves the quality of your sleep because you'll be physically tired at night when you go to bed. Current sleep researchers recommend that most people get at least seven to nine hours per night. Individuals vary, so you need to discover what is best for you. Many adults are chronically sleep deprived and are compromising their health and well-being.

Sleep is always important to your health, but even more so when you're training your body. Because you're actively stressing your muscles, your cells need time to repair. An important hormone for the maintenance and repair of muscle tissue is human growth hormone. Your body naturally secretes this hormone when you sleep. Studies show that supplementation isn't beneficial for healthy individuals so don't go out and buy HGH pills. If you deprive yourself of adequate sleep, you're limiting your opportunity for your muscle tissue to repair itself optimally. Why spend time training only to undermine your hard work by not getting enough sleep? Take care of all aspects of your health for best results.

Detraining: When you're too busy to work out

Last but not least, while you need to make rest a part of your training program, you need to avoid resting too much. Unfortunately for all of us, we can't save or store our fitness. Research evidence suggests that detraining occurs slowly. For example, two weeks after training stopped, study subjects maintained most of their strength and power. However, after eight months of no training, study subjects had lost most, but not all, of their training results. Hear the good news: Maintaining a reduced program can significantly slow detraining.

When your schedule is exceptionally busy and you find it difficult to do your full routine, remember that something is always better than nothing. Even training one day a week, especially if performed at a higher intensity, can be very valuable to prevent a loss of strength over time. Check out Chapter 19 for how to fit in a few exercises on those time-crunched days.

Putting Your Mind into Your Muscle

Shirley is the mind-body spokesperson for IDEA, the largest trade association for fitness professionals in the world. She also writes a monthly column on mind-body news for *IDEA Fitness Journal*. The evidence of the importance of the relationship between the mind and body is strong and clear. In other words, your thoughts and feelings have a significant impact on your physical and mental well-being. Physical and mental well-being have an important bearing on weight training.

Understanding the body-mind connection

Have you ever had an argument with someone and then been so flustered that you stubbed your toe on a footstool in the room? This example shows how your feelings affect your movements. Because you're upset, your heart is racing, your breath is shallow and rapid, and you may even be sweating. That's an example of your mind-body connection.

When you train your muscles, you tap into your mind-body connection through your neuromuscular system. Before you can contract a muscle fiber, the nervous system must run a communication network from the brain through the spinal column and out to the individual muscle fiber. In the early stages of training, before you start seeing visible external results, your body is laying down this neural network. The more extensive your neural network, the more individual muscle fibers contract.

Studies show that by concentrating on the muscles that you're training, you can get results faster. In one study, a group of people performed a simple exercise, another group of people imagined doing the exercise but didn't actually do it, and a third group served as the control and didn't do anything. Of course, participants who actually lifted the weight gained the most strength. However, the people who simply imagined doing the exercise had more gains than those who did nothing.

Physical therapists are also conducting studies on the use of motor imagery with patients who've lost neuromuscular control due to stroke or Parkinson's disease. Patients visualize walking with a perfect gait, as well as practice specific gait exercises. Studies show that this visualization helps improve performance. The bottom line, therefore, is that you have nothing to lose and possibly more effective training results to gain by focusing your mind on your target muscles as you do your exercises.

Psyching up and visualizing yourself strong

Studies also show that psyching up before you perform a weight training exercise can improve performance for people with at least one year of training experience. Psyching up strategies include the use of imagery, positive self-talk, affirmations, and focusing attention. So, when you're ready to train, clear your mind, see yourself going through your workout smoothly and successfully, visualize your strong and toned body, and believe in your ability to lift your weights. It makes a difference.

Organizing Your Long-Term Training: Seeing the Big Picture

After you've been training regularly for at least three months, you're no longer considered a beginner. Congratulations! You can now attend group exercise classes suitable for intermediate to advanced participants. More important, if you want to avoid hitting a plateau and continue to make gains in strength, you need to progress your program.

Studies show that the most effective method to progress your program is through a process called periodization (another bit of weight training jargon that we feel compelled to foist upon you). *Periodization* involves varying volume and training intensity and simply means organizing your program into different *periods,* each lasting about four to eight weeks. Each period has a different theme. For example, one month you may use weight machines, and the next month you may switch to dumbbells and barbells. Or you can change the number of sets, repetitions, and exercises you perform from one period to the next. Athletes use periodization to vary their weight lifting (and other types of training) from their off-season to their competitive season.

Periodization is more than a fun diversion; this strategy gives you better results. The ACSM recommends periodization for experienced exercisers based on the number of research studies that show its benefits. Consider this study of more than 30 women conducted at Penn State University. Half the women did a typical circuit of 12 weight machines (see Chapter 18 for a defin- ition of circuit), performing one set of 8 to 10 repetitions per machine. They continued this workout three times a week for nine months. The second group engaged in periodized training, systematically changing the number of sets, reps, and exercises they performed. Initially, the groups showed compa- rable strength gains. But after four months, the circuit group hit a plateau. The periodization group continued to make steady progress throughout the nine months.

We recommend that an introductory periodization program include five dis- tinct phases, each lasting about a month. (However, depending on your goals, each phase can be as short as two weeks or as long as eight weeks.) You can repeat this cycle over and over again. Here's a look at each phase:

- ✔ **Prep Phase:** During this period, you prepare your body for the chal- lenges ahead with a basic workout. Use light weights, perform one to four sets per muscle, do 12 to 15 repetitions per set, and rest 90 seconds between sets.

- ✔ **Pump Phase:** In this phase, you step up your efforts a bit. You lift slightly heavier weight, perform 10 to 12 reps per set, do three to eight sets per muscle group, and rest only 60 seconds between sets. The pump phase is a good time to introduce a few of the advanced training techniques we describe later in this chapter, such as super sets and giant sets.

- ✔ **Push Phase:** In this period, you do 8 to 10 reps per set, resting 30 sec- onds between sets. You do only two or three different exercises per muscle group, but you do several sets of each so you can use the advanced training techniques, such as pyramids, that we describe later.

- **Peak Phase:** In this phase, you focus on building maximum strength. Do 6 to 8 reps per set, 15 to 20 sets per muscle group, but fewer different exercises. For instance, you may only do one or two leg exercises, but you do multiple sets of each exercise and six to eight repetitions per set. Rest a full two minutes between sets so that you can lift more weight. This phase is your last big effort before you take a break from heavy training.

- **Rest Phase:** In this phase, either you drop back to the light workouts you did in the prep phase, or you take a break from weight training altogether. Yes, that's right, we're giving you permission to stop lifting weights — for as long as two weeks. Resting gives your body (and your mind) a chance to recover from all the hard work you've been putting in. After your break, you move back into your next periodization cycle with fresh muscles and a renewed enthusiasm for your training.

If you're hell-bent on toning or building up your body, you may be tempted to skip the rest phase. Don't. If you never rest, at some point your body starts to break down. You stop making progress, and you may get injured. If you want to get fit, resting is just as important as working out.

We present just one model of periodized training. The possibilities are endless. Depending on your goals, you may want to emphasize or play down a particular phase. For example, if you aim to get as strong as possible, spend more time in the peak phase; if you've been lifting weights for years, shorten the prep phase or skip it altogether. An experienced and well-educated personal trainer helps you design a periodization program to meet your needs.

Periodization in a nutshell

Here's a recap of the five-phase periodization program.

Phases	Weight	Sets Per Phase	Number of Reps Per Set	Rest between Sets
Prep	Light	1–4	12–15	1½ min.
Pump	Moderately light	3–8	10–12	1 min.
Push	Moderately heavy	8–15	8–10	30 sec.
Peak	Heavy	15–20	6–8	2 min.
Rest	Complete rest or light weights	0–2	12–15	1½ min.

Chapter 3

Testing Your Strength, Setting Goals, and Tracking Progress

. . . .

In This Chapter

▶ Testing your strength and endurance

▶ Setting successful goals

▶ Tracking your progress in a workout diary

▶ Testing strength for the few, the proud, the ambitious

. . . .

Y ou need to put your overall fitness, including your strength, to the test from time to time. Strength tests are particularly important when you begin a weight-training program. You need to know your starting point so you can set realistic goals and design a workout program that reflects your current abilities. As you get stronger, periodic strength testing can be a great measure of your achievements and keep you motivated to train. Some people are simply more data oriented than others, so how often you track your progress varies from person to person. For some people, recording daily details are relevant; for others, keeping records of annual tests are sufficiently motivating.

In this chapter, you discover a variety of strength tests appropriate for beginners, a proven strategy for achieving your goals, and a way to track your progress in a workout diary. Just for fun — and for veteran lifters who want to see how they stack up against the nation's finest — we've included the physical fitness requirements for a handful of law enforcement agencies and branches of the armed forces.

Testing Your Strength and Endurance

When you start an exercise program, you need to test more than the strength of your muscles. It's also important to evaluate your cardiovascular fitness (on a stationary bike or treadmill, for example) as well as your flexibility. These additional evaluations provide you with a more complete picture of your fitness instead of only looking at your level of strength. Record the following information in your fitness journal before you begin weight training:

- ✔ Height
- ✔ Weight
- ✔ Resting heart rate
- ✔ Blood pressure
- ✔ Cholesterol levels
- ✔ Waist measurement
- ✔ Body composition
- ✔ Body mass index
- ✔ Blood glucose levels

All these factors give important metabolic indicators of your overall health. Recording the above information helps you track your progress and see proven, documented results, even when you may not be seeing your waistline decrease or biceps increase as quickly as you want. When you do a weight-training program consistently, you'll see improvement in three areas:

- ✔ Body composition
- ✔ Body mass index
- ✔ Blood pressure

All three of these improvements reflect overall in your health. Most fitness facilities offer fitness assessments for their members for a fee. Some clubs include these assessments as part of your introductory membership package.

Research studies tell us that being fit to lower your risk of disease and to improve your quality of life is more important than simply being thin. For example, in a landmark study conducted at the Cooper Institute of Research, people who were both fit and overweight had a lower risk of disease and greater longevity than people who were thin and inactive.

Because this book, *Weight Training For Dummies,* 3rd Edition, focuses on tests of *muscular* strength, consult a qualified medical professional or fitness trainer, or read *Fitness For Dummies* (Wiley) for details about other fitness tests to make sure that you have a well-rounded fitness program.

The term *strength testing* is somewhat of a misnomer. Strictly speaking, your *strength* refers to the maximum amount of weight that you can lift one time — also called your *one-rep max.* For example, if you squeeze out only one shoulder press with 45 pounds, that's your one-rep max for that exercise. In general, it's not such a hot idea to go around testing your one-rep maxes, especially if you're a beginner. Some veterans like to go all out sometimes, but they typically test their one-rep max for just one or two exercises in a given workout. Pushing to the max places a lot of stress on your body parts and can cause extreme muscle soreness even in experienced weight lifters.

A safe alternative to testing all-out muscle strength is testing your *muscular endurance;* you use a lighter-than-max weight and perform as many repetitions as you can. Most health clubs choose to do this type of testing. You can safely test your muscular endurance at home, too.

Table 3-1 contains a list of exercises that you can use to test the muscular endurance of each muscle group. (Actually, you can use any exercise you want, but the exercises in Table 3-1 are some of our favorites.) We haven't included a machine option for abdominals because exercises performed on the floor are more effective. The results simply give you a reference point. Strength improves quickly after you begin lifting weights regularly.

We can't tell you how much weight to use for your strength tests because everyone's abilities are different, but here is a helpful guideline: For each exercise, choose a weight that you think you can lift at least six times. If the weight still feels exceptionally light after six repetitions, put it down and rest a couple of minutes. Then try a weight that's a few pounds heavier.

For exercises that use no weight — such as the abdominal crunch and the push-up — simply perform as many repetitions as you can.

Table 3-1	Sample Exercises to Test Your Strength	
Body Part	*Free Weight Option*	*Machine Option*
Butt and legs	Squat	Leg press
Front thigh	Quad press	Leg extension
Rear thigh	Kneeling leg curl	Lying leg curl
Calf	One-leg calf raise	Standing calf raise
Upper back	One-arm dumbbell row	Lat pulldown

(continued)

Table 3-1 *(continued)*

Body Part	Free Weight Option	Machine Option
Lower back	Back extension	Back extension on a bench
Chest	Push-up	Vertical chest press
Shoulders	Dumbbell shoulder press	Shoulder press
Biceps	Dumbbell biceps curl	Arm curl
Triceps	Bench dip	Triceps dip
Abdominals	Abdominal crunch	None

When you test your strength, create a chart that lists each body part that you need to test. Next to the body part, note what exercise you performed, how much weight you lifted, and how many reps you were able to perform. Be sure to date your chart. Create a file folder for the information, keep it on your computer, or record your stats right away in your workout log. Use the results to design a weight-training program that helps you reach your goals.

Comparing your upper-body strength

Knowing how you stack up against others who've taken similar fitness tests can motivate you to work hard. A commonly administered test for upper-body strength is the push-up test. Men do military push-ups. Women do modified push-ups. Do as many push-ups as you can until you can no longer do another one with good form. The best way to take the test is with a friend, family member, or training partner who counts your reps out loud for you. Record the date and number for your records. Check Tables 3-2 and 3-3 to see how your push-up capability measures up with others.

Table 3-2		**Push-ups for Men**			
Age:	**20-29**	**30-39**	**40-49**	**50-59**	**60+**
Excellent	55+	45+	40+	35+	30+
Good	45-54	35-44	30-39	25-34	20-29
Average	35-44	25-34	20-29	15-24	10-19
Fair	20-34	15-24	12-19	8-14	5-9
Low	0-19	0-14	0-11	0-7	0-4

Table 3-3		Push-ups for Women				
Age:	**20-29**	**30-39**	**40-49**	**50-59**	**60+**
Excellent	49+	40+	35+	30+	20+
Good	34-48	25-39	20-34	15-29	5-19
Average	17-33	12-24	8-19	6-14	3-4
Fair	6-16	4-11	3-7	2-5	1-2
Low	0-5	0-3	0-2	0-1	0

Comparing your abdominal strength

The crunch test is another commonly used assessment that is easy to do at home with a friend, family member, or training partner. Lie on your back on your training mat with your knees bent and arms resting at your sides, palms down. Have your partner mark a horizontal line with masking tape on each side of your body at the end of your fingertips. Place a second piece of tape parallel to the first piece toward your feet — about 2½ inches down the mat.

To begin the test, align your fingertips with the first marking. Crunch upward and slide your fingers along the mat to the second line. Lower completely to the starting position. Continue to do as many reps as you can. Move rhythmically in a smooth, controlled manner. Avoid using momentum and bouncing your body up and down rapidly. Record the date and number of reps for your records. Check Tables 3-4 and 3-5 to compare how you did.

Table 3-4		Crunches for Men		
Age:	**Under 35**	**36-45**	**Over 45**
Excellent	60	50	40
Good	45	40	25
Marginal	30	25	15
Needs work	15	10	5

Table 3-5		Crunches for Women		
	Age:	*Under 35*	*36–45*	*Over 45*
Excellent		50	40	30
Good		40	25	15
Marginal		25	15	10
Needs work		10	6	4

Goal-Setting for Success

A lot of people set goals. Many of them even set realistic ones. But too often, people don't fulfill their ambitions — for many reasons. Researchers have studied why this process is so difficult for people and identified strategies that ensure greater success.

Identifying why your goals are important

You're much more likely to stick to a plan of action if you remind yourself often why it's important to you. For example, if you're starting up a strength-training program because you have borderline osteoporosis, increasing your bone density and preventing fractures is a huge motivator, not to mention avoiding looking like a hunchback. You know your life will be better if you don't end up in the hospital with broken bones on a regular basis. Alternatively, you may be weight training because you want to tone up and have more energy to get through each day. The specific reasons need to be individual and relevant to your life.

Whatever inspires you is key to keeping you on track with your training. Remind yourself of all the benefits you want to enjoy as a result of continuing with your weight-training program. Post your goals (and what you gain from achieving them) on your refrigerator, desk, or computer terminal. Or post pictures of good role models of what you want to achieve. Studies show that the best way to keep you motivated is to remind yourself frequently of the benefits as well as the negative consequences if you don't stay on track with your plans.

Using S.M.A.R.T. goals

People who use a system of setting S.M.A.R.T. (see the following bulleted list for definitions) goals have a much better chance of success at achieving their goals. This system consists of taking small, specific steps toward a particular goal and focuses on changing your habits gradually.

When you set your training goals, check to see if they meet the following criteria:

✔ **Specific:** If you're having a tough time with consistent workouts, set a specific goal that you want to achieve that isn't too extreme. For example, set a specific goal to go through your weight-training program each week.

✔ **Measurable:** A measurable goal is one that you can objectively determine whether or not you met the goal. For example, make a measurable goal be to train at least 2 times per week for at least 25 minutes per session.

✔ **Achievable:** If you've been having a hard time finding a spare hour to train, don't plan to do a one-hour workout. Instead, set a more achievable goal for your schedule such as two 25-minute workouts.

✔ **Reasonable:** If you're having a tough time training twice a week, don't set a goal to train three times a week. First, master finding time to train twice a week and build from there. If even two times a week is tough, start out with a goal of once a week and build from there. Remember, you don't have to achieve your fitness goals all in the first month.

✔ **Timed:** Give yourself a set time to meet your goal. For example, if you set the goal of training at least 2 times per week for a minimum of 25 minutes per session, decide that you want to achieve this over a two-month period. If two months seems too long to you, start with a goal of one-month.

Fifty percent of people typically drop out of a new exercise program within the first six weeks, according to research evidence. Studies also tell us that it takes about eight weeks of doing a new behavior to create a new habit. Know that after you've passed the first eight weeks of consistent training, you're well on your way to successfully achieving your goals and maintaining a lifetime of fitness.

Keep in mind that life happens. If you fall off track, don't waste precious time beating yourself up with negative thoughts. Simply assess what interfered with your regular training, benefit from the experience, and get right back into your program. As the ancient Chinese saying goes, "The journey of 10,000 miles begins with a single step." This wisdom is applicable to your training. Just keep putting one foot in front of the other and believe in yourself.

Getting the support that you need

If you find that you're having a hard time keeping up with your program on your own, consider working with a personal trainer or hiring a lifestyle coach to support you. Chapter 7 provides you with good tips on how to select a personal trainer or group fitness instructor.

Find ways to get the support of friends, family members, co-workers, and training partners. Studies show that social support is the single most important factor for sticking to a workout program. Share your goals with people you're close to and who care about you. Beware of those who may try to sabotage your goals. Let people know how important your training is and why you want to succeed. Share what benefits you expect to achieve and show your appreciation to those around you who do help you to succeed.

Tracking Your Progress

You may find that recording your workout details increases your motivation and helps you keep up with your workout program. Try logging your workouts in a notebook or weight training diary to see if this method works for you.

Recording information in your log

Some people benefit so much from recording their weight routines (and cardiovascular workouts) that they jot down information daily. Other people find the paperwork annoying and prefer to keep a log for, say, one week every couple of months as a reality check. No matter how often you use your log, jotting down many or all the following details is a good idea:

- **Your goals:** At the start of each week, jot down specific workout goals such as, "Push extra hard on back and biceps," or "complete eight push-ups."

- **The name of each exercise:** We're talking specifics. Don't just write "chest"; write "incline chest fly" or "vertical chest press." This way, you know whether you're getting enough variety. Plus, you're forced to know the name of each exercise. We know people who've worked out for years and still refer to the dumbbell shoulder press as "that one where you push the dumbbells up."

- **Sets, reps, and weight:** Note how many repetitions you performed and how much weight you lifted for each set. Suppose that you did three sets of leg curls — first 12 reps with 30 pounds, and then 10 reps with 40 pounds, and then 7 reps with 50 pounds. You can note this by writing "3" in the set column, "12, 10, 7" in the reps column, and "30, 40, 50" in the weight column.

- **How you're feeling:** We're not asking you to pour out your emotions like a guest on *Oprah*. Just jot down a few words about whether you felt energetic, tired, motivated, and so on. Did you take it easy, or did you act as if you were in Basic Training?

✔ **Your cardio routine:** Record how much cardiovascular exercise you did — whether it was a half an hour walking on the treadmill at 4 miles per hour or 15 minutes on the stairclimber at level 6. Also, note whether you did your cardio workout before or after you lifted weights.

✔ **Your flexibility routine:** Record the amount of stretching time and how your stretches felt. If you're feeling ambitious, you can record the names of the stretches or come up with names for your standard stretching routines.

Analyzing your workout log

Your journal gives you positive reinforcement no matter how often you choose to record your information. Watching your progress over time also gives you a big boost. If two months ago you could barely eke out 10 repetitions with 30 pounds on the leg extension machine and now you can easily perform 10 reps with 50 pounds, you know you've accomplished something.

Not only does a diary keep you motivated, but also recording your workouts helps achieve better results. If you're dedicating plenty of time to your weight training but aren't getting stronger or more toned, your workout diary may offer clues as to why you're not seeing results. Scrutinize your diary and ask yourself the following questions:

✔ **Am I getting enough rest?** Maybe you've been lifting weights every other day, but your body actually needs two rest days between workouts. An extra day of rest may give you more oomph when you lift.

✔ **Am I working each muscle group hard enough?** Your log may indicate that you've been neglecting a particular muscle group. Maybe you're averaging only four sets per workout for your legs compared to six or seven sets for your other body parts. Perhaps that's the reason your leg strength seems to be lagging.

✔ **Am I getting enough variety in my workout?** When you flip through your diary, maybe you see the words *biceps curl* three times a week for the past three months, but you rarely see any other arm exercise. Maybe you've fallen into a rut. Add new exercises or vary the number of sets and repetitions you've been doing. Or mix up the order of your exercises.

✔ **Am I lifting enough weight?** Maybe you never write down the words "tough workout." Perhaps picking up the 10-pound dumbbells for your biceps curls has become such a habit that you forgot to notice that those 10-pounders now feel light.

✔ **Am I doing my cardiovascular exercise before my weights or after?** Maybe you've been stairclimbing for 30 minutes before your weight sessions — and, therefore, are pooped out before you even lift a single weight.

Daily Workout Log

Day of the week			Date	
Goals				
Cardiovascular Training	Time			Distance
Strength Training	Weight	Sets	Reps	Notes
Stretching			Notes	

Being All That You Can Be

Arresting thugs, steering a submarine, and pulling people out of burning buildings may not be among your aspirations in life. However, you may get a kick out of knowing whether you're strong enough to be a Marine or a fire-fighter. The following sections include tables that show you the physical fitness requirements for a handful of academies.

U.S. Marines

Marines are looking for a few *strong* men and women. Even after you become a Marine, you must continue to take fitness tests periodically. Tables 3-6 and 3-7 outline the performance requirements for men and women in the Marines.

Table 3-6	U.S. Marines Physical Requirements for Men		
Activity	*Ages 17-26*	*Ages 27-39*	*Ages 40-45*
Minimum performance level			
Pull-ups	3	3	3
Sit-ups (one minute)	40	35	35
3-mile run	28 minutes	29 minutes	30 minutes
Superior scores			
Pull-ups	20	20	20
Sit-ups (one minute)	80	80	80
3-mile run	18 minutes or less	18 minutes or less	18 minutes or less

Table 3-7	U.S. Marines Physical Requirements for Women		
Activity	*Ages 17-26*	*Ages 27-39*	*Ages 40-45*
Minimum performance level			
*Flexed-arm hang	16 seconds	13 seconds	10 seconds
Sit-ups (one minute)	22	19	18
1.5-mile run	15 minutes	16.5 minutes	18 minutes
Superior scores			
Flexed-arm hang	70 seconds	70 seconds	70 seconds
Sit-ups	50	50	50
1.5-mile run	10 minutes or less	10 minutes or less	10 minutes or less

During the flexed-arm hang, you must remain in uppermost chin-up position, with your arms bent. After your chin lowers underneath the bar, the test is finished.

The United States Air Force

The United States Air Force (USAF) has a detailed training program that you can either send away for or download from the World Wide Web at www.usafa.af.mil. See Tables 3-8 and 3-9 for sample tests.

The following list describes the exercises in the USAF physical fitness tests:

- ✔ **Pull-ups:** Start from a full hang and grip the bar with your hands about shoulder-width apart. No rocking, kicking, or cheating allowed.
- ✔ **Sit-ups:** Do as many bent-knee sit-ups as you can do in two minutes.
- ✔ **Push-ups:** Perform military push-ups as described in Chapter 12.

Table 3-8	USAF Candidate Fitness Test Data for Men	
Exercise	*Minimum*	*Average*
Pull-ups	4	10
Sit-ups (two minutes)	49	69
Push-ups (two minutes)	24	41
300-Yard Shuttle Run	*65 Sec	*60 Sec

Maximum time limit

Table 3-9	USAF Candidate Fitness Test Data for Women	
Exercise	*Minimum*	*Average*
Pull-ups	1	2
Sit-ups (two minutes)	46	68
Push-ups (two minutes)	9	24
300-Yard Shuttle Run	*79 Sec	*69 Sec

Maximum time limit

The Seattle Fire Department

Here are the physical requirements that the last American heroes must meet to win the privilege of saving lives and hauling hundreds of pounds of equipment into burning buildings. These standards apply to both men and women. Applicants of the Seattle Fire Department must do the following:

- ✔ Complete a steep incline press (shoulder press about 30 degrees below vertical) with a 95-pound barbell. Arms must extend fully.

- ✔ Perform a biceps curl with an 85-pound barbell, arms fully extended and back and shoulders against the wall.

- ✔ Lift an 80-pound ladder mounted 5 feet high, carry the ladder 40 feet, and place it on a sawhorse.

- ✔ Hoist 80 pounds of equipment to the seventh floor of a building, either alternating hands or yanking with both hands at once.

- ✔ Run up seven flights of stairs with an 85-pound hose while wearing a 25-pound mask.

Chapter 4

Examining Tools of the Weight-Training Trade

*N*o question: The most intimidating thing about weight training is the equipment. You can examine a weight machine for half an hour — looking it up and down, walking circles around it, touching it, prodding it, even reading the instructional plaque posted on the frame — and still have absolutely no clue where to sit, which lever to push, or what possible benefit you derive from using it. Heck, even a simple metal bar sitting on a rack can leave you scratching your head.

Handling the bewildering nature of weight equipment consists of two points.

✔ First, relax. With a bit of practice, weight training contraptions are actually easy to operate.

✔ Second, be happy that you decided to take up weight lifting in the 21st century. Back in the 1800s, fitness enthusiasts lifted furniture, boulders — even cows! Although we personally have never tried hoisting farm animals over our heads, we feel confident that today's weight training devices are a major improvement.

In this chapter, you discover the basic strength-building tools found in health clubs and home equipment stores. You also receive a detailed account of the pros and cons of each equipment category:

✔ Free weights (dumbbells and barbells)

✔ Machines

✔ Rubber exercise bands and tubes

And, with a little guidance, you decide which type of equipment is right for you. This chapter also reveals the answers to the big questions:

- Should beginners stick to machines?
- Do barbells build bigger muscles?
- Can you get strong without using any equipment at all?

Getting Comfortable with Free Weights

Free weights are weights, such as barbells or dumbbells, that aren't attached to any pulleys, chains, or other machinery and are raised and lowered by the use of your hands and arms. Free weights consist of metal bars with weighted plates welded or clipped on the ends. *Dumbbells* are short-barred weights that you lift with one hand. *Barbells* are the long bars that you see Olympic weight lifters pressing overhead with both hands.

Some novices think that free weights are only for advanced weight lifters. Not true. Beginners have as much to gain from using free weights as those guys and gals who look like pros. Beginners can become stronger, improve muscle definition, and increase muscle endurance just like more experienced weight trainers.

Knowing the value of free weights

A friend of ours was lying on a weight bench holding two dumbbells over his head when his cat hopped on the bench. While trying to shoo the cat away by squirming around, our friend kept the weights overhead for so long that he tore a rotator cuff muscle. The point of this story isn't to scare you away from using free weights. In fact, the best approach to strength training combines free weights and machines. Just know that barbells and dumbbells require plenty of concentration. If you follow the safety tips described in Chapter 5 (and if you avoid choosing your pet as a training partner), free weight training is perfectly safe. Here are several good reasons to use dumbbells and barbells:

- **Free weights are versatile.** With barbells and dumbbells, you can do literally hundreds of exercises that work virtually every muscle group in your body. Flip through Part III of this book, and get an idea of just how handy barbells and dumbbells are. Most weight machines, on the other hand, are designed to perform only one or two exercises.
- **Free weights give your muscles more freedom to move.** Suppose that you're lying on a bench pushing a barbell above your chest (this exercise is the bench press, shown in Chapter 12). You can press the weight

straight up over your chest, or you can move your arms a few inches back so you're pressing directly above your neck. Or you can position your arms anywhere between. All these movements are perfectly legitimate ways of doing the exercise and working your pecs, and some motions may feel more comfortable to your body than others.

✔ **Free weights involve several muscle groups at once.** For example, chest press movements (Chapter 12) work your chest, shoulders, and triceps. However, when you perform these movements with a barbell, you also call on your abdominal and lower back muscles to keep your body still and to keep the bar balanced as you press the weight up. With the equivalent weight machine, you don't have to worry about holding the bar still, so your abdominal and back muscles don't get much work.

The more limited action of a machine is sometimes a benefit, as explained in the "Don't Be Afraid of Weight Machines!" section later in this chapter.

Making the choice, knowing the difference: Dumbbells versus barbells

You can perform many movements with both dumbbells and barbells. For example, while sitting on a bench, you can either press a bar overhead (as shown in Chapter 13) or press up two dumbbells (the dumbbell shoulder press, performed in Chapter 13). Which is the better option? Actually, both have their benefits.

Dumbbells and barbells both pose a bit more risk than weight machines because you need to stabilize your own body while performing the exercise, instead of relying on the machine to keep your body in the correct position. But if you follow the safety precautions outlined in Chapter 5, you should have no problem.

Choosing dumbbells

Dumbbells come in pairs, and at most health clubs, they're lined up on a rack from lightest (as light as 1 pound) to heaviest (upward of 180 pounds). By the way, the super heavy dumbbells are mostly for show, considering that about .0000001 percent of the population is capable of lifting them.

Dumbbells come in many shapes and materials. Some have hexagonal ends so they don't roll around the floor. Others have contoured handles so they fit more comfortably in your hand. Dumbbells are made of shiny chrome and gray steel. Others have rubber coating, so if some yahoo drops them, the weights won't dig a hole in the floor the size of Australia. Figure 4-1 shows an array of dumbbells.

Figure 4-1:
Gyms rack
dumbbells
in pairs.

Dumbbells allow each arm to work independently. If one side of your body is stronger than the other — a common phenomenon — this imbalance is apparent when you're working with dumbbells. Your weaker arm may start wobbling or may poop out sooner than your dominant arm.

Using dumbbells helps correct strength imbalances because each side of your body is forced to carry its own weight, so to speak. By contrast, if you use a bar, your stronger side may simply pick up the slack for your weaker side.

Pumping iron with barbells

Like dumbbells, barbells, also called *bars,* come in a variety of designs. The most popular model is a straight bar. At most gyms, these bars weigh 45 pounds and are 6 or 7 feet long. (However, many gyms have bars in a variety of weights, sometimes as light as 15 or 20 pounds. If you're not sure how much a bar weighs, be sure to check with a staff member.) If you want to lift more than 45 pounds, as most people eventually do, you choose from an array of round plates weighing 1¼ to 45 pounds and slide them on either end of the bar. (The plates have a hole in the center.) For example, if you want to lift 75 pounds, you slide a 10-pound plate and a 5-pound plate on each end of the bar.

Some plates have additional holes cut in either side to make them easier to pick up and carry; the holes function like built-in luggage handles. These plates are a brilliant invention and have probably helped prevent many accidents and backaches.

Be sure to use collars, as shown in Figure 4-2, at the gym and at home. *Collars*, cliplike or screwlike devices, temporarily secure weight plates on the bars. The collars prevent the plates from rattling around or sliding off the bar as you push or pull the barbell. Mirrors have shattered from runaway weight plates. Some health clubs require that you use collars.

Figure 4-2:
Using a collar prevents weights from slipping or "running away."

In addition to straight bars, most health clubs and equipment dealers have a number of exotic-looking bars with various twists and bends in them. The most common is a W-shaped bar about 3 feet long called the EZ-Curl, which is designed to make certain triceps exercises more comfortable. Some gyms and equipment stores also have an array of straight and EZ-Curl bars with weight plates welded to the ends. These barbells are convenient to use because you don't have to slide weight plates on and off. If you want to switch from 75 pounds to 85 pounds, you simply put the 75-pounder back on the rack and pick up the 85-pounder. No muss, no fuss.

These welded bars are often shorter and less bulky than the traditional bars, so they're more comfortable for many arm and shoulder exercises. However, you typically won't find these *fixed-weight* barbells weighing more than 150 pounds. For many barbell exercises — particularly certain chest and leg exercises — you may need a lot more weight than 150 pounds. With traditional bars, you can pile on up to 600 pounds (not that we expect you to do this right away).

Some dumbbell exercises just don't *feel* as good as when you use barbells. Any seasoned lifter can tell you that nothing is quite like doing the bench press — the quintessential meat-and-potatoes chest exercise. Many lifters gain a great sense of satisfaction from being able to press so much weight. Even though the dumbbell chest press is a perfectly good exercise, it may not deliver quite the same amount of satisfaction (probably because you can't lift as much total weight). For example, if you can do the dumbbell chest press with a 20-pound dumbbell in each hand, chances are good that you can lift at least a 60-pound barbell because your weaker side always limits you, and it's more difficult to coordinate moving two separate units, instead of one single barbell.

Using a Weight Bench

A weight bench is what you may expect: a sturdy, padded bench that you lie, sit, or kneel on to lift weights. To get the most out of free weights, benches are a must.

Sure, you could lie on the ground and lift free weights, but many exercises come to an abrupt halt when your elbows smack against the floor. As a result, your muscles won't get a chance to work to their fullest through a full range of motion. (Your elbows may not feel so great, either.)

Benches come in a variety of designs. While weight benches come in four different varieties, some benches adjust to serve all four functions.

- **Flat:** A flat bench looks like a long, narrow piano bench, only with padding and metal legs. See the dumbbell chest press exercise in Chapter 12 for an example.

- **Vertical:** A vertical bench looks like a formal chair — with the seat back straight up. You wouldn't want to sit in one of these at the dinner table, but they're quite comfortable for weight lifting. The back support prevents you from straining your lower back muscles during exercises that you perform while sitting up. The dumbbell shoulder press, shown in Chapter 13, uses this type of bench.

- **Incline:** The seat back of an incline bench adjusts so you can lie flat, sit up straight, or position yourself at any angle in between. (The angle you choose determines which muscles are emphasized.) See Chapter 12 for an example of the bench in action with the incline chest fly.

- **Decline:** A decline bench slopes downward so you're lying with your legs higher than your head. Weight lifters primarily use a decline bench to strengthen the lower portion of the chest muscles.

Most lifters don't do much decline work because getting in and out of the position is awkward, especially when you're holding weights. We describe a few decline chest exercises as "options" in Chapter 12. Keep in mind that you should always use a spotter if you feel that you need extra assistance.

Weight lifting accessories

People carry a variety of items in their gym bags. Even if you never set foot in a health club, these weight lifting accessories can make your workouts more comfortable and safe.

✔ **Belts:** The controversy in the fitness community rages on: to wear a belt or not to wear a belt? Proponents of weight lifting belts maintain that belts protect your lower back. Opponents counter that a belt is like a crutch: If the belt does all the work to keep your body stable, then your abdominal and back muscles won't develop to their fullest potential, and you may end up with back problems down the line.

Who's right? We don't know. But we're not fond of belts. Although many casual lifters swear by them, you don't need a belt unless you're a serious powerlifter. Your abdominal and lower-back muscles benefit from the work they do to support you during a lift.

✔ **Clothing:** Suzanne made the mistake of wearing running shorts to her first weight lifting session. The error became apparent when the trainer told her to hop on the outer-thigh machine, which required spreading her legs. The lesson: Wear tight shorts (or at least long ones.) On your top, wear a T-shirt or tank top. Forget the multi-layered, northern Alaska look, and certainly don't wear one of those vinyl exercise suits. Heavy clothing only traps your sweat and leads to dehydration; layers can also impede your movement and hide mistakes in your posture that you'd be able to see if you weren't overly dressed.

✔ **Gloves:** Weight lifting gloves have padded palms, and the tops of the fingers are cut off. Gloves prevent your hands from cal-lusing and slipping off a bar. Wearing hand protection also increases comfort when working with bands or tubing and if you have latex allergies, gloves keep your hands from breaking out.

One alternative to gloves that you may want to use is weight lifting pads — spongy rubber squares or circles (like potholders) that you place in the palm of your hands while you lift. Pads can offer better control than gloves because more of your hand is in contact with the weight. However, lifting pads aren't as convenient as gloves because you have to carry them around as you work out. (Some pads come with clips so you can hook them to your shorts.)

✔ **Shoes:** Wear athletic shoes that have plenty of cushioning and ankle support to protect your feet, your joints, and your balance. On occasion, we see people wearing flip-flops or loafers when they lift weights. If you drop a weight when you're wearing sandals, your toes have *no* protection. And if you wear shoes without rubber soles, your footing won't be secure enough. Some gyms also have policies that prohibit you from training in inappropriate shoes, because it is — an accident waiting to happen.

✔ **Towel:** Do you want to lie down in a pool of someone else's sweat? We didn't think so. Be courteous. Use a towel frequently to wipe off your body and the equipment you use.

✔ **Water bottle:** Every gym has a drinking fountain, but you'll drink more water while weight lifting if you have a bottle by your side. If you exercise at home, a water bottle is a must.

✔ **Weight training log:** Recording your work-outs in a journal keeps you motivated and helps you assess your fitness goals. For suggestions on what to write down, see Chapter 3.

Don't Be Afraid of Weight Machines!

Attach a few bars onto a large metal frame, add a cable and a pulley or two, weld a seat and a few pads onto your creation, and presto! a weight machine is born. Of course, weight lifting machines are a bit more sophisticated than this definition suggests. Keep reading to find out more.

Making weight machines work for you

Like every machine ever invented, from the Cuisinart to the calculator, weight machines provide advantages over the low-tech contraptions that came before. Here are some of the ways that weight machines can top dumbbells and barbells:

- ✔ **Weight machines are safe.** Your movement range is limited and the intended pattern is preset, so you need less instruction and supervision than you do with free weights.

- ✔ **Weight machines are easy to use.** Machines don't require much balance or coordination, so you can get the hang of an exercise more quickly. Also, you're more likely to use proper form because the machine provides so much guidance.

  Machines don't guarantee good form. You can still butcher an exercise on a machine, which can lead to injury or at the very least cheat your muscles out of a good workout.

- ✔ **Weight machines enable you to *isolate* a muscle group.** In other words, machines enable you to hone in on one muscle group to the exclusion of all others. For example, very few free weight exercises isolate your hamstrings (your rear thigh muscles). Usually, you can't exclude other muscles — such as your front thighs, butt, or lower back — from getting involved.

  On the other hand, numerous machines can isolate your hamstrings. This feature of weight machines is helpful if you have a particular weakness or are trying to build up one body part.

- ✔ **Weight machines help you move through your workout in minutes.** You put in the pin, do the exercise, and then move to the next machine. This process also makes working out with a friend, who is stronger or weaker, easier — you don't have to load or unload weight plates off a bar. But keep in mind that you do need to adjust each machine to fit your body. In Chapter 5, we explain how to adjust machines.

✔ **Weight machines challenge your muscles throughout the entire motion of an exercise.** Many (although not all) modern-day weight machines compensate for the fact that your muscles aren't equally strong throughout a particular motion. Consider the triceps kickback exercise, shown in Chapter 14. This exercise is relatively easy at the start, but by the time your arm is halfway straightened out, your muscle is being challenged a lot more. By the end, your triceps again have better leverage, so you finish feeling strong.

Use a kidney-shaped gizmo called a *cam* to manipulate the resistance at various points throughout your exercise. When you're at a weak point during the exercise, the cam lightens the load. When your muscle has good mechanical advantage, the cam gives it more work to do. This way, your muscles are working to their fullest throughout the motion. Otherwise, you're limited to a weight you can move only at your weakest point, as you are with free weights.

Examining specific weight machines

Countless ways exist to put the various elements of weight machines together — flip through Part III and see the wild difference in weight machines. Here's a look at the varieties of machines.

Weight-stack machines

Traditional weight machines have a stack of rectangular weight plates, each weighing 5 to 20 pounds. Each plate has a hole in it; to lift 50 pounds, you stick a metal pin in the hole of the weight plate marked 50. When you perform the exercise — by pushing or pulling on a set of handles or levers — the machine picks up the plate marked 50, plus all the plates above it.

Weight-stack machines save time because changing the amount of weight you're lifting is easier.

Becoming a generic product

Arthur Jones, inventor of Nautilus machines, was the first person to use the cam in exercise machines, and he became a multimillionaire for it. The cam resembled a spiral-shelled nautilus mollusk. Jones sold his first Nautilus machine in 1970. Oftentimes the term *Nautilus machine* is used generically, like *Band-Aid* or *Jell-O* and is now used to refer to any exercise machine that uses cam gear technology. When people refer to Nautilus machines, they may be talking about any one of the major brands, including Cybex, Body Masters, Hammer Strength, Galileo, or Icarian.

Plate-loaded machines

Plate-loaded machines fuse traditional machines and free weights. They have a large frame and protect you from dropping any weight on the floor, but they aren't attached to a stack of weight plates; instead, you place any number of round weight plates onto large pegs.

Some of these plate-loaded machines are gimmicky. They offer no benefits over traditional machines — unless you happen to enjoy carrying weight plates around the gym. However, we do like the plate-loaded machines that let you work each side of your body separately. We also like the varieties that have "free-floating" levers. Instead of forcing you to move through a fixed pathway, the machines let you move any way you want. These machines mimic the feel of free weights (for the most part) while retaining most of the safety benefits of a weight machine.

Hydraulic and air pressure machines

This machine category doesn't have a weight stack either. Hydraulic and air pressure machines have a series of pistons that create resistance by pumping oil, gas, or fluid. These machines are fine — some are very well designed — but some exercisers don't feel motivated when they use them because a weight stack isn't moving up and down or steel isn't clanging. (Some people have quirks about working out.) All you hear is a sound that's similar to a can of hair spray in action. Gyms that offer 30-minute circuit programs often use these machines.

Electronic machines

These high-tech contraptions may be the future of weight machines. Some varieties have computers built right in. You swipe an ID card into the machine, which automatically sets the resistance based on your last workout. As you do your set, the machine sends you technique tips. Other electronic systems attach to regular weight training machines. You punch in a code and the machine retrieves your personal information.

The advantage of electronic machines is the storing of your information. This feature is great for beginners, who may be too overwhelmed to remember how much they lifted last time. These systems also run a variety of extensive reports so you can analyze your training in depth. For instance, you can compare your progress on the leg press to your progress on the leg extension. Serious athletes may find this information useful.

However, what's new isn't always better. Electronic machines slow down the pace of the gym and remove some of the human element involved in working out. Instead of interacting with the staff and other members, you interact with a machine. Also, if the system goes down, the repair process generally takes longer than it does with your basic weight-stack machine. And, the electronic systems aren't connected with free weights, so computer-dependent lifters may be discouraged from experimenting with dumbbells and barbells.

Cable machines: A different breed

Not all machines use a cam. A class of equipment called cable machines uses a typical round pulley. A *cable machine* is a vertical metal beam, called a *tower*, with a pulley attached. You can adjust the height of the pulley to move it close to the floor, up over your head, or anywhere in between. Some cable machines have two towers (for an example, see the cable crossover exercise shown in Chapter 12). Cable machines are more versatile than Nautilus-type machines. Clip a new handle onto the pulley and you instantly create a new exercise.

Consider the triceps pushdown, described in Chapter 14. Pressing down with a rope feels considerably different from pressing down with a V-shaped bar. You may prefer one attachment to the other, or you may want to use both for variety. See the sidebar "Coming to grips with cable attachments," in this chapter for a rundown of the most popular attachments. In Part III of the book, we recommend certain attachments for certain exercises.

Smith machines and power cages

✔ **The Smith machine:** The Smith machine — named for an influential 1970s fitness figure named Randy Smith — features a regular free-weight bar trapped inside a track so that the bar must travel straight up and down. The Smith machine increases the safety of exercises such as bench presses, overhead lifts, and squats because you don't have to worry about the bar wobbling or slipping from your grip. At the same time, the machine retains the feel of free weights. Many Smith machines possess another safety feature: self-spotting pins jutting out from the frame. These pins prevent the bar from being lowered below a certain point, so there's no chance you'll get crushed under the bar if the weight is too heavy.

Smith machines use a traditional 45-pound bar, but in some cases, the bar balances on springs to negate most or all of its weight.

The purpose is to add smoothness to the movement. Many lifters don't like this feature because it takes away from the macho spirit of weight lifting. Also, the movement is a bit too smooth, removing all the coordination and extra muscle usage associated with lifting free weights.

✔ **The power cage:** A power cage is a large steel frame with a series of stanchions affixed to the sides. You stand in the center of the cage and place your bar on the stanchions that are at the right height for your lift. A power cage doesn't offer as much safety as a Smith machine because after you lift the bar from the stanchions, you're on your own. Still, the cage does offer an extra measure of protection during heavy lifts or lifts that require a lot of balance. And if your muscles give out, the stanchions catch the weight before it crashes to the floor.

Coming to grips with cable attachments

At most gyms, you see a large heap of metal bars and handles sitting in a plastic container or milk crate. This pile may look like junk but, actually, it's more like a treasure chest. By attaching these handles to a cable pulley, you create an unlimited variety of exercises.

Some people are afraid to go near this pile, so they simply use whatever bar happens to already be attached to the cable. But if you frequently switch the handles, your workout can be more fun. Here's a rundown of the most popular cable attachments:

✔ **Ankle collar:** You clip this wide leather ankle bracelet to the pulley to perform exercises such as leg lifts, back kicks, and leg curls. The ankle collar can strengthen your inner and outer thighs while you're standing. We don't use the ankle collar in this book, but a trainer can fill you in on the details.

✔ **Curved short bar:** Some of these are U-shaped and some are V-shaped. Both varieties are used almost exclusively for triceps exercises, such as the triceps pushdown.

✔ **Long bar:** These bars come in various lengths and are commonly used for back exercises that involve pulling the bar to your chest, such as the lat pulldown shown in Chapter 11. You can pull these bars with an underhand or overhand grip, and you can place your hands as far apart or as close together as you like.

✔ **Rope:** This attachment is most commonly used for triceps exercises such as the triceps pushdown.

✔ **Straight short bar:** This bar is used in triceps exercises, biceps curls, and rows. We especially like to use this bar for the triceps pushdown and the seated cable row.

Buckling Down on Bands and Tubing

Giant rubber bands and rubber tubes provide a muscle resistance workout for just pennies. These inexpensive items can't make you as strong or measure your progress as precisely as machines and free weights, but bands do challenge your muscles in different and effective ways. For example, because bands don't rely on weight or gravity for resistance, bands provide a challenge during both the up and down motions of an exercise. With most free weight and weight machine exercises, on the other hand, you typically feel most of the resistance during the lifting portion of the exercise, because gravity assists in the lowering portion.

Rubber bands and tubes are also convenient and portable. (You can't exactly pack dumbbells in your overnight bag.) If you don't have access to machines, bands are a great supplement to free weights because they allow you to do exercises that aren't possible with dumbbells and bars. Chapter 24 shows you ten exercises that you can perform with bands and tubes.

Lifting your body weight

Why is it that certain exercises can be quite challenging even though you're not holding any weights or using a machine? (The lunge, shown in Chapter 16, is a good example.) In these cases, you're not lifting *zero* weight; you're lifting your body weight. With a number of exercises, moving your own body weight offers plenty of resistance, especially for beginners.

The effectiveness of an exercise without equipment depends on how much of your weight you actually have to move and how hard you have to work to overcome the force of gravity. Consider the push-up, shown in Chapter 12. In the military version of the push-up, you have to push your entire body upward, directly against the force of gravity. The modified push-up, where you're balanced on your knees rather than your toes, factors out the weight of your legs so the exercise is easier. Neither exercise requires you to hold a weight, but both versions can be tough.

Chapter 5

How to Avoid Dropping a Weight on Your Toe (and Other Safety Tips)

In This Chapter

▶ Discovering the universal laws of weight lifting

▶ Perfecting the art of spotting and being spotted

▶ Avoiding injury while lifting weights

▶ Seeking help if you're injured

*F*orget what your Grandma told you. Truth is — there's nothing inherently unsafe about weight machines or barbells. It's what you *do* with these contraptions that can leave you with smashed toes, ripped hamstrings, and torn tendons. If you pay attention, use proper form, and don't get too macho about how much weight you lift, you can go for years without even a minor injury. In fact, one of the best reasons to lift weights in the first place is to *reduce* your risk of injury in daily life by strengthening your muscles and bones. Follow the safety tips in this chapter, and you'll walk out of the weight room the same way you entered it: in one piece and under your own power.

Remembering the Safety Laws of Weight Lifting

We said that weight training is safe and that you can go a lifetime without a minor injury, but with that said, you may feel occasional muscle soreness — especially if you're new to the game or haven't worked out in a while. A little bit of post-workout soreness is okay; chances are, you'll feel tightness or achiness 24 to 48 hours after your workout, rather than right away. (This postponed period is called Delayed Onset Muscle Soreness, for those of you who feel more comfortable when your pain has a name.) But there are ways to reduce your amount of discomfort so you can be a normal, functioning human being after your workout. The following guidelines can help you keep this soreness to a minimum.

Warming up before you lift

Before you start your training session, warm up your body with at least five minutes of easy aerobic exercise (see below for suggestions). Your warm-up increases circulation to and the temperature of your working muscles, making them more pliable and less susceptible to injury. Your warm-up also lubricates your joints. The pumping action of your bones at the joints stimulates the release of synovial fluid, which bathes your joint and keeps it moving smoothly, as if you're oiling a mechanical joint. If you have a particularly heavy-weight workout planned, warm up for ten minutes.

Warm up your muscles by using *Active isolated stretching (AI)*. AI involves tightening the muscle opposite to the one that you're planning to stretch and then stretching the target muscle for two seconds. You repeat this process 8 to 12 times before going on to the next stretch. See Chapter 8 for an in-depth explanation of AI.

Walking, jogging, stairclimbing, and stationary biking are also excellent aerobic warm-up activities for the muscles south of your waistline. But to prepare your upper body muscles, you need to add extra arm movements to these activities.

- ✔ Vigorously swing your arms as you walk, jog, or use the stairclimber.
- ✔ When you ride the stationary bike, gently roll your shoulders, circle your arms, and reach across the center of your body.
- ✔ Use an aerobic machine that exercises your entire body, such as a rower, cross-country ski machine, or stationary bike with arm handles. (Many gyms have the Cybex Upper Body Ergometer [UBE]; ask a trainer where you can find the UBE.)

Starting with lighter weights

If you're planning to do more than one set of an exercise, start by performing eight to ten repetitions with a light weight. A warm-up set is like a dress rehearsal for the real thing — a way of reminding your muscles to hit their marks when you go live. Even monstrous bodybuilders do warm-up sets. Sometimes you'll see a human hunk of muscle bench-pressing with just the

45-pound bar. Just as you're thinking, "What a wimp," he piles on so many weight plates that the bar starts groaning. Then you realize that the first set was just his warm-up.

If you get too cocky and head straight for the heavy weights, you risk injuring yourself. With weights that are too heavy for you, you're playing with some risky behaviors.

- ✔ Losing control of the weight
- ✔ Dropping the weight on yourself or on someone else
- ✔ Straining so hard to lift the weight that you tear a muscle
- ✔ Ending up so sore that you can barely lift your feet up high enough to climb stairs

One or a combination of these accidents can cause a lapse in your workout as you may have to take time off to recover. Be smart and start with lighter weights — weights that you can lift for more reps before you reach fatigue. Check out Chapter 2 for workout lingo and training concepts. Then challenge your body by increasing the weight over time. Check Chapter 18 to relate the percentage of intensity that you're working with the number of repetitions that you can lift that weight. A personal trainer at the gym can also help you target a starting weight for your repetitions.

Lifting weights too quickly doesn't challenge muscles effectively and is a pretty reliable way to injure yourself. When you're pressing, pushing, lifting, or extending at the speed of a greyhound, you can't stop mid-rep if weight plates come loose, you're positioned incorrectly, or something just doesn't feel right. So take at least two seconds to lift a weight and two to four seconds to lower it. Some experts feel that you should move even slower than that. If you're banging and clanging, slow down your pace.

Breathing properly

Breathing is often the most overlooked and least understood component of weight training. If you're a competitive lifter, you probably already know that your breathing can either make you or break you come contest time.

We're not suggesting that you're a competitive or powerlifter, but we also don't suggest inhaling and exhaling with the gusto of a Lamaze student. Relaxed breathing while exercising is the best technique. Don't hold your breath either.

Lifting weights temporarily causes your blood pressure to shoot up, which normally isn't a problem. But when you hold your breath, your blood pressure rises even higher — and then suddenly comes crashing down. Holding your breath creates intra-thoracic pressure — pressure in the chest cavity — that stops the circulation of blood from your muscles, but can increase blood pressure. When you relax, the muscle relaxes, the blood begins to flow again, and your blood pressure drops. This drastic drop may cause you to pass out and drop your weight. And if you have a heart condition, you could be in serious jeopardy.

Using proper form

In addition to heeding the general safety tips we present here, be sure to follow the specific tips we give you for each exercise. Even subtle form mistakes, such as overarching your back or cocking your wrist the wrong way, can lead to injury.

The main goal is to adjust your body so that when you move you don't place any undue strain on any of your joints or muscles. It's important that you understand that form is everything in weight lifting. Poor form ultimately leads to injuries.

Before you start building muscle, you need to establish correct form and balance — and especially before you add more weight. When you start using heavy poundage, bad form ultimately leads to injuries to muscles and joints.

Don't get discouraged because form adjustment is something all weight lifters must do. If you start with bad form, you carry that form forward, until you find out the hard way that you've been moving incorrectly. Old habits are hard to break!

Follow these tips:

- ✔ Don't jerk or bounce any weight around.
- ✔ Don't be afraid to ask for help while you're in the gym.
- ✔ Ask gym employees for help if you're having trouble with certain exercises. Staff is usually helpful and answers any questions you may have.
- ✔ Follow a beginners' weight lifting routine consistently for two to three months before moving on to more challenging exercises. Be patient, you'll eventually start to pile on weight plates; but for now, think form and balance.

Water, water everywhere: Drink it!

Drink at least two 8-ounce glasses of water before starting your weight lifting routine and two–four glasses while working out. In order to move your muscles, you need water. Muscle is considered an active tissue and water is found in the highest concentrations in active tissue. Your muscles are 72 percent water. If your body is only slightly dehydrated, your performance will decline.

Signs and symptoms of dehydration include the following:

- Dry mouth
- Fatigue
- Loss of appetite
- Lightheadedness
- Headache
- Dry cough
- Dark yellow urine

You have to train your neuromuscular system before you start increasing muscle tone and size. In other words, you need to improve the connection between your brain and your body so that more muscle fibers will fire with each contraction. This process of developing muscular control simply takes time. Star quarterbacks weren't born throwing touchdown passes in the Super Bowl. Excellent form took many, many years of disciplined practice and training to develop that level of skill and expertise. Training takes time.

Cooling down

If you've done a fairly fast-paced weight workout (described in Chapter 18), complete the workout with five minutes of slow aerobic exercise. The aerobic cool-down gives your pulse, blood pressure, and breathing a chance to slow down before you hit the showers. If you've been lifting weights at more of a plodding pace, with plenty of rest between sets, a few minutes of stretching suffices as a cool-down. Ending your workout with an easy set also helps you cool down.

Resting your muscles

You can lift weights on consecutive days — just don't exercise the *same muscle* two days in a row. Forty-eight hours is usually the ideal waiting period before exercising the same muscle group again. Lifting weights tears apart your muscle cells. Your muscles need a day to rest and repair so they come back even stronger.

If you ignore this rule, weight lifting may make you weaker rather than stronger. At the very least, your muscles feel too tired to perform at peak operating levels. In Chapter 21, we explain how you can lift weights four to six days a week without ever hitting the same muscle group on consecutive days.

Heeding Some Advice: Weight Lifting Safety Tips

Weight lifting is a safe activity that involves a risk of injury. You can minimize your risk of hurting yourself by following the basic common sense tips: Always respect the equipment, stay alert, and focus on your task at hand. You should be able to enjoy a lifetime of training.

Free weight safety tips

We know a police officer who arched his back so severely over years of bench-pressing that he finally was forced to retire. So keep in mind the following during your free weight workouts:

✔ **Use proper form when you lift a weight off the rack.** When you lift a dumbbell or barbell off a rack or when you lift a weight plate off a weight tree, always

- Bend from your knees — not from your hips.
- Get in close to the rack.
- Keep your arms bent.

Figure 5-1 shows you how *not* to lift a weight off the rack.

✔ **Pay attention when carrying weights around.**

- Hold heavier weight plates with *two* hands.
- Keep the plates close to your body when you carry them.
- Watch where you're going when you carry barbells.

    Making a U-turn while hauling around a 7-foot bar can cause serious destruction.

- Keep your elbows slightly bent when carrying a dumbbell in each hand.

✔ **Use collars.** As we explain in Chapter 4, a collar is a clamplike device that you use to secure a weight plate onto a bar. Often, when you perform a barbell exercise, the bar tilts slightly to one side; without a collar, the plates may slide right off and land on somebody's toes or crash into the mirrors on the wall. We know one woman who was knocked unconscious when a collar flew off a guy's weight bar and hit her in the head.

✔ **Don't drop weights on the floor.** After you complete a dumbbell exercise on a bench (such as the chest fly or dumbbell chest press, described in Chapter 12):

- Bring the weights to your chest.

- Gently rock yourself up into a sitting position.

- Some people simply let go of the weights, which isn't only unnerving to the other gym members but also unsafe because they can land anywhere, roll, and create hazards for others. Weights always need to be controlled.

✔ **Safely return weights to the rack.** When you finish using dumbbells, barbells, or weight plates, don't just lean straight over with locked knees and plunk the weights back on the rack.

- Bend your knees.

- Pull your abdominals in.

- Hold the weights close to your body before you release them.

Be careful not to smash your fingers when placing the weights back on the rack. We've done that. Ouch!

Figure 5-1:
The wrong way to lift weights from the rack.

Weight machine safety tips

One of the selling points of weight machines is that they're safer than free weights. And it's true — you're in no danger of being crushed by a 100-pound barbell. The way that machines create a safer environment is that they put your body in the correct position and direct the movement pattern. Still, if you're not careful, you can injure yourself.

Follow these safety tips to keep yourself (and others) out of harm's way:

✔ **Custom fit each machine.** Some machines require a single adjustment, such as the seat height. Others require two or more adjustments: For instance, with some versions of the leg extension machine exercise, shown in Chapter 16, you have to adjust the back rest as well as the leg bar. Don't worry; you don't need a mechanic's license to adapt these machines to your body. Usually, you just pull a pin out of the hole, lower or raise the seat, and then put the pin back in place. Some machines are so simple to adjust that they don't even involve a pin. With practice, fitting the machine to your body becomes second nature.

Don't get lazy about making adjustments. Using a weight machine that doesn't fit your body is like driving a car while sitting in the back seat: uncomfortable, if not downright dangerous. When you strain to reach a handle or sit with your knees digging into your chest, you're at risk for pulling a muscle or wrenching a joint. After you make an adjustment, jiggle the seat or the backrest to make sure that you've locked it securely in place. You don't want the seat to drop suddenly to the floor with you on it.

✔ **Watch your fingers.** Occasionally, a machine's weight stack gets stuck in midair. Don't try to rectify the situation yourself by fiddling with the plates. Instead, call a staff member for help.

We once saw a gym member try to fix a weight stack himself. The stack came crashing down, sandwiching his fingers between the weight plates. We've seen other people get clumps of hair caught in the stacks, and even one guy got his genitals stuck between the weight plates. We don't know the details and don't want to, but we did hear the story from a reliable equipment dealer who witnessed the ordeal.

✔ **Buckle up.** If a machine has a seat belt, use it. The belts are there for a reason. Use them! The seat belt prevents you from wasting muscle power squirming around to stay in place as you move the bar or lever of the machine. You're most likely to find seat belts on older models of the inner/outer thigh, pullover, seated leg curl, and triceps dip machines.

✔ **Don't invent new uses for the machinery.** You wouldn't use your favorite sweater to dust the house, right? You wouldn't use your television as a step-stool to reach the top cupboard. So don't use a chest machine to strengthen your legs.

People are constantly inventing new — and unsafe — ways to use weight machines. For example: In order to release the chest bar on the vertical chest press machine (described in Chapter 12), you must use your feet to press down on a bar near the floor. Well, we've seen people ignore the chest press altogether and use this floor bar to exercise their thighs or arms. If you dream up new uses for a machine, you may be asking for injuries.

The Art of Spotting

A *spotter* is someone who stands close by you when you're lifting weights. This person is ready to grab your weights in case your muscles give out. The spotter can be your lifting partner that you go to the gym with or a stranger in the gym that you enlist for one or two exercises.

Going to the gym with a friend is a good way to hold each other accountable. You can spot each other during lifting, and while you rest in between repetitions, your partner can perform the same exercise. Friends can encourage you in the last few reps, and keep you motivated. Your well-known lifting buddy also knows what you're capable of and when you've had enough.

If you're in the gym lifting weights alone, you may not need a spotter hovering over you for *every* free weight exercise because you may feel smothered, as if your mom is chaperoning you on a date. But do call on a spotter when you're alone and doing the following:

- **Trying an exercise for the first time.** Even if you're not lifting significant weight, the weights may wobble when you perform a new movement. A spotter gently guides you through the motion until you have the confidence and the muscle memory to do it yourself.

- **Attempting a heavier weight than usual.** If you've never bench-pressed 100 pounds, try the exercise first in the presence of a spotter. The moment the bar comes crashing down on your chest isn't a good time to find out you weren't ready for the lift (or the time to try gasping for air to yell for help). Lifting heavy weights without a spotter is a lot like a trapeze artist working without a safety net. You may be fine the first nine times, but the tenth time. . . .

- **Wanting to eke out extra reps.** Sometimes you're just not sure whether you have one more repetition in you. If you have a spotter, the repetition is worth trying (there's no danger in trying). A spotter also can help you with machine exercises and assist you, for instance, on the last few inches of a heavy leg curl or arm curl.

Briefing your spotter

Your spotter can be your friend or a training partner that you meet at the gym. If you don't know anyone, you can usually ask a staff person who is working on the weight-training floor. If you work with a personal trainer, she'll spot you. Regardless of who you choose, prepare your spotter for the mission ahead:

- ✔ Explain how many repetitions you're aiming to complete. Think about how many reps you think that you can do before you'll need the spotter's assistance. Be honest! If you think that you may need a spot on the sixth repetition, say so. This way, your spotter can start paying extra close attention around the fourth rep.

- ✔ Make it clear to your spotter whether you need help lifting the bar off the rack or getting the dumbbells into position.

- ✔ Set up a specific plan. Will the spotter help you *on* the count of three or *after* the count of three? Tiny misunderstandings can lead to big injuries.

- ✔ Offer your gratitude both before and after your set. Don't forget to tell your spotter *thank you*. An attitude of gratitude makes you a reputable person in the gym.

Being the spotter

When people recruit you as a spotter, you have a big responsibility to perform your job correctly. Be realistic. If you weigh 90 pounds soaking wet, don't attempt to spot someone doing a 350-pound bench press. If you have any doubt you can pull it off, don't take on the assignment. The moment that the lifter's arms give out isn't the moment to realize you're out of your league.

If you do accept the job, pay close attention so you're ready at the precise moment your partner needs help. Step in to help on these situations:

- ✔ The weight stops moving for more than a split second and it's immediately apparent that the person is no longer in control of the movement.

- ✔ The weight begins traveling in the wrong direction.

- ✔ The lifter screams, "HELP!"

- ✔ Your partner can't complete a rep.

The do's and don'ts of spotting

When the time comes that you're in the gym and someone calls on you to help them with a few exercises, remember the do's and don'ts of being a responsible spotter.

- ✔ Don't impose a lift-or-die mentality upon your lifting partner. Just because he may have planned to complete five reps doesn't mean that you should withhold assistance if he starts struggling after three.

- ✔ Don't offer too much help too soon. This eagerness defeats the purpose of spotting, because the person only needs a spotter because they're trying to test the edge of their limits. If you prevent that person from testing that edge, you'll annoy the heck out of the person being spotted.

- ✔ Don't lean so close to your spottee that you impede or distract his movement. Bench-pressing isn't enjoyable when someone's face is directly over yours, and you can see up the person's nose.

- ✔ Be a cheerleader! Now put your pom-poms away. You don't have to jump up and do the splits, but people appreciate support — and may even lift more weight — if you offer enthusiastic encouragement: "You're almost there!" or "It's all you! You've got it!"

Exercises that need spotters

Where you stand when spotting someone can make the difference between being helpful and being useless in an emergency. The following list offers spotting tips for a variety of common exercises:

- ✔ **Bench press:** Stand behind the bench with your hands above or underneath the bar but not touching it. When the lifter needs you, lean in and get a quick grip on the bar.

- ✔ **Chest fly and dumbbell chest press:** For these dumbbell exercises (and versions performed on an incline bench) place your hands close to the person's wrists, not close to the weights. (You may see people spot underneath the elbows, which isn't a crime but not as safe, either.) When spotting flat-bench chest exercises, kneel on one knee behind the bench and follow the movement with your hands. For incline exercises, you may find it more comfortable to stand with your knees bent.

- ✔ **Barbell squat:** Stand behind your spottee, and be prepared to assist at the hips or underneath the arms. Your spottee may not want to be spotted at the hips unless you happen to be that person's significant other. If you're squatting with a particularly heavy weight, you may want two spotters, one standing on either side of the bar.

- ✔ **Pull-up and dip:** Stand behind your spottee and offer assistance by holding his or her shins or waist and guiding them upward.

- ✔ **Machine exercises:** Spot at the bar or lever of the machine. For example, if you're spotting someone on the cable row (pictured in Chapter 11), stand slightly behind and to the side of your spottee. Grasp one of the handles and gently assist it the rest of the way.

Never spot machine exercises by placing your hand underneath the weight stack. That's a good way to get a squashed hand!

Common Weight Training Injuries

Accidents happen, even to careful lifters. So, here's a primer on weight training injuries in case you do run into one.

When you *strain* or *pull* a muscle, you actually overstretch or tear the *tendon,* the tough, cordlike tissue at the end of the muscle where the muscle tapers off and attaches to the bone. A strain can happen when you push up the bar too forcefully during the bench press or stand up too quickly out of the squat. Strains are often accompanied by a sudden, sharp pain and then a persistent ache.

A *sprain* is something different altogether. This injury happens not to a muscle but to a joint, such as your ankle or wrist. When you sprain a joint, you've torn or overstretched a *ligament,* the connective tissue that attaches one bone to another. You may feel pain and throbbing and notice some swelling and bruising. You can sprain just about any joint in your body; ankles and wrists seem to take the most beating.

Depending on the severity of the injury, the healing process may take anywhere from a couple of days to a couple of months. If your injury doesn't appear to be healing, see your doctor. Some of the common injuries caused by lifting weights include the following:

- ✔ **Torn rotator cuff:** The muscles of your rotator cuff (described in Chapter 13) are often injured during bench presses and shoulder presses. You may have torn your rotator cuff if

  - You feel a persistent ache or a sharp pain deep within your shoulder at a specific point during the exercise.

  - You're unable to raise your arm in front of you and over your head.

If you've injured your rotator cuff

- Stop performing any exercises that cause you pain or soreness in that area.

- Skip all overhead pressing movements for as long as your health-care provider recommends that you rest. You shouldn't exercise while you have any pain.

- Lighten up your load on the bench press to a weight where you don't feel any pain.

- Limit the distance you move the bar.

- Or skip the exercise altogether.

Review your form: Make sure that you're not bouncing the weights up and down or taking the exercise past your natural active range of motion that you can control.

The rotator cuff exercises shown in Chapters 13 can help prevent injuries to these muscles. These exercises are a must if you lift heavy weights, if you lift regularly two to three times a week, or if you participate in a sport that uses the upper body, such as tennis, rock climbing, or swimming.

✓ **Sore knees:** Pinpointing the source of the problem can be difficult with knee injuries because the injury can come in so many varieties and have so many different causes. Often, the injury is caused by something you did outside of the weight room. Still, certain weight training mistakes, such as those described in Chapter 9, are likely culprits. Runners, walkers, and cyclists can ward off many common knee injuries by performing quadriceps exercises.

- If any leg exercise causes you pain, skip it or modify it by following our instructions. Some people try to protect their knees from injury by wrapping them in yards of bandages. We don't love the idea of knee wraps unless you're into some serious power lifting. A wrapped knee may mask a problem that needs immediate attention.

- To help protect your knees, make sure that you strengthen both your front and rear thigh muscles — the muscles that support your knee joint. Stretching is also helpful to keep all the muscles that surround the knee loose and limber.

✓ **Sore wrists:** Some people injure their wrist muscles by bending their wrists too much when they lift weights, so pay attention in Part III when we describe the proper wrist position for various exercises.

To prevent wrist injuries, do regular wrist curls and reverse wrist curls (see Chapter 14).

✔ **Lower back pain:** If you have a history of back problems, you can just as easily throw out your back reaching for an apple in the fridge as you can pumping iron. But because the weight room constantly challenges your ability to stabilize your spine and maintain good form, it increases the risk of triggering an old injury — or developing a new one.

If you have a history of back issues, be sure to study the core exercises in Chapter 17 and follow a core routine as described in Chapter 20.

Always take precautions for your lower back when you lift weights. One key preventive measure (that we mention repeatedly throughout this book) is to pull your abdominals inward. By tightening your abs, you create a natural girdle to support and protect your lower back.

Overcoming Injuries

We don't yet have a cure for the common cold, but we do have a reliable remedy for most minor sprains and strains: RICE, an acronym for Rest, Ice, Compression, and Elevation. RICE is most effective if you begin the process within 48 hours of injuring yourself. RICE includes the following four components:

✔ **Rest:** Stop performing activities that aggravate your injury. (Notice that we didn't say stop all activity — that's rarely the solution.) Wait until you've had two completely pain-free days before doing exercises that involve the injured area.

✔ **Ice:** Contrary to popular belief, ice, not heat, helps reduce the pain and swelling of most common injuries. Ice your injury for 15 to 20 minutes, 3 or 4 times a day, for as long as you feel pain. You can apply ice with a store-bought pack, a plastic bag full of ice cubes, and even a package of frozen strawberries. But don't allow ice to sit directly against the skin. (You may end up with ice burns.) Instead, wrap whatever is holding your ice in a thin towel.

Throw out the berries after they've been used as an ice pack a few times. The thawing and refreezing renders the berries less tasty than they would've been before.

Two areas may not respond well to icing: your neck and back. These injured areas may be so sensitive to the cold that you may tense up. If that's the case, a moist heating pad or wet, warm towel is best for treating the injury and allowing your muscles to relax.

✔ **Compression:** Put pressure on the injury to keep the swelling down. Use a damp elastic bandage or buy a special brace or wrap for your knee,

> elbow, or wrist. Wrap the bandage tightly enough so you feel some tension but not so firmly that you cut off your circulation or feel numb.
>
> ✔ **Elevation:** Elevating your injured body part drains away fluids and waste products so swelling goes down. If you've hurt your ankle, you don't need to lift it up over your head. You only need to elevate it higher than your hip so gravity assists the blood flow downward. Propping up your ankle on several pillows or books does the trick (pillows will be more comfortable, of course).

Sometimes RICE isn't enough to treat an injury. If the pain is truly excruciating or is bothersome for more than a few days, your injury probably needs more aggressive treatment and possibly medical attention. If you experience excessive swelling, discoloration, or bleeding, you may need a trip to the emergency room. Use your judgment. If you see a bone fragment sticking out of your ankle, don't simply stick an ice pack over it.

Part II

Weighing In with Weight Training Wisdom

The 5th Wave   By Rich Tennant

"READ THE ASSEMBLY INSTRUCTIONS" I SAID, BUT NOOOOoo...: ONLY AN IDIOT READS THE INSTRUCTIONS," HE SAID.

HANG IN THERE, SIR. THE JAWS-OF-LIFE WILL BE HERE ANY MINUTE.

In this part . . .

This part helps you set up a home gym for lifting weights on your own, and you're introduced to strength equipment that fits every budget. If you want to train at a fitness facility, you're guided through the selection process and how to get the right health club deal for you and your budget. If you're joining a gym and also want a personal trainer or group fitness instructor, you'll find that information in this part of the book as well. For gym goers, you receive guidance on weight training etiquette: Just because you're wearing tight shorts, dripping with sweat, and stinking up the joint doesn't mean that you can't show some courtesy.

To complement your weight training and make sure that you get a safe and effective workout, this part also gives you an overview of the subject of stretching and why it's an important addition to your weight training program. Also in Part II, you're reminded of the most common weight lifting mistakes that interfere with progress or lead to injury and how to avoid those mistakes.

Chapter 6

Exercising at Home: Setting Up Your Own Gym

*I*s lifting weights better at a health club or at home? That's like asking whether it's better to drive a half-ton pickup truck or a four-door sedan. The answer depends on your personal needs.

In this chapter, you discover how to create a training environment at home. A home gym is a great option if you never plan to go to the gym or if you want to complement your gym workouts with a home program. You also discover how to invest in weight equipment, which includes buying gadgets and how much to spend.

Lifting Weights at Home

Exercising at home is the perfect solution for many people. Here are the main reasons why working out at home makes sense:

> ✔ **You live too far from a gym.** Although more than 13,000 fitness centers exist in this country, not everybody lives near one of them. If you don't live or work within ten minutes of a club, lifting weights at home may be your best option. Or if you can afford it, not only join a club that you can get to on days when you have time, but also invest in some basic weight

equipment at home for days when you're too busy to walk, bike, or make the drive (preferably choose an active way to get to the gym; that way you'll already be warmed up).

✔ **Your schedule.** If your club doesn't have childcare or you can't leave the house for some other reason, buying your own equipment makes sense. The same applies if you work unusual hours and the gym's schedule doesn't jive with yours. If your den is equipped with dumbbells and a bench, you can exercise at 6 a.m. on Sunday if you want.

✔ **You're self-conscious.** If you can't bear the thought of exercising in front of other people — or just need a little time to get used to what you look like in a pair of athletic shorts — by all means, work out at home. Videos, DVDs, or personal trainers give you instruction and help keep you motivated. However, don't let self-consciousness keep you away from a club for too long if you have other compelling reasons to go. For the most part, health club members are too busy looking at themselves in the mirror to notice what you look like.

✔ **You don't like crowds.** Some people simply like to be alone with their dumbbells.

Designing a Home Gym

Exercise equipment lasts a long time, takes up space, and serves a variety of purposes. Put some time and thought into creating your home gym. Keep in mind that this is a long-term commitment. You're investing in a healthy lifestyle and a better quality of life for years to come. You want to create a space that you'll enjoy and look forward to using regularly.

This section deals only with weight training equipment; you need to consider separately any cardiovascular equipment, such as a treadmill or stationary bike. Shirley recommends that you purchase a jump rope for a great investment in cardio equipment. You can find one on sale for as little as $5 and it can last a lifetime. Jumping rope regularly improves endurance, agility, and coordination and helps keep bones strong while burning as many calories as cycling. Quite a bargain for a few dollars!

Before you purchase any equipment, consider the following questions.

✔ **How much space do you have?** If you have virtually no space for weight equipment, your best bet is a set of rubber exercise tubes that come with door handle attachments. However, we think that you build greater strength and size by using dumbbells and a weight bench, so make room for these gadgets if possible. Conserve space by buying clever dumbbell products such as power blocks, smart locks, or plate mates, which are all described in the "Nifty dumbbell products" sidebar in this chapter.

✔ **What are your goals?** Make sure that you buy equipment that helps you reach your goals. If you're a big guy and you want to build some serious muscle, a couple sets of dumbbells aren't going to cut it. In fact, you may need to buy a dozen pairs of dumbbells and purchase a free weight bench. Just make sure that your goals jive with the amount of space you have available: If you live in a tiny apartment but want to live in a body like Sylvester Stallone's, you may have to get rid of your bed, coffee table, television, refrigerator, and stove in order to make space for your weight equipment. (We know people who've done this.) If your goal is to develop moderate strength and muscle tone, your best bet is to buy an adjustable weight bench and several pairs of dumbbells.

✔ **How much money can you spend?** The cheapest (and smallest) weight training gadget you can buy is a rubber exercise band, which sets you back about $5. But your development of muscle strength is limited to the price of a McDonald's Happy Meal. On the other hand, you don't need to raid your retirement account in order to build a firm, strong body. For $200 to $500 you can buy an adjustable weight bench and more than enough dumbbells. You may be able to find equipment at an even cheaper price if you search used sporting goods stores or shop on eBay. If you have an extra thousand or two lying around, go ahead and purchase a multigym for variety. By the way, if you're tight on money, don't even think about buying any weight training gizmo off of the TV. Most of the gadgets are gimmicks that don't offer any training advantages over traditional equipment.

✔ **Will you be using videos or DVDs?** If you plan to use weight training videos or DVDs, we suggest that you invest in dumbbells and an adjustable weight bench (or at least a step aerobics platform, which doubles as a bench). Many videos and DVDs also use rubber exercise bands, ankle weights, barbells, or stability balls. So when you buy new tapes or DVDs, make sure that you have (or are willing to buy) the necessary equipment.

Choosing Free Weights

If you're just starting out, dumbbells are a more practical purchase than barbells because they're more versatile. You may want to save barbells for your next shopping spree. In terms of quality, where you buy free weights — a sporting goods store, department store, specialty shop, or garage sale — doesn't much matter. A specialty weight shop may offer the best selection, but prices may be higher. For great bargains, check out stores that sell used sports equipment. In many cases, the equipment is almost brand new.

Before purchasing weights online or through mail-order catalogs, be sure to check the shipping price. You may be better off buying products from a local store that includes free delivery or where you can bring the weights home on your own. Shipping costs for weights are expensive.

Strength training on the road

If you're looking for an excuse to skip your weight training workout, vacations and business trips won't cut it. You can keep your muscles strong no matter where you go, whether your destination is Caribou, Maine, or the Mongolian desert.

Of course, you may not always find a health club with 16 shoulder machines and aromatherapy baths. While touring Micronesia, Suzanne worked out at Yap Island's only gym — a tin shack where the locals hoist rusty barbells while chewing betel nut, a mild narcotic that stains your teeth red. In Nairobi, she lifted weights at a club where staff members had to boil water on a stove in the weight room because the water wasn't safe to drink. The bottom line: You can always make do.

Strength training on the road is well worth the effort. Even fitting in one short workout a week can help you maintain the strength you've worked so hard to build. Here are some tips for getting in a strength training workout away from home:

✔ **Book a hotel with a gym, if possible.** Some hotel gyms have facilities that rival those at regular health clubs, including personal trainers, towel service, and massage. And these days, even many of the less posh hotel gyms offer a decent array of free weights and weight training machinery.

✔ **Look for a gym in the neighborhood.** If your hotel doesn't have a gym, ask the concierge, or simply open up the phone book and look under "health club" or "fitness." Expect to pay $15 to $20. Some upscale Los Angeles and New York clubs charge as much as $35 or more.

✔ **Stick to free weight exercises and machines that you recognize.** If you're in a gym that's foreign to you, unless you ask someone on staff to help you, this isn't the time to test whether you have a knack for figuring out how weight training contraptions work. When you work out away from your home club, expect to sign a waiver essentially saying that any torn muscle, broken bone, or smashed toenail you sustain is your fault and yours alone.

By the way, one of the best reasons to find a local gym has nothing to do with your muscles. "You get to meet the locals and find out about the least crowded beaches, and the best place to go for a beer," says Alec Boga, an avid traveler from California, who's lifted weights in Thailand, Costa Rica, Zimbabwe, Venezuela, and Fiji, just to name a few countries. "The equipment might be good or bad, but you just ad-lib and enjoy talking to the people."

✔ **Pack an exercise band.** If you have no access to weight equipment, you can perform dozens of exercises with a single band, which takes up about as much space as your travel toothbrush. Shirley never travels without exercise tubing and a stretch strap. See Chapter 24 for band exercises.

✔ **Lift your own body weight as a last resort.** If you get stuck without even a band, you can do equipment-free exercises such as push-ups, triceps dips, crunches, back extensions, squats, and lunges. Shirley creates outdoor circuit workouts in local parks, combining walking with stops at trees, stairs, and park benches for push-ups, dips, lunges, and squats for a workout that combines aerobic training and toning. Outdoor workouts are a great way to see the sights and experience local flavor, enjoy the outdoors, and keep up your fitness program.

Buying dumbbells

The biggest mistake people make when buying dumbbells is investing in a pair of 10-pound weights and then using them for every exercise. We suggest that you start with eight pairs. If that seems overwhelming, buy up to four pairs on the lower end and add the heavier weights as you become stronger.

For women who're beginning lifters:

- Buy dumbbells weighing 2, 3, 5, 8, 10, 12, 15, and 20 pounds.

- Look for brands of dumbbells with narrow handles (so you don't have to buy as many weights). This way, you can hold two dumbbells in one hand, for example, a 5-pound weight and a 3-pound weight to create 8 pounds.

For novice men:

- Buy 8, 12, 15, 20, 25, 30, 35, and 40 pounds. As explained in Chapter 2, to get good results you need to lift precisely the right amount of weight for each exercise.

- Another alternative to buying so many dumbbells is to buy adjustable dumbbells with weight plates, similar to barbells.

If you're short on space or money and buying eight pairs of dumbbells is impossible, consider an adjustable dumbbell kit. You get two short bars and a number of round plates that you clamp on with collars. Just beware: The plates tend to rattle around, and you may find it annoying to constantly pop off the collars and add or subtract weight plates. Making these adjustments can add precious minutes to your workout. Worse, you may be tempted to skip the adjustments and use the same weight for several exercises. See the sidebar "Nifty dumbbell products" for clever alternatives to the ones we discuss in this section.

Figuring the cost

So what's all of this going to cost? The answer depends on how fancy you want your weights to be. Dumbbells cost about $.50 to $2 per pound ($150 to $300 for the women's set and $300 to $600 for the men's), depending on which part of the country you live in, where you buy them, and whether you catch a good sale. Hexagonal dumbbells (called *hexes* or *hex heads*) tend to be less expensive. Plastic-coated dumbbells are cheaper, but the plastic tends to rip over time.

Liz once owned a pair of dumbbells that started to leak; every time she pressed the dumbbells overhead, a few grains of sand fell in her mouth or eye. The most expensive dumbbells are the shiny chrome ones with contoured handles. You can see your reflection in the ends of the top-drawer ones. You find chrome dumbbells in ritzier health clubs and in home gyms that try to emulate ritzy health clubs.

Nifty dumbbell products

If you're in the market for dumbbells and want to save money and/or space, here are a few inventive gadgets that might suit your needs.

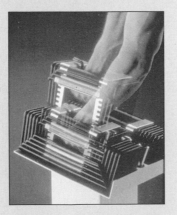

- **Plate mates:** This product is like an oversized refrigerator magnet that you stick on both ends of a dumbbell to increase the weight. Plate mates come in four weights: $\frac{5}{8}$ pound, $1\frac{1}{4}$ pound, $1\frac{7}{8}$ pound, and $2\frac{1}{2}$ pounds. Prices range from $19 to $28 per pair. Plate mates save you big bucks on dumbbells because you have to buy only half of the weights you would otherwise. For instance, transform a set of 5-pounders into $6\frac{1}{4}$-pound dumbbells or $7\frac{1}{2}$-pounders simply by sticking a plate mate on each end. Plate mates bond to the weights quite well. Try to shake the dumbbell up and down and the magnet won't fall off. Removing a plate mate requires nothing but a quick twist.

- **Smart locks:** Smart locks are a nice improvement to adjustable dumbbells. They're short bars that come with spring-loaded collars that easily pop on and off. The collars lock the plates on the bars so tightly that they don't rattle around or slide off. For less than $200, you can buy a set that builds up to two 40-pound dumbbells.

- **Power blocks:** These dumbbells are clever and adjustable but strange looking. Each block consists of a series of weighted, rectangular frames, each smaller one nesting inside one slightly larger. Holes run along the outside frame: You stick a two-headed pin in the hole that corresponds to the amount of weight you want to lift, and the pin locks in the number of frames you need to lift. Power blocks save you time — it's a lot quicker to stick a pin in a hole than it is to clamp on new weight plates. For about $600, you can buy a set that builds up to two 90-pound dumbbells. They fit into a corner of the room and take up no more space than your nightstand. A similar product, Probells, is easier to use but only goes up to 30 pounds. Probells usually sell for $299 a pair; their stand costs an additional $149.

Storing your equipment

Buy a rack to store your dumbbells. Racks save space, and they keep your house looking tidy so your mother won't have to step over your weights if she stops by unannounced. Also, a rack can save you from injury because you don't have to constantly bend over and lift the dumbbells off the floor. Don't be surprised if a rack costs more than the dumbbells you're storing. A $200 to $300 rack is adequate, but you can shell out up to $800 for a three-tiered, chrome rack.

Buying barbells

Unless you're related to the Sultan of Brunei, you'll probably find it too expensive and too space consuming to buy a whole array of fixed-weight barbells, as recommended with dumbbells. It's more practical to buy an empty bar and clip on the weights yourself. You can buy bars that weigh 15 to 45 pounds, although the most popular bars are the heavier bars used in health clubs.

Figuring the cost

Barbells cost about the same per pound as dumbbells, but if you're lucky, you may find them as low as a nickel a pound. Most stores sell variety packs, often called Olympic packs, which come with a whole assortment of plates weighing a total of 200 to 300 pounds.

We also recommend buying collars to keep the weight plates from sliding off the bar. MCR makes the sturdiest and most user-friendly collars. You slip the collars on the bar and twist a small lever, locking them in place. They cost $20 a pair.

Storing your equipment

As with dumbbells, we recommend buying a barbell rack. Vertical racks ($100 to $200) take up less space and cost less than horizontal racks ($300 to $700). However, it's more awkward to place a bar on a vertical rack. Store your plates on a weight tree — a contraption that has several rungs. Weight trees come in an astonishing variety of shapes and sizes and typically cost $75 to $200.

Buying a bench

If you have a dedicated space for your home gym and want to buy a bench, your best bet is an adjustable incline bench — one that adjusts from a flat position all the way up to vertical. Make sure that the incline mechanism is secure and easy to manipulate. With some cheap brands, the pin that holds the backrest upright tends to slip out or, even worse, break off. The decline feature shouldn't be a high priority because you won't use it very often, if at all. Before you buy a bench, sit on it, lie on it, drag it around, adjust it, and inspect it. Look for a high-quality Naugahyde, leatherlike material used to cover all seat and back pads.

Figuring the cost

Good flat benches start at around $100 and run upward of $500 for extra-thick padding and high-quality hardware. Adjustable incline and decline benches range from $200 to $600. Good bench brands include Hoist, York, Icarian, Paramount, and Tuff Stuff — the brands you're likely to encounter at the gym — along with Galileo, Cybex, and Body Masters.

Storing your equipment

Storing your bench is nearly impossible. Benches that fold up and go under your bed or fit neatly in a closet don't exist. For this reason, you should have a dedicated space for your home gym that's roomy enough for a bench (and all of your equipment). If you can only fit in the weights, skip the bench.

Investing in Weight Machines

Obviously, it's not practical to put an entire line of weight machines in your home, unless you're willing to take out a second mortgage to pay for the weights and for the new wing of the house you'll need to build. A more reasonable alternative is a multigym (see Figure 6-1), which combines several weight lifting stations into one frame. Most multigyms have one or two weight stacks, meaning that one or two people can work out at a time. Good multigyms give your muscles a sufficient workout, although most models don't feel as smooth or as solid as health club machines.

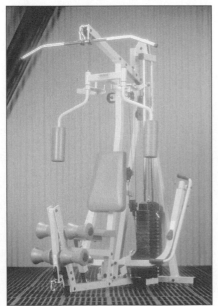

Figure 6-1:
You can buy
a multigym
to work out
at home.

A decent multigym costs between $300 and $1,000. Buy from equipment specialty stores, not from department stores and certainly not from TV infomercials. Visit several stores to compare prices. If you don't live near a specialty store, call the manufacturers and ask for the dealer closest to you. Most top brands have a dealer in every nook and cranny in the country, as well as in many parts of Europe, Asia, and Africa. In some cases, buying directly from the manufacturer is cheaper. Good multigym brands include Parabody, Paramount, Universal, Vectra, Pacific, Hoist, and California Gym. Here are some tips for buying multigyms:

- ✔ Look for sturdy and thick padded seats filled with dense foam. Seats covered with durable material clean easily. The pad is the part of the equipment that has the most body contact, which includes your sweaty body. With a cleanable cover, you can wash away your workout sweat after each use.

- ✔ Look for machines that use plastic-coated cables as opposed to chains or giant rubber bands. Check all cables for imperfections and fraying.

- ✔ Try out every exercise station. Some may feel comfortable, while others make you feel like your arm is about to be ripped out of its socket. Look for a weight stack that moves smoothly up and down. Some machines that move smoothly at heavier weights become wobbly and sticky when you're lifting only one or two plates.

- ✔ Make sure that the parts are easy to adjust. You don't want to waste half your workout fiddling with the arm and seat adjustments to make the machine fit your body.

- ✔ Look for free assembly. Forget about those "easy-to-follow" directions. Trying to put some of these contraptions together yourself is like trying to build a space shuttle with a step-by-step manual.

Buying Bands or Tubing

Make sure that you buy bands or tubes specifically designed for exercise, rather than the kind you use to keep your mail together in the office. Office rubber bands aren't strong enough for constant stretching, so you have a pretty good chance of getting popped in the face when one breaks. See Chapter 24 for a complete band workout and helpful tips on using bands and a description of our favorite band products.

Join your own home gym

Even if you're not interested in joining a health club, you may want to incorporate aspects of the gym experience into your home workouts. Adding the following health club features to your home gym boosts your motivation and sense of purpose.

- **Sign-in sheet:** When you go to the health club, you have to sign in at the front desk to prove you were there. If you're the type of person who's motivated by measuring your accomplishments, record your attendance at your home gym in a workout log or even create your own attendance sheet and tape it to the door or keep it on top of your file cabinet. Signing in at the beginning of your session reinforces your commitment to weight training.

- **Mirror:** The purpose of a mirror isn't to develop anxiety over the shape of your body. You need a mirror to check your form, especially when you're doing free weight and band exercises. Just make sure that you watch where you put your dumbbells and barbells. If you leave them on the floor, they may roll around and crack the mirror. The best way to avoid this problem is to invest in a dumbbell rack. Any mirror suffices as long as it's big enough for you to see your entire body when you're standing with your arms spread wide.

- **Comfortable mat:** A mat is useful for doing strength training exercises on the floor, such as abdominal crunches and side-lying leg lifts. And, of course, it's useful for stretching and doing yoga or Pilates exercises. You can substitute a towel or blanket, but these substitutions tend to bunch up. Most exercise mats fold or roll up and can be placed in a corner or underneath your weight rack. A good mat costs $20 to $100.

The differences between a cheap mat and a more expensive one are many:

- The thickness and quality of the padding
- The quality of the surface covering
- The antibacterial and antifungal materials
- The size of the mat
- The way the mat stores

The mat should be long enough so it fits your body from the top of your head to your tailbone. The padding should be cushy enough so your knees don't dig into the floor when you do the modified push-up and other exercises that require kneeling. Shirley recommends combining a towel over a mat for strength training exercises as the towel absorbs perspiration and extends the life of your mat.

- **Rubber mat:** A rubber mat, placed under the equipment, looks like the rubber mats on the floor of your car. They help cut down on noise and vibration to the floors below, and they help protect your floors and rugs from sweat and wear and tear. Mats are particularly good to put under equipment that leaks oil, such as multigyms and treadmills. Some mats are custom designed to fit under specific pieces of equipment.

- **Proper attire:** Health clubs require you to wear freshly laundered exercise clothing so the grime from your jeans, leather belts, and work shirts doesn't soil the pads on the weight equipment. Follow the same rule at your home gym, too. You'll prolong the life of your equipment. Plus, it's a lot more motivating to work out when you're wearing clean, comfortable clothes that allow your skin to breathe.

Chapter 7

Exercising Away from Home: Clubs, Trainers, and Classes

*T*he gym can be an intimidating setting for the inexperienced. How do you decide which club to choose? And, after you join a club, how do you select a trainer, decide which class to attend, and act in training sessions and around the weight room?

This chapter demystifies the gym environment. You discover whether to invest in a gym membership and how to size up a health club's equipment, staff, atmosphere, and facilities. We explain how to choose a personal trainer or group fitness instructor. We inform you who's qualified to coach you and who isn't and what you can expect to gain from a trainer or a class.

Deciding to Join the Club

You may feel overwhelmed when you walk in a health club, but don't let feelings of anxiety stop you from signing up. Within a few sessions, your terror of the machines will seem unwarranted, and the club starts to seem as familiar as your own neighborhood. Here are a few reasons to become a health club member:

✔ **Equipment choices:** At a health club, you may have dozens of machines for each muscle group including newfangled contraptions that haven't yet reached the consumer market or are too expensive or too large for home use.

✔ **Advice:** A gym that is invested in you has staff members walking around who can remind you how to do the perfect back extension or how to adjust the calf machine.

✔ **Safety:** Weight training isn't inherently dangerous, but if you do happen to get stuck underneath a 100-pound barbell, at least you have people around to rescue you. You also have plenty of spotters to choose from.

✔ **Motivation:** After you're inside a health club, you eliminate all your excuses not to exercise. Besides, the atmosphere of a club may make you *want* to work out. You see people of all shapes and sizes pumping and pushing and pulling, and you can't help but be inspired to do the same.

✔ **Cost:** A typical yearly health club membership costs between $250 and $2,000, depending on where you live and what type of facilities the club offers. Home weight equipment may cost you less over a period of years, but unless you're a Silicon Valley multimillionaire, you probably can't afford to update your equipment as often as health clubs replace their contraptions. In order to stay competitive, many gyms turn over at least some of their equipment every year, if not more often.

✔ **Relaxation:** Ironically, a health club may be just the remedy for busy people who say that they don't have time to go to one. At the gym, you're free from stress and distractions. The phone doesn't ring. Your kids don't beg you to watch *A Shark's Tale* for the 127th time. Your boss can't assign you a last-minute report.

✔ **Other facilities:** Weight training is only one component of fitness. At a gym, you have treadmills, stationary bikes, stairclimbers, and other elliptical trainers. You may also find a sauna, steam room, swimming pool, vending machine, and even a snack bar (eat the healthy food, of course).

Choosing a Health Club

Many people have no choice. If your neighborhood has only one club, that's the club you probably need to join, even if the facilities aren't top-notch. You're more likely to use the mediocre fitness center around the corner than the first-rate gym that's 45 minutes away. If you have a routine of basic exercises, you can get a good workout in just about any facility that calls itself a gym.

Don't be scared off by the name of a health club or the size of the people who work out there. Among the general public, Gold's Gym franchises seem to have a reputation of catering only to serious bodybuilders. In reality, Gold's clubs — like any other chain clubs — cater to people of all ages and ability levels. We know a 94-year-old woman who is an avid attendee at Gold's Gym in Sacramento. Some gyms attract more serious lifters than others, but believe us, at virtually every gym in America, people like you attend. Besides, you can gather a lot of information from hanging around veteran lifters.

If you're lucky enough to have your choice of clubs, weigh your options carefully. You may want to tour each club to discover the variety of machines and mechanisms offered. You also want to notice if the staff is friendly and helpful. When you tour a club, bring the following checklist for consideration for your membership:

- **Hours of operation:** Some gyms are open 24 hours a day; others close at noon on weekends. Make sure that the hours of operation fit your schedule.

- **The cancellation, freeze, and refund policies:** Many gyms let you put your membership on hold for medical or maternity leave (freeze). Some clubs refund your remaining membership if you move more than 25 miles away. Most states have laws that allow you to cancel within three days of joining with a full refund.

- **Qualifications of the staff:** When you visit, ask what the club's requirements are for staff certification. Nationally recognized certification organizations include the American College of Sports Medicine, the American Council on Exercise, and the National Strength and Conditioning Association, among others.

- **Cleanliness:** Make sure that there are no strange growths in the showers. Check the weight benches and equipment for sweat residue. Most gyms have squirt bottles with bleach cleaner and towels handy for cleaning equipment before and after you use it. Remember that you're joining a gym to *improve* your health, not destroy it.

- **Equipment quality:** The quality of free weights doesn't vary much, but it's *not* a good sign if the plates on the dumbbells rattle around or you see lots of "Out of Order" signs scattered around. High-quality weight machine brands include Cybex, Nautilus, Galileo, Body Masters, Hammer Strength, and Icarian. Try out a few machines. Do they move smoothly? Is the weight stack rusted? These subtle signs relate to how well the management takes care of the gym.

- **Friendliness of management:** Does the staff at the front desk greet you with a smile, or are they standing in a clique gossiping about the members? If the staff isn't accommodating before they've made a sale, think about how they'll act *after* you sign on the dotted line.

- **Cost:** Cheaper isn't always better. If the club's machinery is always broken or the bathrooms are cleaned monthly instead of daily, you may pay more in doctor's bills for injuries and infections than you do for your monthly membership.

- **Extra conveniences:** Some gyms have hair blow dryers in the locker rooms, Internet access on the cardiovascular equipment, membership competitions, and special guest instructors — little extras that keep you motivated over the long haul.

- **Affiliation with other clubs:** If you travel a lot, consider joining a club that is affiliated with gyms around the country. Large chains may not have the most qualified staff or offer the most personalized attention, but you can save money on guest passes.

WARNING!

When a "deal" isn't a steal

Getting the facts you want from a health club often requires persistence and savvy. Here are some tips to prevent you from getting ripped off:

- **Stand your ground.** Health club salespeople may quote what seems like a reasonable price, but by the time you get finished adding in all the options like locker space and towel service, they've doubled the price of admission.

- **Ask what the price includes.** If it doesn't include an item you want, such as an extra training session, ask if the salesperson will toss it in to make the sale. Also, don't let the salespeople cheat you out of the advertised price. If you see an ad in the paper, bring it with you to the club. If you heard an ad on the radio, note the station and the time it aired.

- **Don't be insulted.** Some salespeople try to assault your self-esteem by telling you how much better you'll look and feel if you lose ten more pounds to get you to join or to sign up for extra training sessions. Remember, many health club salespeople work on commission, so they say just about anything to make a sale.

- **Don't rush into your decision.** The gym will be there tomorrow. And if it isn't, you'll be glad you didn't sign up, right? Take your time.

- **Don't pay an initiation fee if you can help it.** An initiation fee is an upfront payment to join and doesn't cover any monthly dues. Some gyms waive this fee during certain times of the year or if you join with a family member — or if you're persistent enough.

- **Don't sign up for more than a year.** Many states have laws that forbid lifetime and long-term memberships. Loopholes exist in the law, and even when there aren't these holes, disreputable salespeople may try to snow you. You don't know where you'll be a year from now — and more important, you don't know where the gym is going to be a year from now. Many gyms have monthly memberships that are slightly more expensive than buying a whole year, but these month-to-month deals may be a better deal for you if your life is in flux.

- **Join with a friend and ask for a discount.** Know that the best sales are usually in the slower times — all the summer months and right after Christmas. Some clubs give you a rebate or free months if you recommend a friend who joins.

Researching Trainers

This book offers detailed instructions for dozens of exercises and plenty of ideas for designing your own workouts. Still, we think that getting personal instruction at least three times is valuable for anyone who lifts weights. If you join a club, you should automatically get a free training session on top of a fitness evaluation. Ask in advance, and you may even get extra free sessions. If you lift weights at home, you can hire a trainer for a couple of sessions to get you up and running. (If a trainer isn't an option for you, a good video or DVD can augment what you gather from this book, although when you're an absolute beginner, a video or DVD is no substitute for hands-on instruction.)

Finding fitness help: What a trainer can do for you

While standing in line at your local grocery store, you read about the stars who spend thousands of dollars on fitness trainers who mold bodies into divas and studs for upcoming performances. Personal trainers are famous for performing award-winning actions to firm bodies quickly with amazing results for prizefighters, action heroes, and models, but a good fitness trainer can do that for *you* too. For example, one of Shirley's training clients — a woman in her 30s — lost 20 pounds in just 3 months of supervised exercise.

Perfecting your technique

A trainer can offer subtle pointers to improve your weight lifting form. Even if you do your best to follow instructions like, "Keep your arm parallel to the floor," you may not be able to tell whether your arm is in precisely the right position. After you know what it feels like to correctly perform an exercise, you're likely to keep using good techniques when you're on your own.

Showing you alternative exercises

A trainer can help you build on the exercises in this book, showing you additional moves that meet your specific needs and preferences. If you're pregnant, a trainer can show you how to perform abdominal exercises without lying on your back and hamstring exercises without lying on your stomach. If you suffer from arthritis, a personal trainer can show you how to stretch and strengthen your muscles while alleviating some pain and fatigue.

Introducing you to the equipment

Each brand of equipment has its own quirks. The seat adjustment for one lat pulldown machine (see Chapter 11 for a description) may work by a different mechanism than it does for another, even though the machines strengthen your back muscles in the same way. A trainer can tell you about the intricacies of each machine in your health club or home gym.

Designing or updating your program

If you wanted to, you could come up with a new routine every day for the rest of your life. A trainer can help you expand on our workout suggestions and design routines that fit your specific schedule, whether you work out 3 days a week for 20 minutes or twice a week for an hour. For example, many of Shirley's training clients are executives who travel frequently for business. She provides on-the-road-training plans, as well as airplane stretches to alleviate stiffness. Trainers also come in handy if you're working toward a specific goal — preparing for ski season requires a different type of routine than getting ready for a backpacking vacation.

Keeping you motivated

Some people wouldn't even consider getting out of bed, let alone lifting a weight, if they didn't have a trainer standing over them saying, "Okay, Larry, ten shoulder presses, now!" Others manage with a motivational boost every month or two, working out on their own the rest of the time. And then some people rely so much on their trainers for inspiration that they actually bring them along on vacation.

Finding a qualified trainer

Fitness trainer is about as meaningful a term as *Internet consultant* or *marketing liaison.* In terms of skills and education, the term doesn't mean a darn thing. We know a group of private trainers who hang a large sign outside their gym that says, "World Class Personal Trainers." Only one of the group's six trainers is even certified by a single professional organization. Find a trainer that you can trust.

Looking for the certification

Although no laws exist on the books requiring trainers to have any particular training or certification, professional organizations and university programs are certifying more and more trainers. Many health clubs now require their trainers to have at least one certification, and as the personal training profession becomes increasingly competitive, many private trainers are earning certifications in order to stay ahead of the competition.

A number of certifications require several days of seminars taught by fitness experts and a passing grade on a written exam. But beware: We recently came across a certification offered over the Web that involved answering a few questions and paying $90. You could take the test as many times as you wanted and didn't have to pay until you passed — at which point you would be issued a fancy certificate saying that you're a "Certified Kickboxing Instructor" or "Certified Personal Trainer." The Web site even bragged "No teaching experience necessary!"

The following organizations are among the most reputable certifying agents:

- ✔ American College of Sports Medicine (ACSM)
- ✔ National Strength and Conditioning Association (NSCA)
- ✔ American Council on Exercise (ACE)

Hiring an experienced trainer

Don't be shy: Ask for references and call a few. Do as good a job screening potential trainers as you'd do checking out potential employees. Ask for a resume.

Making sure that your personalities mesh

Trainers are human beings, which means that they come in all different personality types. Some are enthusiastic. Some are downright perky. Others are drill sergeants.

Interview a few trainers and choose one who makes you feel comfortable. Your trainer doesn't need to be your best friend. In order to act as an objective professional, your trainer — like your doctor or lawyer — may need some distance from you.

Expecting good teaching skills

Even if your trainer has a PhD in physiology and is more congenial than Oprah, there's no guarantee that he can show you how to perform a push-up correctly. The ability to get a point across is a skill in and of itself. Good trainers speak to you in your native tongue, not in jargon. If you don't understand something, a trainer should be able to find another way of explaining the point. Also, good trainers prepare you to venture out into the world alone. They make sure that you understand not only how to adjust the seat on the Leg Extension machine, but also why you're adjusting it that way.

Getting personal attention

Your trainer should shower you with questions about your goals and should thoroughly evaluate your health, strength, cardiovascular fitness, and flexibility. Look for evidence that you're getting a custom-designed routine. Many trainers specialize in certain types of clients, such as seniors, children, pregnant women, multiple sclerosis patients, or ultra-endurance athletes. If you have a specific goal in mind or have special circumstances, it's wise to seek out a trainer who has the training and experience to meet your needs.

Paying a hefty fee

Hollywood stars may pay $200 per weight training session, but you don't need to. Fees vary widely depending on what part of the country you live in, but in many places, you can find a trainer for about $35 an hour. Expect to pay between $75 and $150 per hour if you live in big cities such as Chicago, Los Angeles, or New York City. More experienced trainers generally receive a higher rate. You may spend less money by purchasing five or ten sessions at once, but highly qualified trainers often don't discount their rates. You also can save cash by hiring a trainer who works at your health club, but don't forget that you're also paying the club's monthly dues. Many trainers offer semiprivate sessions for a reduced fee. If you go this route, try to hook up with a buddy whose goals and abilities are similar to yours.

Be sure to weigh all factors when you hire a trainer because the least expensive person may not be the best choice for you, especially if you need someone with extra qualifications. Trainers with additional education in working with people with certain medical conditions or women who're pregnant usually charge higher rates. Yoga and Pilates instructors often charge more, too.

Insisting on liability insurance

Make sure that your trainer carries liability insurance. Of course, we hope you never find yourself in a position where insurance matters. But you do need to face the realities of the modern world. If you get hurt, you may be looking at thousands of dollars in medical bills, even if you have medical insurance. A trainer's liability coverage may foot the bill if you can prove your injury is a direct result of the trainer's negligence. Many insurers award coverage only to trainers who're certified, so liability insurance is often an indication that your trainer has some credentials.

Being on your best behavior

Just like you expect a trainer to meet certain qualifications and protocol, you too need to be up to the standard, aligning your behaviors with a willing participant and one that trainers can work with. Take an active role in your training sessions, especially if you're going to have just a few of them. Follow these tips to get the most out of your training sessions:

✔ **Show up on time.** Trainers are professional people with busy schedules and bills to pay, so show them courtesy. Honor your trainer's cancellation policy (and avoid chronic cancellations). Most trainers require at least 24 hours notice when you can't make it to your session. They may let you slide the first time, but they do have the right to charge you for missed sessions.

✔ **Have a good attitude.** Your trainer doesn't want to hear you whine about your boss or your latest speeding ticket.

✔ **Speak up.** The more questions you ask, the more information you're likely to remember. When you perform the lat pulldown, don't feel stupid about asking why you pull the bar down to your chest rather than to your belly button. A good trainer has coherent answers on the tip of her tongue.

✔ **Listen to your trainer.** When you're advised to perform 12 repetitions per set, don't say, "My stockbroker says that it's better to perform 40 repetitions." Trust that your trainer has more experience than you do (or your stockbroker for that matter). Of course, you should always ask questions if you don't understand something and if your trainer's advice sounds out of line. If you don't get your questions answered the way you hope or you have poor results from your training sessions, the time has come to find another trainer who better meets your fitness goals.

Working in a Group: An Introduction to Weight Training Classes

Some people thrive on one-on-one instruction. Others really respond to the atmosphere of a class, even if they can afford a private trainer. If you're uncomfortable with someone scrutinizing your every move, as a personal trainer does, then taking a class is a good way for you to discover weight-training techniques while still blending into the crowd. And if you're short on self-motivation, your classmates hold you accountable and keep you pumping weights when you'd prefer to go home and watch TV. Even if you're the type of person who enjoys working out alone, you can pick up new moves by taking an occasional class.

Conditioning your muscles

Muscle conditioning or body sculpting, sometimes called *body shaping,* is the classroom buzzword for weight training and calisthenics. We think that teachers started these terms because they figured *weight training* would scare away people who're afraid of lifting weights. Some people say, "Oh, I hate weight training, but I love body sculpting," which is like saying that you hate sweet potatoes but love yams. It's all in the delivery!

Group classes use dumbbells and exercise bands, as opposed to weight machines. A class typically lasts between 45 and 90 minutes and works all the major muscle groups in the body. Most clubs also offer 15 to 30 minute toning classes, such as "Abs Only" or "Lower Back Care," that focus on particular areas of the body. If you take a focused class, just make sure that you don't neglect the rest of your body.

Although we wholeheartedly endorse group training, we do want to point out two flaws that commonly plague these classes: performing too many repetitions and failing to use enough weight. Just because you're in a classroom doesn't mean that the basic rules of weight training go out the window. You still need to lift enough weight for each exercise so that the muscle in question is fatigued by the 15th repetition.

Expecting quality from your instructor

In general, the quality of instruction has drastically improved in recent years, because most clubs demand certification and because poorly attended classes get dropped from the schedule. If you don't like one instructor, try another one if your schedule permits. Look for the following when evaluating an instructor:

- ✔ **Certification:** The American College of Sports Medicine, the American Council on Exercise, or another nationally recognized organization should certify your teacher as an exercise instructor. Instructor certifications are different from personal training certifications. Typically, the exams aren't as difficult in the areas of fitness assessment and individual program design as they are for personal trainers, but the tests focus more on the skills that instructors need for group training situations.

- ✔ **Concern for newcomers:** A good instructor asks whether anyone is new to the class and whether anyone has any injuries or special problems. If you fit the bill, you may want to arrive a few minutes early and explain your situation to the instructor. The teacher may give you a special place to stand so she can keep an eye on you. At the very least, you should get a little extra attention.

✔ **Clear instructions:** A good instructor acquaints you with important terminology without overloading you with jargon. We know one instructor who says things like, "Raise up on your phalanges," which in English means, "Stand up on your tiptoes."

✔ **Concern for safety:** Don't be afraid to walk out of any class that doesn't feel right. Liz once bailed on a "step 'n' sculpt" class because the teacher had class members flying all over the step with weights in their hands. The uncontrolled activity caused a near collision between Liz and the student next to her. Don't worry about hurting the teacher's feelings. Your priority is keeping your body intact.

✔ **Motivation:** Instructors shouldn't act like they're on autopilot. Your instructor should be one of the reasons that you look forward to going to class and someone who keeps you interested in your training program. The teacher should model correct form and demonstrate a variety of options for people of different levels in the class. Your responsibility is to choose the correct level. If you're not sure which level that is, ask the instructor.

✔ **Individual technique tips:** Instructors can't possibly give a personal training session to all 20 members of the class, but they should offer some individual tips. They need to let you know if you hold your arms too wide during chest fly exercises or if you throw your body around when you do biceps curls. If you have questions about any exercises, take the initiative and come to class a few minutes early or speak to the instructor after class. Be courteous. If your instructor is busy that day, ask when a convenient time for you to ask a question is.

✔ **A warm-up, cool-down, and relaxation stretch:** Every weight training class should have a warm-up that consists of at least six minutes of light aerobic exercise to warm up muscles and joints. The class should end with three to five minutes of light movement at a lower intensity to cool down followed by a stretching and relaxation segment lasting between five and ten minutes. Take advantage of the instructor-led relaxation and stretches. Focus on deep breathing, releasing muscular tension, and achieving a good stretch. So often, people skip this part of training. More and more evidence from research supports the importance of learning how to relax to improve health and well-being. Enjoy these few moments to relax both your body and mind.

✔ **An intensity check:** During the class, the instructor should check to make sure that people aren't pushing themselves too hard (or taking it too easy to benefit from the workout). The *intensity check* can be something as casual as "Hey, how's everyone doing so far?"

Class etiquette

Remember that "Gets Along Well with Others" category on your grade-school report card? Well, no one is going to grade your behavior in a weight training class, but the principle still applies: You must be courteous to your fellow students. Win friends and the teacher's approval in class by following these rules:

✔ **Follow the teacher.** You're not just renting the weights for an hour; you're there to participate with the group. When the class is trying to listen to the instructor's explanation of the shoulder press, you shouldn't be off in your own world doing a set of biceps curls. Your deviation can be distracting to both the class members and the instructor.

✔ **Choose the appropriate class level.** If you're a flat-out beginner, don't venture into the Monster Muscles advanced muscle conditioning class. Your presence isn't fair to the students or the teacher, who is supposed to be challenging the other students, to have to stop to explain the basics to you. (Also, your safety is at risk.) On the flip side, if you're an advanced student slipping into a beginner toning class, know that you won't be as challenged. Don't bother complaining to the instructor that the class is too easy for you.

✔ **Don't disorganize the weights or benches.** We sometimes see class members arrive early, pick through weights to find the ones they want, and reserve their favorite spot in the class. This behavior wouldn't be a problem if the classmates didn't throw their reject equipment all over the floor. Don't create any hazardous conditions.

✔ **Respect other students' personal space.** Place your equipment far enough from your neighbors so you don't smack into them during the exercises. If the class is too crowded, the teacher is obligated to turn people away or modify the routine so nobody ends up injured.

✔ **Don't show up late.** Most teachers don't let students in after the warm-up period. You shouldn't miss this segment, anyway.

✔ **Respect the teacher's instructions.** A group fitness instructor's most important job is to ensure the safety of everyone in the class. Respect the teacher's exercise instructions as well as guidance regarding where to position yourself in class and what to wear.

Mastering Gym Training Etiquette

Even at a health club — a place where tank tops, profuse sweating, and mild grunting are perfectly acceptable — rules of etiquette should be followed. Sure, the social graces expected in a weight room are a bit different from those expected at the symphony or the Louvre, but manners are important just the same. In this section, we explain the rituals and customs unique to gyms. Some habits may seem odd at first, but after you understand how you're expected to act, you'll feel a lot more at home in your club.

If you witness a flagrant etiquette violation, don't be afraid to inform the club staff. You're not being a snitch. The rules are for everyone, whether you're the Queen of England or one of her loyal subjects.

Sharing equipment

In a gym, weight equipment is considered communal property, so don't sit on a machine while you rest between sets. Especially don't sit there reading a magazine, talking on your cellphone, or rehearsing an opera. (We've witnessed all three.) Instead, stand up and let a fellow gym member *work in* — let the member alternate sets with you. The same rule applies if you're using a pair of dumbbells. When you complete a set, place the weights on the floor so someone else can sneak in a set while you rest.

The only time you should retain possession of weight equipment while you rest is when you're using a barbell stacked with weight plates. Suppose that you're bench-pressing 75 pounds — a 45-pound bar with a 10- and 5-pound weight plate on each side. Someone else, meanwhile, wants to bench-press 225 pounds — the bar plus two 45-pound plates on each side. You can see what a hassle it would be for the two of you to work in with each other; between each set, you'd need to slide eight plates on and off the bar. So you're under no obligation to let the other person work in with you. (However, if people are waiting for the equipment, have the courtesy not to perform 15 sets.)

Unloading your weight bar

After you finish using a bar, leave it completely empty. Don't assume that everyone can lift the same amount of weight you can. Removing weight plates from a bar takes a fair amount of strength as well as good technique. Don't assume that the next person who comes along has the ability (or desire) to clean up after you.

By the way, this clear-the-bar rule doesn't just apply to heavy lifters. Even if you're using only a 10-pound plate, you still need to clear your bar. If the next person who comes along wants to use 45s, he shouldn't be bothered with removing your 10-pounders.

Putting weights back where you found them

When you've removed a weight plate from a bar or when you finish using a pair of dumbbells, return the weights to their designated spot on the rack. Typically, clubs have dumbbells sitting in order. On a weight plate tree, the light plates usually sit on the top rungs while the heavier ones go on the bottom. When people pile the plates indiscriminately on top of one another, invariably they've made you slide off three 45-pound plates and two 25-pounders just to get to the 10-pound plate (that is if you're able to lift those weights). You may have to find a trainer to help you, consequently wasting more time.

Never leave dumbbells or barbells on the floor when you're finished using them. Someone may trip on the weights. If you leave dumbbells on the floor between sets, criss-cross them or butt them up against the wall or the bench so that they can't roll away.

Keeping your sweat to yourself

Carry a towel and wipe off any bench or machine you use. Nothing is quite as gross as picking up a slippery weight or lying down in a stranger's pool of sweat. If you forget to bring a towel, use your sweatshirt or the paper towels provided by the club.

Extra Credit: Wipe up the pool of perspiration you may have left on the floor surrounding your machine or bench. Otherwise, the next person may inadvertently do a third-base slide into the machinery.

Helping the flow of traffic

Don't block the traffic flow. As mention earlier, you shouldn't camp out on the equipment while you're resting between sets. However, neither should you clog the pathways between machines or congregate with a dozen of your buddies in the free weight area. Not only is this inconsiderate, but also it can create a hazardous condition. In general, weight rooms are crowded with little room between machines. If you block space, someone may walk around you and inadvertently bump someone who's working out on a machine, causing the person to lose control and to drop a weight. This has happened before with serious consequences. The weight room is for training. If you want to visit with friends, go out into the hallway.

Hogging the drinking fountain

Don't stand at the drinking fountain trying to catch your breath when the line behind you is longer than the line for World Series tickets. Take a drink, and get back in line. Better yet, carry a water bottle in the weight room. For some reason, many people who use a water bottle on the stationary bikes and stair-climbers don't think of carrying one around the strength training area. When you do fill up your bottle, let everyone else in line get a drink first; don't hold up the entire gym membership while you fill a gallon-sized water jug.

Don't spit your gum into the drinking fountain — this tip should be obvious, but club staffers report otherwise. Actually, don't spit *anything* into the fountain. No one wants to stick his face into a wad of your spit.

Toting around your gym bag

Some people carry their bag from machine to machine. You know those large hollowed-out cubes called lockers? That's where you store your gym bag. At most gyms, the machines are only a few feet apart; by dumping your bag on the ground you're hogging precious floor space. In addition, you're creating a hazardous condition because someone may trip and fall over your bag. Many gyms forbid members to bring their bags into the weight room because less honest members may walk out with lovely parting gifts, like dumbbells, cable handles, and other small items. Someone recently stole all the collars from a gym that Liz manages, creating a real safety issue until the collars were replaced. (We define collars in Chapter 4.)

Treating the locker room like your own bathroom

Even more so than the weight room, the locker room is the place where your true colors emerge. Women are on equal standing with men in this arena: Men may be more likely to hog dumbbells in the weight room, but women can stand for hours in the only available shower stall with the best of 'em.

Follow these suggestions for locker room etiquette to maintain good relations with your fellow gym mates:

- ✔ **The shower:** Don't take a marathon shower if people are waiting. With the exception of sweat, what you take into the shower should come out with you when you leave. Make sure that you remove all your shower supplies and that little pile of your hair from the drain. (Carry a latex glove or two in your shower supplies if picking up your own hair freaks you out.)

- ✔ **The vanity area:** Don't hog the mirror or the hair blow dryer. If you brush your hair and 200 strands of hair fall on the counter, wipe them off with a paper towel (wipe them into the towel or in the trash, not on the floor).

- ✔ **The locker area:** Don't take up three lockers and spread your clothing over the entire bench. Share with others. Shut your locker when you leave.

Don't leave your belongings in lockers overnight unless you have permission from your gym to do so. Most gyms empty out unsanctioned lockers at the end of every day and won't guarantee the safe return of your personal items.

If the lockers at your gym require a key, return the key at the end of your workout. Keyed lockers are a convenience to members so they don't have to carry a lock of their own. However, members often walk away with the keys, rendering the lockers unusable and creating a big expense for the facility, which has to keep replacing the keys.

✔ **The laundry and trash areas:** Limit yourself to one or two towels. After you finish using your towels and other paraphernalia, place them in the laundry or trash bin instead of dropping them on the floor.

Chapter 8

Stretching: The Truth

- -

- -

Stretching seems like such a straightforward topic that you may expect us to explain it in a sentence or two and then show you a stretching routine. Well, as it turns out, a lot of confusion surrounds the subject of stretching. The American College of Sports Medicine (ACSM), one of the most respected sports and fitness organizations in the world, provides guidelines on how to stretch, but the organization still admits that more research is needed to determine exactly what stretching can and can't do for you. This chapter explains that stretching maintains freedom of movement and enhances muscular performance and that stretching isn't just about isolated muscle fibers. This chapter outlines the ACSM guidelines for stretching and covers other promising stretching methods (considered promising by exercise experts).

Knowing Why and When to Stretch

Stretching lengthens your muscles and loosens up the joints that your muscles connect to so you can move more freely but still keep your joints stable. Too much flexibility leads to unstable joints; too little flexibility leads to restricted movement. When your muscles are at their ideal length, you can walk without stiffness, reach down to tousle a toddler's hair, or turn around when someone calls your name — everyday movements that you take for granted until you have trouble doing them. When your muscles and joints lack flexibility, you feel *tight*.

Two stretching methods we describe in this chapter, Active isolated and PNF, actively stimulate the nervous system to increase the release of muscular tightness. With these methods, you hold stretches for a shorter period of time than you do with traditional stretching, and you contract the muscle ultimately to encourage more relaxation.

Lengthening your muscles

This muscular tension isn't simply a result of tight muscle tissues. For example, if you were under anesthesia, your body would be much more flexible. The neuromuscular system regulates muscular tension. So, when you stretch, you aren't simply pulling on muscle fibers. Instead, you're stimulating your nervous system to signal the muscle to rest in a longer position.

Several studies show that the optimal amount of time to hold a stretch is between 20 and 30 seconds. Holding a stretch for 60 seconds doesn't seem to make you more flexible. In fact, it's better to do two stretches of 30 seconds each or three stretches of 20 seconds each than to do a one-minute stretch. Theory states that stimulating your nervous system multiple times to encourage your muscle to be longer leads to a greater likelihood of "re-setting" the resting muscle tension length in a longer position. Studies show that the greatest increases in flexibility come from the first four repetitions.

Alleviating muscular tension

Another important concept to understand is muscular balance affects the resting length of your muscles. In other words, the back of your leg doesn't exist in isolation from the rest of your body. For example, the tightness you feel in your calves relates to the strength of your shins. If your calves are relatively stronger than your shins, the calf muscle dominates the pair and your calf feels tight. To decrease this muscular tension, you need to strengthen your shin.

Stretching alone can't eliminate muscular tension. To address tight muscles, your weight lifting program must consist of both strengthening exercises for the opposing muscle group and stretching exercises for the tight muscles.

Preventing injuries

Stretching has been widely recommended to prevent injury and ease muscle soreness, but many recent studies find that traditional methods of stretching may not accomplish either goal and may, in fact, *cause* injuries (like muscle tears from overstretching). A University of Hawaii study of more than 100 runners found that the nonstretchers performed better, reported fewer injuries, and experienced less muscle soreness after their running workouts than those runners who stretched regularly. Why? Perhaps tighter muscles better stabilize the joints, thereby protecting knees and hips from the trauma of running.

However, having tighter muscles for stability may be true only to a point. If muscles are too tight, the risk of injury appears to increase. For instance, runners who sit a lot during the day — and therefore have tight hamstrings — are prone to herniated disks because their hamstrings pull on the pelvis, rotating it backward. Over time, tension from tight hamstrings creates a flat-back posture; the disc fluid moves toward the back of the disc, creating pressure and a bulge. Inflexible runners aren't the only ones who can be troubled by inflexibility. A recent study found that, two and three days after moderately heavy weight lifting, less flexible exercisers feel more muscle tenderness than more flexible subjects.

Keep in mind that these studies are just a few among many, and that little research exists to prove or disprove previous studies. So, we're left with a hodgepodge of studies that seem to compare apples to oranges.

The truth about stretching

How do you achieve and maintain your muscles at their ideal length so that you can move easily and freely? According to the ACSM, stretching is important to achieve this goal.

The ACSM's position stand on exercise for health, last published in 1998, states that growing evidence supports stretching for the purpose of improving range of motion and joint function and enhancing muscle performance, as well as substantial "real-life" reports to support its role in preventing injuries. The ACSM issues the following guidelines on how to stretch:

- Hold each stretch for 10 to 30 seconds and repeat up to four repetitions.
- Perform at least one stretch for each major muscle group.
- Stretch at least two to three times a week, preferably every day.
- Stretch to the point of discomfort but not beyond.
- Don't hold your breath while stretching.

An important concept to understand when it comes to stretching is the *stretch reflex mechanism*. This mechanism defends against overstretching and tearing and signals the muscle to shorten and tighten when stimulated. An example of the stretch reflex: when your doctor taps your knee with a little hammer and your leg kicks up. To avoid stimulating the stretch reflex, never stretch to an extreme length or stretch quickly as in a bouncing movement.

To date, most stretching studies have looked at traditional stretching. Other varieties of stretching, which we describe later, show some promise in the areas of preventing injuries and easing muscle soreness. But no major studies that we know of have compared the various stretching methods head to head. In fact, more and more studies show that there isn't necessarily one best way for all people because we each have different body types, experiences, and goals. Experiment with a variety of stretching methods, and find out which stretches feel most comfortable to you. You may even want to combine a number of stretching methods. You may find, for example, that you enjoy doing Active isolated stretches (covered later in the chapter) for your *hamstrings* (rear thigh muscles) but traditional stretching for your shoulders.

Celebrating Traditions: Traditional Stretching

What it is: You hold each stretch for 10 to 30 seconds without bouncing. (Traditional stretching, also called *static* stretching, holds your body still.) As you hold the position, you feel a pull that spreads up and down the length of the muscle. Traditional stretching is the method performed at the end of many exercise classes and in exercise videos. While it may not achieve as much increase in flexibility as some of the other methods, it's very safe, easy to understand, and has a low risk of injury.

Traditional stretching has some definite advantages:

✔ Almost anyone can perform some static stretches; you can easily modify the position to suit your level of flexibility.

✔ Many people find this method of stretching a good way to relax and to cool down after a workout.

✔ If you perform traditional stretches at least three days a week, you'll probably notice an increase in flexibility after a few weeks.

On the other hand, some cons coincide with traditional stretching:

✔ If you're inflexible, this type of stretching may be far from relaxing. In fact, it may be so uncomfortable that you end up skipping your stretches altogether.

✔ Separating one muscle group from another with traditional stretches is difficult; you often are forced to stretch several different muscle groups at once. This situation is a problem if one of the muscles being stretched is tighter than the others.

Contrary to popular belief, you should never perform traditional stretching before you warm up. Stretching in and of itself doesn't constitute a warm-up. See the sidebar, "Stretching guidelines," to find out what constitutes a proper warm-up.

If you're a stretching neophyte, start with 10 seconds of stretching and gradually work your way up to a full 30 seconds. Don't bounce. Jerky movements may actually make you tighter. Get in the proper stretching position slowly and smoothly and then stay there. After you've held the stretch for a few seconds, slowly stretch a bit further.

POSTURE PATROL

Stretching guidelines

Follow these simple guidelines, which apply to all methods of stretching:

✔ **Aim to stretch daily, but make sure that you stretch at least three times per week.** You improve your flexibility the same way you get to Carnegie Hall: practice, practice, practice. Your muscles will "remember" to stay loose and flexible if they're reminded often enough.

✔ **Stretch after your workout, not before.** Follow this rule whether you're doing aerobic exercise, weight training, or both. On days when you do only weight training, you need to do at least five minutes of rhythmic, low-intensity aerobic exercise such as walking, jogging, cycling, or stepping. Warming up gets your blood flowing and raises your body temperature so your muscles are more receptive to the stretch. Never stretch a cold muscle. (This rule doesn't apply to Active isolated stretching (covered at the end of this chapter), which can safely be included as part of a warm-up.)

✔ **Never force a stretch.** Stretch to the point at which you're right on the edge of discomfort, never to the point of "Ouch!" There's no optimal amount of flexibility, so stretch within the limits of each individual joint.

✔ **Don't forget to breathe.** Deep, natural breathing increases your flexibility by helping you to relax and by sending oxygen-rich blood into your muscles. Inhale deeply just before you go into a stretching position, and exhale through your mouth as you move into the stretch. Breathe deeply several times as you hold the stretch.

✔ **Don't just go through the motions and declare, "There, I've stretched."** Concentrate. Focus. Do you feel the stretch where you're supposed to? Are you using correct form? Do you need to back off or push a little further? You don't need to quiz yourself with the intensity of a prosecutor; stretching is supposed to be relaxing, after all.

✔ **Give priority to the muscles you use the most in your workouts and in everyday life, but don't neglect any major muscle group.** For instance, cyclists should perform a few extra sets of stretches on their thighs, calves, and lower back, but they shouldn't skip upper body stretches altogether. You want your entire body to be flexible so that you can reach across the bed to snag the remote control from a spouse who inexplicably watches reruns of "The Iron Chef" on Food Network.

Hold each of the following positions for 10 to 30 seconds.

Quadriceps (front thigh): Lie on your left side with your legs out straight and your head resting on your outstretched arm. Bend your right knee so your heel is close to your butt, and grab your ankle or toes with your right hand. Pull your heel back and toward your butt, taking care to keep your hips stacked directly on top of one another. Try to keep your knees together, not separated. Don't arch your back (see Figure 8-1) or allow your butt to stick out. Use the image of trying to press your pocket forward and flat. After you stretch your right quadriceps, turn over (to lie on your right side) and stretch your left.

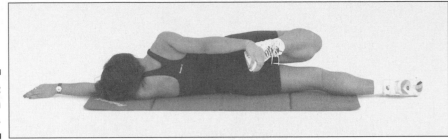

Figure 8-1:
Don't arch
your back.

Hamstrings (rear thigh): Lie on your back with your left knee bent and your left foot flat on the floor. Straighten your right leg out in front of you along the floor, and flex your toes toward yourself. Slowly raise your right leg off the floor as high as you can without allowing your back or butt to lift up. As you hold this position, you feel a stretch through the back of your thigh. Clasp your hands around your thigh above your knee (see Figure 8-2) or use a stretching strap with loops to help raise your leg. (Using your hands or a stretching strap to help is an especially good idea if you're not very flexible.) Lower your leg slowly and repeat the stretch with your left leg. Before you hold the stretch, you can use the strap to lower and lift your leg and explore your active range of motion. Be sure to relax your thighs and use the strap for support to maximize your stretch (see Figure 8-3).

Figure 8-2:
Hold this
position to
feel the
stretch.

Figure 8-3: Remember to keep your thigh muscles relaxed.

The pretzel stretch (butt, lower back, and outer thigh): Lie on your back and bend your knees. Lift your legs up so that your knees are directly over your hips and your calves are parallel to the floor. Cross your left ankle over the front of your right thigh. Clasp both hands around the back of your right thigh and pull back with gentle, steady pressure. See Figure 8-4. Keep your butt in contact with the floor. Don't round hips up and off the floor. As you hold this position, you should feel the stretch spread through your left buttock and outer hip and through the center of your lower back. Repeat this stretch with your right ankle over the front of your left thigh.

Figure 8-4:
Pull back
with gentle,
steady
pressure.

Reach up (entire upper body and lower back): Sit up tall either cross-legged on the floor or in a chair. Make a loose fist with your hands, and raise your arms directly over your shoulders. Lengthen your right arm upward, as if you're trying to touch an object above you that's just out of reach. Hold this position for two to four slow counts. Without relaxing your right arm, stretch your left arm upward. Sit up tall and keep your shoulders relaxed (see Figure 8-5) as you alternate stretching each arm upward five times. Try to reach a little higher each time — without hunching your shoulders up to your ears. You should feel this stretch throughout the length of your spine, in the "wings" of your upper back, and in your shoulders and arms.

Figure 8-5:
Keep your
shoulders
relaxed.

Hand clasp (chest, shoulders, and arms): Sit up tall either on a chair or cross-legged on the floor. Lean a few inches forward from your hips (see Figure 8-6) and clasp your hands behind your back. Drop your shoulders and shoulder blades downward as you lengthen your arms out behind you. You should feel the stretch across the top of your chest, in your shoulders, and along the length of your arms. If you don't have enough flexibility to clasp your hands together, hold an end of a towel in each hand.

Figure 8-6:
Lean
forward a
few inches.

Stretching with Assistance

What it is: Assisted stretching is a traditional-type stretch that requires a partner. Your partner helps you into position and then gently helps you stretch further than you can by yourself. As with traditional, or static, stretching, you hold the position for 10 to 30 seconds without bouncing. The best way to figure out how to perform assisted stretches is from an experienced fitness trainer. While the ACSM's guidelines don't offer strategies for this type of stretching, the organization does reference it as promising and possibly effective.

The pros of assisted stretching are as follows:

✔ Having someone else do a lot of the work for you is relaxing. This technique is particularly valuable for a tight muscle that you have trouble stretching yourself.

✔ If have trouble mastering some of the common stretching positions, assisted stretching helps you understand the techniques while you develop enough flexibility to do them more comfortably on your own.

✔ A partner tends to push you a bit further than you can push yourself.

Assisted stretching also comes with its cons:

✔ If you don't have a partner, you're out of luck (although some assisted stretches can be mimicked by using a towel or stretching strap).

✔ If your partner overstretches you, you may end up injured.

✔ Assisted stretching requires less muscle awareness than the other techniques, so you may not gain much from doing it. (We discuss muscle awareness in "Proprioceptive Neuromuscular Facilitation [PNF]" later in the chapter.)

Sample assisted stretch (see Figure 8-7): This stretch focuses on your lower back and butt. Lie on the floor with your partner standing in front of your feet; relax your arms at your sides, and keep your head on the floor. Lift your legs, and bend your knees into your chest. Have your partner place her palms on your thighs and gently press down and in so your knees move even closer to your chest. As you hold this position, you should feel the stretch spread from your butt into your lower back.

Figure 8-7:
An assisted
stretch.

Proprioceptive Neuromuscular Facilitation (PNF)

What it is: The term *Proprioceptive Neuromuscular Facilitation* sounds like some high-tech, life-saving medical procedure used by doctors on "ER," but really, it's a simple method of stretching. You get into a stretch position, tighten a muscle for about 6 seconds, allow it to relax, and then hold a static stretch for 10 to 30 seconds. In theory, when the muscle is stimulated by contracting, more of the muscle fibers are triggered to relax. Some PNF stretches work best with the assistance of another person; others you can perform yourself. The best way to be taught PNF stretches is from a trainer who is familiar with the technique.

Check out these pros to PNF stretching:

✔ Many studies, including some referenced by the ACSM, show that PNF stretching is a good way to increase your flexibility.

✔ The tightening part helps strengthen the muscle being stretched. This is especially true if the muscle is injured and you can't do the bending and straightening necessary to perform strength-training exercises.

✔ Some studies have found that PNF stretching increases blood flow into joints and muscles, especially if they've experienced a recent injury.

✔ PNF teaches you about your muscles. If you're doing a PNF hamstring stretch, you need to know where your hamstring is and how it feels to tighten this muscle. This knowledge also comes in handy when you perform weight training exercises.

The cons of this type of stretching are

✔ Many people find PNF stretching uncomfortable or even painful.

✔ You need extra motivation to tighten a muscle as hard as you can for six seconds. Not everyone has the strength or the patience for this.

✔ If you do PNF stretches with a partner, your buddy may be overenthusiastic and try to force the stretch beyond your capabilities, and then *snap!* Pay attention so that this doesn't happen.

✔ Avoid PNF stretches if you have high blood pressure, because the stretches may result in sharp, sudden increases in blood pressure.

Sample PNF Stretch (see Figure 8-8): This PNF stretch loosens up your hamstrings. Lie on your back with your left knee bent and left foot flat on the floor. Have your partner kneel on one knee in front of your feet. Raise your right leg, and place the back of your heel on top of your partner's shoulder. Have your partner place one hand on your thigh, just above your knee, and the other hand on top of your shin. Forcefully press your heel down into your partner's shoulder, and concentrate on tightening your hamstring as much as possible for six seconds. Relax the muscle, and have your partner gently push your leg up and back without allowing the knee to bend. Hold the stretch for 10 to 30 seconds and repeat the stretch four times. Switch legs.

To do the previous stretch without a partner, wrap a towel or stretching strap around your ankle or the back of your calf, and then pull your leg toward you as you tighten your hamstring and press it downward.

Figure 8-8:
A PNF
stretch.

Active Isolated (AI) Stretching

What it is: *Active isolated (AI) stretching* involves tightening the muscle opposite to the one that you're planning to stretch and then stretching the target muscle for two seconds. You repeat this process 8 to 12 times before going on to the next stretch. By stretching for such a brief period of time, you don't give the muscle enough time to trigger its stretch reflex. (We define the stretch reflex earlier in this chapter, in "Knowing Why and When to Stretch.") What's the purpose of tightening the muscle opposite the one you're stretching? When a muscle tightens, the opposing muscle has no choice but to relax.

Although Active isolated stretching has been around since the 1950s, it's just now gaining popularity — largely through the efforts of father-and-son physiologist team Phil and Jim Wharton, authors of *The Whartons' Book of Stretching* (Times Books). Many sports teams and elite athletes, including one of the world's fastest humans — sprinter and Olympic gold medalist, Michael Johnson — also favor the AI method. Researchers are currently studying this method and may soon offer more insight into its benefits.

AI stretching has its advantages:

- Many AI stretching exercises do a good job of isolating one muscle group at a time. For example, with an AI stretch, you can stretch the hamstrings without involving the lower back and hip muscles.

- If you're particularly weak in one area or are rehabilitating a muscle from injury, the tightening may help strengthen that muscle.

- Many people find AI stretches less painful than traditional stretches.

This method of stretching also has disadvantages:

- The technique is harder to master than traditional stretching, and some of the positions are difficult to get into.

- AI stretching is time consuming. You need about 20 minutes to stretch your entire body, whereas you can do an adequate traditional stretch routine in 5 to 10 minutes.

Sample AI Stretch (see Figure 8-9): This move stretches your calf muscles. Hold one end of a belt or towel in each hand. Sit on the floor, and lift your left leg a few inches off the floor, positioning your right leg in the most comfortable position. Loop the center of the belt around the instep of your left foot. Point your toes away from you to tighten your calf muscles and then pull your toes back to stretch your calf muscles. Hold the position for two seconds. Repeat 8 to 12 times and then stretch your right calf.

Figure 8-9:
An AI
stretch.

Chapter 9

Avoiding Common Weight Lifting Mistakes

Some awfully strange things happen in weight rooms. Not long ago we saw a guy attempting the shoulder shrug (see Chapter 11), but instead of shrugging his shoulders, he simply bobbed his head back and forth. Another guy performed the lat pulldown (see Chapter 11) in a way that resembled an attempt to slice a giant wedge of cheese. And we saw a third person, a woman, doing some martial arts-type punching movements with 8-pound weights in her hands. One wrong move and she would've flown into the mirror. Some of these mistakes simply make the exercises ineffective; other goofs can result in serious injury. Avoid the following weight training mistakes.

Cheating Your Abs

To listen to abdominal gadget infomercials, you'd think that performing an abdominal crunch correctly without some sort of machinery was impossible. The truth: You're perfectly capable of crunching correctly without any equipment. But first, you must realize the common mistakes of the crunch to know how to do the exercise properly.

Crunching incorrectly

Many people complain that crunches cause neck pain. They do — but only if you yank your head and neck instead of lifting your torso by the power of your abdominals. Another mistake is lifting your torso straight off the floor, rather than curling it upward. How do you know whether you're curling or just lifting? Do the basic crunch, described in Chapter 15, and freeze at the top of the movement. Your torso should be in a slightly rounded, almost C-shaped position. A third crunch error: forgetting to breathe. See photo A of Figure 9-1.

Crunching properly

To avoid jerking your neck, place your fingertips and thumbs behind your head and don't lace your fingers together. Hold your elbows out wide and keep your shoulders relaxed. Your arm placement is correct if you can barely see the points of your elbows out of the corners of your eyes. As you curl up, keep your head, neck, and arms frozen in position. When you curl the right way, your head, neck, and lower back feel nearly weightless. Finally, breathe correctly. As you lift your torso, exhale forcefully through your mouth; as you lower, inhale through your nose. See photo B of Figure 9-1.

Figure 9-1: As you curl up, keep your head, neck, and arms frozen in position.

Squatting Too Far

The squat strengthens virtually every muscle in your lower body: your butt, front thighs, rear thighs, and lower back. The squat even improves your sense of balance. That's good for a move that essentially mimics getting in and out of a chair. But if you don't do this exercise correctly — and many people don't — you're asking for an injury.

Squatting incorrectly

We know one guy who spread his legs practically into the splits and lowered his butt all the way to the floor when squatting. Then he'd pop back up into a standing position so forcefully that he was close to being airborne. After a few months, this guy began showing up at the gym with ace bandages wrapped around his knees. Small wonder! When you do squats with such incorrect form, it's easy to injure your knees. Another common error is leaning too far forward and letting your knees shoot out past your toes. Two other problems: dropping your knees inward or letting them bow to the outside. These mistakes put incredible pressure on the delicate tendons, ligaments, and cartilage that hold the knee in place and lead to knee injuries. See photo A of Figure 9-2.

Squatting properly

Start with your feet hip-width apart and point your toes straight ahead or angled slightly outward — whichever foot position is more comfortable and allows your knees to travel over your feet. As you squat down, your knees should travel in a straight line, in the direction that your toes are pointed. Never squat so low that your thighs are lower than parallel to the ground. When you stand up, press through your heels, and finish with your legs straight but relaxed. Snapping your knees places pressure on your knees and sends your lower back into an extreme arch. See photo B of Figure 9-2.

Practice doing the squat sideways in front of a mirror so you can see your form by turning your head. Alternatively, you can ask a friend or spotting partner to watch and correct you, or work with a personal trainer. Don't add weight to your squat until you're positive that you can do the movement properly. Always check and make sure that your knees travel in the same direction as your toes.

Don't lean forward; instead, stand up tall.

Figure 9-2:
Never squat
so low that
your legs
are lower
than parallel
to the
ground.

Arching Your Back

In general, you don't want to over arch your lower back during any strength training exercise. Your lower back already has a natural curve. Over-arching creates tremendous pressure to the discs in the lower back and creates a high risk of injury. In particular, you don't want to arch your back when you do the bench press. Note that when you do a back extension exercise, the curvature of the back should be distributed along the entire length of your spine rather than focused in the lower back.

Bench-pressing the wrong way

Some weight lifters think that anything they do to pile on poundage — including arching their back and squirming around — is fair game. In reality, how much weight you hoist above your chest isn't necessarily related to how strong your chest muscles are. When you arch your back, you simply increase your mechanical advantage (and your injury risk); more muscles pitch in to move the bar upward. We know one guy who convinced himself that arching was an essential part of the bench press. We produced several anatomy textbooks before we convinced him that we hadn't fabricated this bit of information. See Figure 9-3.

Figure 9-3:
Keep your
back in
contact with
the bench
throughout
the
exercise.

Bench-pressing the right way

Keep your back in contact with the bench throughout the exercise. You don't need to force your back into an unnaturally flat position — it's okay to have a small, natural arch under your lower back. If you can't plant your feet flat on the floor because the bench is too high, place your feet on the bench. For more information on the bench press, head to Chapter 12.

Lowering Your Elbows Too Far

We hate to pick on chest exercises again, but they're often the victims of multiple mistakes. The mistake we discuss in this section applies to the dumbbell chest press, the bench press, and the chest fly, all described in Chapter 12.

Lowering your arms the wrong way

When doing chest exercises, some people drop their elbows so low that they practically touch the floor. The resulting stretch in your chest muscles may feel good, but at this point, your chest muscles and your shoulder ligaments are in danger of snapping, much like a rubber band that's pulled too far. Also, when you lower your arms too far, you shove the head of your big arm bone — the humerus — way up into your shoulder socket. The rotator cuff muscles and nearby ligaments and tendons must twist themselves in unspeakable ways to accommodate this unnatural position. You may not feel pain immediately, but sooner or later, all this twisting may catch up to you and result in shoulder pain and injury to your shoulder joints. See photo A of Figure 9-4.

Lowering your arms the right way

When you perform the dumbbell chest press, bench press, or chest fly, stop lowering your arms when your elbows are slightly below chest level. Depending on the build of your body, the bar may touch your chest on the bench press. See photo B of Figure 9-4.

Figure 9-4:
When you perform chest exercises, stop when your elbows are slightly below chest level.

A   B

Pulling a Fast One

Pulling a bar down to your chest isn't as simple as it may appear. To give your back muscles a workout and to protect yourself from injury, you need to make sure that the bar travels in a specific path.

Pulling down a bar the right way

Here are tips for performing a perfect lat pulldown (described in Chapter 11). Choose a weight that's challenging but not so heavy that you feel like you're dangling off the end of a helicopter ladder. Sit down — taking the bar with you — and wedge your thighs under the thigh bar. Now lean just a few inches backward and keep your abdominal muscles pulled in to support your lower back. Pull the bar toward the top of your chest, lifting your chest to meet the bar. Take your time so that the bar remains level throughout the movement. Don't sway back and forth: Rock and roll is dead here.

When you've completed your set, stand up and gently deposit the bar back where it belongs. If you open your hands and let the weight plates come crashing down, you'll startle everyone else in the weight room and you may damage the equipment. The exercise isn't finished until you've completely lowered the weight stack with control. See photo B of Figure 9-5.

Pulling down a bar the wrong way

One common mistake — a mistake that places your shoulder joint and muscles in jeopardy — is pulling the bar straight down toward your lap rather than toward your chest. A second error occurs when you pull the bar down unevenly — one end of the bar may be 6 inches lower than the other. But perhaps our biggest pet peeve is leaning *way* back as you pull the bar down and then rocking forward as the bar travels upward. Generating this type of momentum helps you move a lot of weight, because you're using your body weight instead of your muscles to help you pull down the bar. Because you're not using your muscles to move the bar, this "trick" doesn't improve your back strength. See photo A of Figure 9-5.

Figure 9-5:
Don't sway back and forth as you pull down the bar. Rock and roll is dead here.

Letting Your Butt Stick Up in the Air

The leg curl, described in Chapter 16, is the most popular hamstring (rear thigh) exercise; unfortunately, performing this exercise incorrectly is also quite popular. In general, you don't want to allow your butt to stick up in the air as you exercise (with the exception of the downward-facing dog exercise in yoga). When you're doing an exercise such as the push-up or plank, if your butt is in the air, it means that you're relying more on your legs instead of your abdominals to stabilize your torso. In the case of certain machine exercises, sticking your butt up in the air means you're not isolating the correct muscle group.

Using the leg curl machine the wrong way

Watch people use the leg curl machine and you'll see that as they kick their legs toward their butt, their hips lift off the support pad, and their butt sticks up about 2 inches. This mistake is subtle, but it's a sneaky way of taking work away from your hamstrings and transferring the effort to your hip muscles, allowing the hamstrings to avoid doing the work that they need to do to get stronger. See photo A of Figure 9-6.

Using the leg curl machine the right way

To prevent your hips from popping off the pad, raise your upper thighs just a hair off the pad before you bend your knees for the kick upward. In this position, you feel your hamstrings working a lot harder. See photo B of Figure 9-6.

Figure 9-6:
Don't let
your hips
pop off the
support pad.

Exaggerating the Row

If you sit hunched over in a chair most of the day, you're a good candidate for goofing up the seated cable row, described in Chapter 11.

Rowing the wrong way

One common mistake found in rowing is rounding your back or allowing your shoulders and neck to droop forward. This slumped posture puts your neck and lower back in a pressure cooker. Another problem: leaning way back like someone involved in a game of tug of war. See photo A in Figure 9-7.

Rowing with poor posture reinforces bad postural habits. Rather than becoming more fit, you're risking back injury and practicing bad posture. What you train is what you get, according to specificity of training. Train with good posture to develop good posture.

Rowing the right way

Sit up tall with your abdominals pulled in. Your upper body, from the top of your head to your belly button, should be perpendicular to the floor. Bend your knees as much as you need to in order to maintain this posture. Allow your arms to stretch fully out in front of you without losing that perpendicular posture. Then when you pull the bar toward your chest, sit up even taller and bring your hands into your body, just below your chest. Squeeze your shoulder blades together as you pull, and drive your elbows straight back behind you. See photo B in Figure 9-7.

Sitting Up Improperly from a Weight Bench

Liz was spotting a woman who was performing a textbook-perfect set of the dumbbell chest fly (see Chapter 12). The set was truly a thing of beauty — until right after her final repetition. Suddenly she extended her arms straight out, lowered the weights toward the floor, opened her hands, and let the weights roll off her palms. She then jerked herself upright and popped up off the bench. Overall, she managed to make about a half dozen mistakes on movements that weren't even part of the actual exercise. Realize that you can't let your guard down until you've safely gotten yourself out of the exercise position.

Figure 9-7:
Don't lean
way back
like
someone
involved in a
game of tug
of war.

Sitting up the wrong way

In this book, many exercises that you perform while lying on your back on the floor or on a weight bench are shown. When you sit up after doing these exercises, don't jerk straight back up into a sitting position, especially if you're holding weights. When you get up suddenly, you can adversely impact your blood pressure and experience a moment of dizziness. You want to avoid any type of sudden or jerky movement when you're holding weight because the weight can create momentum and cause you to lose control over your movements. Another no-no: bringing your arms straight out to the sides and dropping the weights, or twisting to either side to drop a weight. See photo A of Figure 9-8. You never want to drop weights. You always want to put weights down slowly and with control to avoid hurting yourself and others.

Sitting up the right way

To protect your lower back when you get up off the floor, roll to the side and then use both arms to push up into a sitting position. Or you can hug one knee into your chest and gently rock yourself up. After performing an exercise involving dumbbells, such as the chest fly, bring the weights down into your chest, and then roll up. (When you begin the exercise, do the opposite: Bring the weights into your chest and rock yourself back on the bench.) See photo B of Figure 9-8.

Figure 9-8: After an exercise, don't jerk straight back up into a sitting position, especially if you're holding weights.

Spotting Too Much — Or Not Enough

Most weight-training mistakes made don't affect anyone but you. However, if you mess up while spotting someone else, you may be putting your friend (or soon-to-be ex-friend) at risk for injury. Or, at the very least, you may be depriving your buddy of an enjoyable and effective workout. When acting as a spotter, you need to walk that fine line between not helping enough and getting too involved.

Spotting the wrong way

Don't zone out while you're spotting someone. Spotting isn't the time to contemplate peacekeeping solutions in the Middle East. If your buddy poops out in the middle of a set and you're even a split second too late to grab the weight, your friend may get clunked on the head, chest, or some other body part. Your spottee may also tear a muscle or ligament while trying to do your job for you (that is, to save the weight from crashing). Pay attention. You would want the same courtesy paid to you. See Figure 9-9.

Figure 9-9:
When acting as a spotter, walk that fine line between not helping enough and getting too involved.

Spotting the right way

Tune out everything in the universe other than your spottee. Put your hands in the right place (see Chapter 5 for details), and watch your buddy like a soldier guarding Buckingham Palace. Don't wait for your spottee to scream, "Dude! Where are you?!"

Carrying a Weight Plate Too Casually

We often listen to exercisers gripe that their backs hurt after they perform the bench press. Yet when we go to check out their technique, it looks impeccable. We're baffled — until these people pop off the bench, slide the weight plates off the bar, and put them back on the weight tree. Ah ha! Mystery solved. It's not the bench press or any other exercise that's giving them an aching back; the way exercisers carry around those big, heavy weight plates is the culprit. (See Chapter 4 for descriptions of weight plates and weight trees.)

Carrying a weight plate the wrong way

Sometimes we see people carrying weight plates around the gym floor as if the plates were super-size Frisbees. Other lifters tuck plates under their arms as if they're clutching a purse. Or they hold the plate on the edge of their fingertips with a straight arm and locked elbow, as if they're carrying a bowling ball.

Carrying around a lot of weight with one hand tied behind your back may be the ultimate display of macho, but even if you're a big, strapping fellow, this sort of behavior puts your body in a terribly unbalanced position because you're adding all the weight only on one side of your body. Your elbows and shoulders bear more of the burden than they're designed to handle. See photo A of Figure 9-10.

Carrying a weight plate the right way

Hold the plate close to your chest with both hands. Stand as close as you can to the bar, line up the hole in the plate with the bar, and then slide the plate on. Don't just extend your arms out straight and toss the plate as if you're performing some sort of ring-tossing circus act. When you pick up a plate off the floor or from a low rung on a weight tree, bend your knees as if you're doing a squat, bring the weight in close to your chest, and stand up using your leg muscles, not your lower back. All this advice goes for lighter weights, too. See photo B of Figure 9-10.

Figure 9-10:
Always hold weight plates close to your chest with both hands.

Part III
Tackling the Exercises

The 5th Wave By Rich Tennant

YOUR WEIGHTS ARE TOO LIGHT...

...if on any one routine you're doing more than 700 repetitions...

...if you can use them to play fetch with your toy poodle...

...if they keep getting stolen and used as body ornaments by a sickly street gang...

...if they keep getting lost in your wife's/husband's jewelry/cuff link drawer.

YOUR WEIGHTS ARE TOO HEAVY...

...if any part of your body explodes during a routine...

...if people refuse to spot for you without the aid of a forklift...

...if anywhere on your weights there appears the name of a ship and the word, "BALLAST"...

...if transporting them requires a vehicle with flashing lights and a flat bed.

In this part . . .

Part III is the meat and potatoes of this book. It's where you determine exactly how to tone those triceps or build that butt. The format for the exercise instructions is introduced first, and you're familiarized with the muscles you'll be working. Each chapter focuses on one body area.

You'll have a high school flashback when you receive a brief physiology lesson for each of your major muscle groups. Riveting! And a vocabulary section (important slang) helps you become seasoned so you can go around saying things like "I had a killer lat and delt workout." After that, exercises that use both free weights and machines are shown. Throughout this part of the book, you're reminded to use good form and to prevent injuries. Follow the instructions like "Don't arch your back," "Tighten your abdominals," and "Don't eat too much bread, or you'll spoil your dinner." Just kidding on that last one.

Chapter 10

Interpreting the Exercise Instructions

In This Chapter

▶ Introducing you to the exercises

▶ Explaining pet phrases

▶ Incorporating breathing techniques into your routine

Don't be alarmed by the fact that an entire chapter is devoted to how to read the exercise instructions. This doesn't mean that the instructions are complicated. You won't feel like you're struggling through a tax preparation guide or one of those do-it-yourself shelving manuals. This chapter simply introduces some basic terms used frequently in this part of the book. You also determine what the differences are between the various exercise options.

Tackling the Basic Info

For every muscle group presented in this book (such as back, chest, or shoulders), first we show the non-machine exercises — moves involving dumbbells, barbells, or no equipment at all. Next are exercises that do require weight machines. Explanations include at least one machine per muscle group (except the abdominals, for reasons we explain in Chapter 15). Figures 10-1 and 10-2 show you the major muscle groups in your body.

If we tried to show you every exercise in existence, this book would be thicker than the unabridged edition of the Oxford English Dictionary. So, we've chosen to present the most common, basic exercises — classic moves that not only are safe and appropriate for beginners but also are standard moves for veteran exercisers. New to this edition is Chapter 17, which features moves that strengthen the core muscles. Core muscles stabilize the torso, improve posture, and help prevent back pain.

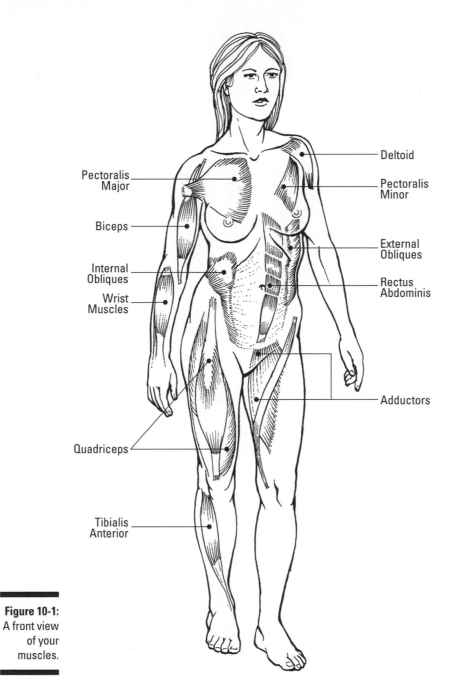

Pectoralis Major

Biceps

Internal Obliques

Wrist Muscles

Quadriceps

Tibialis Anterior

Deltoid

Pectoralis Minor

External Obliques

Rectus Abdominis

Adductors

Figure 10-1:
A front view
of your
muscles.

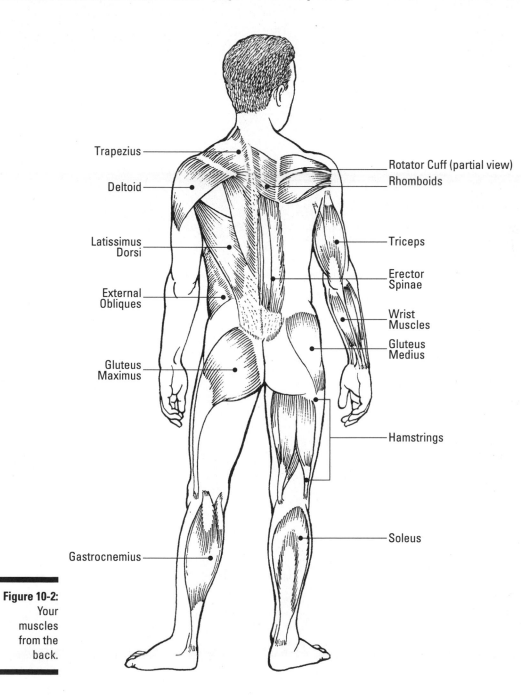

Trapezius

Deltoid

Latissimus Dorsi

External Obliques

Gluteus Maximus

Gastrocnemius

Rotator Cuff (partial view)

Rhomboids

Triceps

Erector Spinae

Wrist Muscles

Gluteus Medius

Hamstrings

Soleus

Figure 10-2:
Your muscles from the back.

If you have knee, hip, back, or other orthopedic problems, look for the Joint Caution icon; this icon alerts you to exercises that you may want to avoid or modify. Instructions are given on how to adjust many of the exercises to work around your joint problems.

After presenting each exercise, the "Other options" section describes a number of other versions of the workout. Some of the options are easier than the basic version, requiring less coordination or strength. Others are tougher. Some options, neither easier nor harder than the basic version, simply work the muscle from a different angle.

After you feel comfortable with the basic version, expand your horizons by experimenting with the options. You may discover, for example, that you prefer to do the dumbbell shrug (explained in Chapter 11) with a barbell instead. Or maybe you enjoy both versions and want to alternate them in your workouts. However, don't get overly enthusiastic and try all options of an exercise in a single workout. Experiment with one or two new versions each time you work out, and concentrate on mastering the movement.

Explaining Our Favorite Phrases

Everyone has pet phrases. Parents like to say "Eat your vegetables!" and "Don't forget to take a jacket!" (even if their children are 45 years old). Dentists like to say "Don't forget to floss!" and "Brush in all the corners!" Fitness experts have their favorite sayings, too, such as "Pull in your abdominals!" These phrases aren't meant to annoy you (we'll leave that job to parents and dentists) but to keep your joints and muscles from getting injured and to make the exercises more effective. Here's a rundown of phrases used repeatedly in Chapters 11 through 17. Chances are, you'll hear these same phrases in exercise videos and classes and when you work out with a fitness trainer.

Pull in your abdominals

Place your hand over your belly button and gently pull your belly button in and away from your hand; that's what it feels like to pull in your abdominal muscles. Don't try to create a vacuum or suck your stomach into your ribs as if someone was going to punch you. Just hold your abs slightly in toward your spine. Tightening your abs helps hold your torso still when you exercise and keeps your back from arching or rounding — mistakes that can lead to back injury.

Stand up tall with square shoulders and a lifted chest

Keep your head centered between your shoulders, and don't round your shoulders forward. In other words, avoid slouching. Your chest should be comfortably lifted, not forced; you needn't stand like a soldier at attention. Avoid arching your upper back and pushing your ribs forward.

Don't lock your joints

The phrase "Don't lock your joints" refers to your elbows and your knees. *Locking a joint* means straightening it so completely that it moves past the point where it normally sits at rest. For example, you don't usually stand with your quadriceps (front thigh muscles) as tight as can be with your kneecaps pulled up; that's a locked knee. Locking your knees isn't only bad news for your knee joints, but it also causes lower back pain. It can even lead to more serious injuries. One of our friends actually knew someone who passed out when he was singing at a choir concert because he locked his knees — he fell right off the back of the riser. And locking the knees is a way of cheating when you perform exercises in a standing position, such as the lateral raise (shown in Chapter 13) and the barbell biceps curl (check out Chapter 14).

Locking your elbows places excessive pressure on your elbow joints, tendons, and ligaments. Constant elbow locking causes *tennis elbow* (an inflammation of the elbow tendons), even if you've never held a tennis racket in your hand. Locking your elbows also contributes to *bursitis* through the rupturing of the *bursa* (little lubrication capsules) located in your joints. Bursitis results in swelling, pain, and tenderness at the elbow. Snapping your elbows also is a form of cheating because the weight is temporarily shifted off your muscle and on to the bone. When you snap your elbows, your muscles fail to get the proper workout.

Keep your shoulders and neck relaxed

If your shoulders are hunched up near your ears, you need to relax. Hunched shoulders may be linked to holding the phone to your ear or sitting at your computer all day long, absorbing workday stress. If you're prone to hunching, think about lengthening your shoulder blades, as if they're dropping down your back, and try to keep them there as you perform the exercise. Strengthening your shoulder stabilizer muscles, such as the mid-upper back and external rotators, improves your ability to keep your shoulders down.

Tilt your chin toward your chest

Tilt your chin just enough to fit your closed fist between your chest and your chin. This position lines up the vertebrae of your neck with the rest of your vertebrae. (Because your neck is a continuation of your spine, it should stay in the same general line as the rest of your vertebrae.) So don't tilt your chin back or drop it toward your chest like you do when you sulk. These two movements strain your neck and place excess pressure on the top vertebrae of your spine.

Don't shoot your knees past your toes

"Don't shoot your knees past your toes" and similar phrases are used often when describing butt and leg exercises, such as the squat and lunge (head to Chapter 16 for examples). If your knees are several inches in front of your toes, you're placing your knees under a great deal of pressure. Also, you probably have too much weight distributed on your toes and not enough on your heels, which means that the exercise doesn't strengthen your butt as effectively.

Don't bend your wrists

When you bend your wrists too far inward or outward (that is, when you don't keep your wrists in line with your forearms), you cut off the blood supply to the nerves in your wrists. If you do this frequently enough, you can give yourself a case of carpal tunnel syndrome. The phrases "Keep your wrist in line with your forearms, or keep your wrists flat," describe the same position.

Maintain proper posture

Proper posture is an all-encompassing phrase that includes everything that we've mentioned in this section. This phrase is used often because good posture is so important — and because our posture often goes down the tubes when we focus on lifting and lowering a weight.

Good posture isn't automatic for most of us, so give yourself frequent reminders. And if you exercise with correct posture, you'll train your muscles to hold themselves correctly in everyday life. Throughout these chapters, the Posture Patrol icon reminds you to maintain good posture. And Chapter 17 is entirely dedicated to exercises that improve posture. See Figure 10-3 for an example of good posture.

Figure 10-3:
For good posture, align ears, shoulders, hips, knees, and ankles.

Studying Breathing Techniques for Exercise

The exercise descriptions in this book don't include breathing instructions because too many extra instructions amounts to information overload. Nevertheless, proper breathing technique is important, so to spare you the overkill, we're only going to say this once. You'll thank us later. But don't forget to breathe. Promise? Okay. Here are the general rules:

- ✔ Inhale deeply through your nose to bring in a fresh oxygen supply during the less difficult part of an exercise (such as when you lower the weight during a bench press). Inhaling provides the spark of energy for your next repetition.

- ✔ Exhale deeply through your mouth during the most difficult part of the exercise, also known as the *exertion phase* or the *sticking point*. During the bench press (explained in Chapter 12), for example, pressing the bar up is the exertion phase, so exhale as the bar travels upward.

  Exhaling protects your lower back by building up pressure that acts as a girdle to hold your spine in place. Exhaling also ensures that you don't hold your breath so long that you pass out.

Before the hard-core weight lifting contingency sends irate letters, note that these breathing directions are for *non-maximal lifts*. World-class powerlifting isn't discussed here. If you plan to compete in powerlifting, you need to use a slightly different breathing technique than the one described above. Because we don't think that many of you plan to enter such competition (at least not immediately), we won't bore you with the details.

Chapter 11

Working Your Back

More than 80 percent of adults in North America experience back pain during their life. Back pain is the leading cause of disability from work in the United States. With this much back pain going around, you need to be proactive and strengthen your back to prevent pain and injury. Staying healthy and pain free will go a long way toward improving your quality of life. And a strong back is important for many daily activities, including recreation, fun, and work.

This chapter divides into two sections: upper back and lower back. Even though these muscle groups reside in close proximity to each other, they have different job descriptions and require different workout routines. Many upper back exercises involve lifting a fair amount of pounds; lower back exercises, on the other hand, require more subtle movements, usually without any free weights or machinery. You realize why you need to perform both types of exercises and which moves get you the best results.

Understanding Upper Back Muscle Basics

Pull up a chair and let's talk about your upper back muscles. There. You just used 'em. No, that wasn't a trick. In fact, you use your upper back muscles whenever you pull anything toward you, whether it's a piece of furniture, a stubborn golden retriever on a leash, or the mountain of chips you won at your Thursday night poker game.

Your upper back consists of several muscles (Figure 11-1 highlights the muscles of your upper back).

✔ *Latissimus dorsi (lats):* The largest muscles in your back run from just behind each armpit to the center of your lower back. Olympic swimmers, particularly those who swim butterfly, have well developed lats. These muscles give swimmers that V-shaped torso. The main purpose of your lats is to pull your arms (and anything in your hands) toward your body.

✔ *Trapezius (traps):* Above the lats are your two traps. Together, your traps look like a large kite that runs from the top of your neck to the edge of your shoulders and narrows down through the center of your back. Your traps enable you to shrug your shoulders (like when your spouse asks how you could've forgotten to pay the phone bill). More important, your lower traps stabilize your shoulders and help prevent shoulder injuries and your upper traps help you to move your head to the back, side, or to look behind you.

✔ *Rhomboids:* Your rhomboids cover the area between your spine and your shoulder blades. Along with your traps, you use your *rhomboids* for squeezing your shoulder blades together. You have to call them your *rhomboids,* because *boids* somehow never caught on. Most people who work long hours at computers or in other seated positions have overstretched and weak rhomboids.

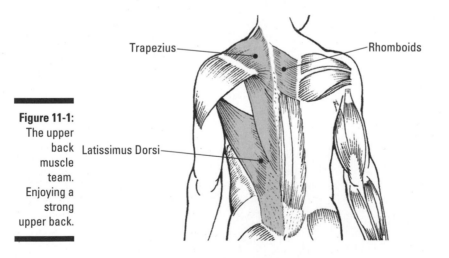

Trapezius——

——Rhomboids

Figure 11-1:
The upper back muscle team. Enjoying a strong upper back.

Latissimus Dorsi——

Strengthening your back muscles has important advantages.

✔ **Real-life benefits:** With a strong upper back, you'll find it easier to drag your kids into the dentist's office or lug your suitcases through endless airport terminals. You'll say goodbye to slouching as your posture improves and get rid of tension in your neck and shoulders.

✔ **Injury prevention:** Strong upper back muscles play a significant role in keeping your shoulders healthy. Your lats handle most of the work in pulling movements, so you don't overstress your shoulders. For example, well-developed upper back muscles could save you from injury when unfolding the sofa bed for a houseguest.

✔ **The "Feel Good" factor:** Upper back exercises make your back more broad, which, in turn, slenderizes your lower body. These exercises also improve your posture by helping you stand straighter and taller, open up your chest, and give up slumping as a pastime.

Getting an Upper Back Workout

Upper back exercises fall into three general categories: pulldowns and pull-ups, rows, and pullovers. Later in this chapter, you discover a variety of exercises in each category. For the most complete upper back workout, perform at least one exercise from each category, although you needn't do all these exercises in the same workout.

✔ **Pulldowns and pull-ups:** With a pulldown, you grab a bar attached to an overhead pulley and pull it down; with a pull-up, you grasp a bar above you and pull yourself up. If you exercise at home, use an exercise band to mimic the pulley machine and do the band lat pulldown (exercise bands are covered in Chapter 24). Pulldowns and pull-ups are grouped in one category because they work your back in the same way. Both types of exercises involve your lats, traps, and rhomboids, but they also rely heavily on your biceps, shoulders, and chest muscles.

If you're looking to develop a broader back and improve your posture, emphasize pulldowns and pull-ups. For example, you can do a pulldown with a band (see Chapter 24).

✔ **Rows:** What I am about to tell you may be shocking, but rowing exercises are similar to the motion of rowing a boat. (I know. You're amazed.) You may perform rows with a barbell or dumbbell, a set of machine handles, a bar attached to a low cable pulley, or an exercise band. Rowing exercises use the same muscles as pulldowns and pull-ups except that they don't involve your chest. Rows are particularly helpful if you want to find out how to sit up straighter (to perform a row correctly on a machine, you have to sit up tall).

✔ **Pullovers:** When you do a pullover, your arms move up and down in an arc, like when you pull an ax overhead to chop wood. Pullovers rely mainly on your lats, but they also call upon your chest, shoulder, and abdominal muscles. Like the other upper back exercises, pullovers help with posture. A pullover is an ideal transition exercise from a back workout to a chest workout. In other words, use a pullover as the last exercise of your back workout and as a prelude to your chest exercises because your chest will be warmed up.

Whether you're performing pulldowns, pull-ups, rows, or pullovers, remind yourself that these exercises first and foremost strengthen your back muscles, not your arms. Think of your arms merely as a link between the bar and your back muscles, which should do the bulk of the work. Concentrate on originating each exercise from the outer edges of your back. This bit of advice may be difficult to relate to at first, but as you get stronger and more sophisticated, your body awareness improves and you know exactly where you should feel each exercise.

Most of the upper back exercises in this chapter involve weight machines or cable pulleys. If you work out at home and you don't have a multigym (a home version of health club machinery, described in Chapter 6), use a rubber exercise band to mimic the pulley machine. See Chapter 24 for an example of a back exercise performed with a band.

Avoiding Mistakes When Working Your Upper Back

The upper back is one area where we see a lot of attempted heroics. With pulldowns and rows, people tend to pile on more weight than they can handle and end up trying to throw their entire body weight into the exercise to move the weight. This sort of behavior won't train your back muscles and may result in injury.

Follow these tips to avoid injury when training your upper back:

- **Don't rock back and forth or wiggle around.** In an effort to pull the weight toward them, many people squirm around to build up momentum, but that's the last thing you want; instead, rely on your own muscle power. If you find yourself shifting around in order to lift and lower the weight, drop down a few plates.

- **Don't lean too far back.** You may be able to lift more weight when you lean way back, but that's because you have better leverage and you're using your body weight to cheat, not because your back muscles get a better workout. A more upright posture ensures that your back muscles are in the prime position to do maximum work. Any time you pull something toward you, slide your shoulders down, squeeze your shoulder blades together, and sit up tall. With pulldowns, you can lean back ever so slightly, but for rows you need to be sitting as tall as you do when your flight attendant demands that you return your seat back to its full upright position with your seat belt fastened and tray table locked.

✔ **Don't pull a bar down behind your neck.** There are endless variations of the pulldown exercise, but one now frowned on by many exercise experts is the behind-the-neck pulldown. Critics of this exercise say that your arms twist so far back that your upper arm bones get jammed into your shoulder sockets, which could overstretch your ligaments and strain those delicate rotator cuff muscles we describe in Chapter 13. Unless you're a rock climber, an avid rower, or a swimmer who favors the butterfly stroke, front pulldowns will suffice.

Becoming Skilled at Upper Back Exercises

Upper back exercises that you can do with dumbbells and machines are previewed in this section. You'll move from dumbbell to barbell to machine exercises. Here's a preview of the upper back exercises shown in this chapter:

✔ One-arm dumbbell row

✔ Dumbbell shrug

✔ Machine row

✔ T-bar row

✔ Lat pulldown

✔ Cable row

✔ Assisted pull-up

One-arm dumbbell row

The one-arm dumbbell row targets your back but also emphasizes your biceps and shoulders.

Be careful with this exercise if you have lower back problems.

Getting set

Stand to the right of your weight bench and hold a dumbbell in your right hand with your palm facing in. Pull your abdominals in and bend forward from your hips so your back is arched naturally and roughly parallel with the floor. Bend your knees slightly. Place your left hand on top of the bench in line with your left shoulder for support and let your right arm hang down underneath your right shoulder. Tilt your chin toward your chest so your neck is in line with the rest of your spine. See photo A in Figure 11-2.

The exercise

Pull your right arm up, keeping it in line with your shoulder and parallel to the ceiling. Lift your arm until your hand brushes against your waist. Lower the weight slowly back down. See photo B in Figure 11-2.

Do's and don'ts

- ✔ DO remember that, although your arm is moving, this is a back exercise. Concentrate on pulling from your back muscles (right behind and below your shoulder) rather than just moving your arm up and down.

- ✔ DO keep your abs pulled in tight throughout the motion.

- ✔ DON'T allow your back to sag toward the floor or your shoulders to hunch up.

- ✔ DON'T jerk the weight upward.

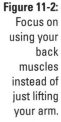

Figure 11-2: Focus on using your back muscles instead of just lifting your arm.

Other options

Rotation row: As you lift the dumbbell, rotate your arm so your palm ends up facing backward. This position gives the exercise a different feel and places extra emphasis on your biceps.

Barbell row: Place a barbell on the floor and stand about a foot away from it. With your knees bent, bend down and grasp the bar in an overhand grip with your hands a little wider than your shoulders. Pull your abs in tight and don't let your back arch. Keeping your hips bent so that your torso is at a 45-degree angle to the floor, pull the bar toward the lower part of your chest and then slowly lower it back down. You can also perform this exercise with an underhand grip or with your hands a bit closer together.

Dumbbell pullover

The dumbbell pullover is mainly a back exercise, but it also works your chest, shoulders, biceps, and abdominals.

If you have shoulder or lower back problems, you may want to skip this exercise because the dumbbell pullover requires raising your arms overhead, while stabilizing your spine.

Getting set

Holding a single dumbbell with both hands, lie on the bench with your feet flat on the floor and your arms directly over your shoulders. Turn your palms up so one end of the dumbbell is resting in the gap between your palms and the other end is hanging down over your face. Pull your abdominals in, but make sure that your back is relaxed and arched naturally. See photo A in Figure 11-3.

The exercise

Keeping your elbows slightly bent, lower the weight behind your head until the bottom end of the dumbbell is directly behind your head. Pull the dumbbell back up overhead, keeping the same slight bend in your elbows throughout the motion. See photo B in Figure 11-3.

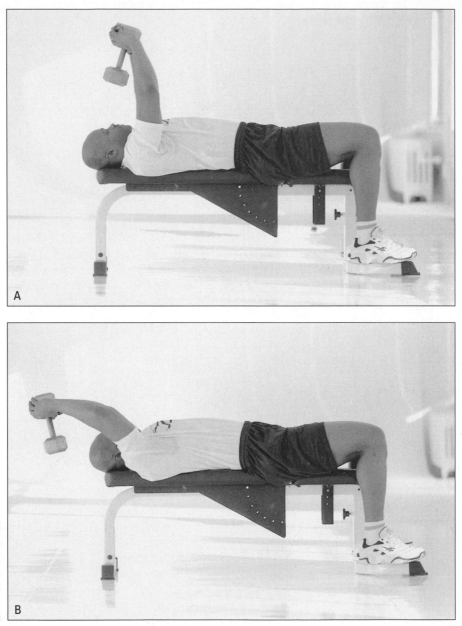

Figure 11-3:
Don't let
your back
arch off the
bench.

Do's and don'ts

- ✔ DO make sure that you grip the dumbbell securely.

- ✔ DO concentrate on initiating the movement from the outer wings of your upper back rather than simply bending and straightening your arms.

- ✔ DON'T arch your back up off the bench, especially as you lower the weight.

- ✔ DON'T lower the weight too far behind you.

Other options

Barbell pullover: Do this same exercise with a bar, holding the bar in the center with your palms facing up. Another variation on the same theme: Hold a dumbbell in each hand with your palms facing in.

Machine pullover: Many gyms have a machine that mimics the action of a dumbbell pullover while you're in a seated position.

Cross bench pullover (harder): Perform this exercise squatting in front of the bench and resting your shoulders on the top. Because your body isn't supported by the bench, you have to work extra hard to maintain good form; this variation kicks in all the deep muscles in the back and abs.

Dumbbell shrug

The dumbbell shrug is a small movement with a big payoff: It strengthens your shoulders and the trapezius muscles of your upper back.

Be careful if you're prone to neck problems.

Getting set

Stand tall and hold a dumbbell in each hand, arms straight down, palms in front of your thighs and facing in. Pull your abdominals in, tuck your chin toward your chest, and keep your knees relaxed. See photo A of Figure 11-4.

The exercise

Shrug your shoulders straight up toward your ears the same way you do if you don't know the answer to the $500 geography question on *Jeopardy!* Slowly lower your shoulders to the starting position. See photo B of Figure 11-4.

Figure 11-4:
Shrug your shoulders straight up instead of rolling them in a circle.

A   B

Do's and don'ts

✔ DO keep your neck and shoulders relaxed.

✔ DON'T roll your shoulders in a complete circle — a common exercise mistake that places too much stress on your shoulder joint.

✔ DON'T move body parts other than your shoulders.

Other options

Barbell shrug: Hold a bar with your hands shoulder-width apart and in front of your thighs, palms facing in. Do the exact same movement as in the basic version.

Shrug roll (harder): Shrug your shoulders upward as in the basic version, squeeze your shoulder blades together, and then lower them back down. This version brings the trapezius and rhomboids (two back muscles) into the mix.

Modified upright row: Stand tall with your feet hip-width apart and hold a barbell in front of you at waist level. Place your hands about 6 inches apart. Bend your elbows to raise the bar upward until the bar is just above the level of your bellybutton. Slowly return to the start.

We don't recommend the full upright row, which involves pulling your arms up until the bar is directly underneath your chin. This movement can be hard on your shoulder joints, rotator cuff, tendons, and ligaments.

Machine row

The machine row focuses on your back, with additional emphasis on your shoulders and biceps.

Take special care performing this exercise if you've had lower back or shoulder injuries.

Getting set

Sit facing the weight stack of the machine with your chest against the chest pad. Adjust the seat so your arms are level with the machine's handles and you must stretch your arms fully to reach them. This adjustment is important — and one that many people forget to make. If you can't fully straighten your arms when you grasp the handles, you'll end up using your arm muscles a lot more than your back muscles. Grasp a handle in each hand, slide your shoulders down, and sit up tall. See photo A in Figure 11-5.

The exercise

Pull the handles toward you until your hands are alongside your chest. As you bend your arms, your elbows should travel directly behind you, not out to the side. At the same time, squeeze your shoulder blades together. Slowly straighten your arms, feeling a stretch through your shoulder blades as you return the handles to their original position. See photo B of Figure 11-5.

Do's and don'ts

- ✔ DO sit up even taller as you pull the weight.
- ✔ DON'T lean back so far that your chest comes off the pad as you bend your arms.
- ✔ DON'T round your back or lean forward as you return the handles to the starting position.
- ✔ DON'T stick your neck forward as you pull the weight.

Other options

Other machines: Although each manufacturer has its own version of the machine row, the same basic rules apply. Depending on the brand, the handles may be parallel, perpendicular, or diagonal; some machines have all three grips. Experiment with different grips to get a different feel from this exercise.

Advanced machine row (harder): Do this exercise without keeping your chest on the chest pad. Without the support, you have to work harder to sit up straight.

A

B

Figure 11-5:
Sit up
tall as you
perform the
machine
row.

Lat pulldown

The lat pulldown is primarily a back exercise, although your shoulders and biceps also see some action. Try switching grips and attachments to give this exercise a different feel.

When engaging in the lat pulldown, be careful if you have shoulder or lower back problems.

Getting set

Before you start, sit in the seat and adjust the thigh pads so your legs are firmly wedged underneath the pads with your knees bent and your feet flat on the floor. Stand up and grasp the bar with an overhand grip and your hands about 6 inches wider than shoulder-width apart. Still grasping the bar, sit back down and wedge the tops of your thighs (just above your knee) underneath the thigh pads. Stretch your arms straight up, keep your chest lifted, and lean back slightly from your hips. See photo A in Figure 11-6.

The exercise

In a smooth, fluid motion, pull the bar down to the top of your chest. Hold the position for a moment, and then slowly raise the bar back up. When you've completed the set, stand up in order to return the weights to the stack. Don't just let go of the bar while you're seated — the sudden release causes the weight stack to come crashing down. See photo B in Figure 11-6.

Figure 11-6: Don't lean more than an inch or two back as you pull the bar down.

A   B

Do's and don'ts

- ✔ DON'T rock back and forth in an effort to pull down the weight.
- ✔ DON'T lean way back as you pull the weight down. Keep that inch-or-two lean that you had at the beginning of the movement.
- ✔ DON'T move so quickly that you jerk your elbows or shoulders.
- ✔ DON'T bend your wrists.

Other options

Changing your grip: Experiment with the width of your grip and the orientation of your palms to give this exercise a different feel. For example, use the triangle attachment for a **triangle-grip lat pulldown.** Or use an underhand grip (**reverse-grip lat pulldown**) and hold near the center of the bar for a pulldown that feels similar to a chin-up. Avoid pulling the bar behind your neck (see "Avoiding Mistakes When Working Your Upper Back" in this chapter for the reasoning). Experiment with other attachments of varying lengths and curves, such as the short straight bar and rope.

Cable row

The cable row strengthens your back, along with your biceps and shoulders.

Be careful with the cable row if you've had lower back or shoulder problems.

Getting set

Hook the short straight bar attachment onto a low pulley. Place a riser from a step bench (or box of similar length) directly against the base of the cable tower. (Some machines come with a foot bar so you don't need to add a box.) Sit facing the tower with your legs slightly bent and hip-width apart, and your feet firmly planted against the riser. Grasp the handle and straighten your arms out in front of your chest. Sit up as tall as you can, sliding your shoulders down, pulling your abdominals in and lifting your chest. See photo A in Figure 11-7.

The exercise

Sitting up tall, pull the handle toward the lower part of your chest, squeezing your shoulder blades together as you pull. Your elbows should travel straight back, arms brushing lightly against your sides as you go. Without stretching forward, straighten your arms slowly back to the start. See photo B in Figure 11-7.

Figure 11-7:
Feel this
exercise in
your back,
not just in
your arms.

Do's and don'ts

- ✔ DO feel this exercise in your back, not just in your arms. Concentrate on starting the pull with the outer edges of your back.
- ✔ DON'T arch or round your back.
- ✔ DON'T rock back and forth to help you lift and lower the weight.

Other options

Extended row: The basic version of this exercise is excellent for targeting the upper back muscles. However, you can strengthen your lower back at the same time by leaning forward a few inches at your hips as you stretch your arms out and by leaning back slightly as you pull the handle toward you. Some exercise purists scorn this version because it doesn't "isolate" your upper back, but the extended row works the upper and lower back work together and is great for people who do a lot of rowing or activities: weeding, dancing, or climbing. However, skip this version if you have a history of low back pain.

One-arm cable row: Attach a horseshoe handle and perform this row one arm at a time.

Assisted pull-up

The assisted pull-up targets your back, with additional emphasis on your shoulders and biceps.

Be careful if you have lower back or shoulder problems.

Getting set

Step up on the platform of an assisted pull-up machine (sometimes called a gravitron) and carefully kneel onto the kneepads. (Some versions require you to stand.) Grab the handles that place your palms facing forward and straighten your arms. Pull your abdominals in and keep your body tall. See photo A in Figure 11-8.

The exercise

Pull yourself up until your elbows point down and then slowly lower your body back down. See photo B in Figure 11-8.

Figure 11-8:
Don't cheat
by rocking
your body.

Do's and don'ts

- ✔ DO relax your shoulders so they don't hunch up by your ears.
- ✔ DON'T rock your body to help move you up and down.
- ✔ DON'T arch your back or round forward.
- ✔ DON'T dawdle at the bottom of the exercise. Move steadily until you finish your reps.

Other options

Different grips: Some assisted pull-up machines have a choice of wider or narrower grips. Experiment with your hand placement to see which ones you like best.

Bar pull-up (harder): Using a Smith machine or power cage, set the bar so that it is securely resting against the stops set in the center of the frame. Grasp the center of the bar with your hands a few inches apart and palms facing you. Kick your legs out in front of you so that your torso forms a 45-degree angle with the floor. Bend your arms and pull yourself upward until the top of your chest touches, or nearly touches, the bar. Slowly lower to the start position.

Understanding Lower Back Muscle Basics

Your lower back muscles have two main jobs: bending your spine backward and bracing your torso when you move some other part of your body. (Your lower back muscles perform this stabilizing job in tandem with your abdominal muscles, located directly in front of them.) The exercises in this section strengthen the moving function of the back. Chapter 17 focuses on the bracing function of the muscles with stabilization exercises. The main lower back muscles you need to know about are the *erector spinae.* Feel along either side of your spine just above your hips and you have a handle on your lower erector spinae. Figure 11-9 points out your lower back muscles.

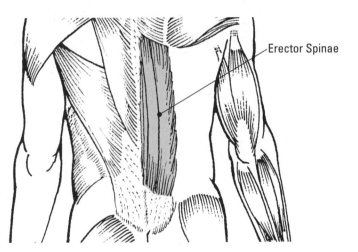

Figure 11-9:
A look at the lower back.

Erector Spinae

Enjoying a Strong Lower Back

Most lower back exercises — particularly those appropriate for beginners — don't involve free weights or machines. Usually, it's just you and the floor. Here's what you can accomplish without any equipment at all:

- ✔ **Real-life benefits:** Sitting puts your spine under a lot of pressure, much more pressure than if you stood all day, and particularly compresses your lower spine. That's why your lower back feels sore after a day in front of the computer. When your back muscles are weak, you tend to slouch or arch your back, which places the spine under even more stress.

In addition to strengthening and stretching your lower back on a regular basis, you should get up a few minutes every hour when you're sitting throughout the day.

✔ **Injury prevention:** Ironically, even people with chronic lower back pain tend to neglect lower back exercises, often because they're afraid of inflicting even more damage. Also, while people have gotten the message that abdominal exercises help alleviate back pain, many don't realize that lower back exercises are equally important in this pursuit. When one of these sets of muscles is stronger or more flexible than the other, your posture is thrown off kilter, and you're more prone to back pain. This scenario is common.

✔ **The "feel good" factor:** Strengthening your lower back helps you stand up straight, which, in turn, makes you look taller, as much as 5 pounds slimmer, and gives you a more confident, commanding presence.

Getting a Lower Back Workout

We often take for granted the role that our lower back muscles play in our everyday mobility. So, while your lower back muscles need to be strong, they also need to be flexible.

This balance between strength and flexibility is particularly important with your lower back. That's why we include the pelvic tilt, which both strengthens and lengthens out the muscles attached to your spine. With the widespread incidence of lower back pain among adults, everyone should practice this exercise. The same goes for back extension exercises.

However, if you're experiencing back pain right now or have a history of back trouble, check with your doctor before performing any extension exercises.

When you do a lower back exercise, you should feel a mild pull or pressure build within the muscle, *not* a sharp pain. If you do feel a piercing pain, back off. Review the exercise description to make sure that you haven't pushed your body too far and then try the movement again. If you still feel pain, seek medical advice before proceeding.

You may feel a dull ache in your back a day or two after you've worked your lower back. This is normal. But if the pain is sharp and so debilitating that your most upright posture looks like you're trying to duck under a fence, you've either pushed yourself too far or you have a back problem.

Avoiding Mistakes When Training Your Lower Back

Few people make mistakes when they do lower back exercises. That's because few people actually take the time to do these exercises, which is a big mistake in itself. Here are a few other common errors:

- ✔ **Bending too far back.** On back extensions, raise your body just a few inches, and lengthen out as much as you can. With pelvic tilts, the point is to isolate your lower back muscles while keeping your back planted on the floor.

- ✔ **Performing back exercises quickly. Always perform your back exercises slowly and carefully.** If you race through them, you may cause the very back problems you're trying to prevent.

Becoming Skilled at Lower Back Exercises

In this section, you follow two lower back exercises, along with several variations of the exercises:

- ✔ Pelvic tilt
- ✔ Back extension

Pelvic tilt

The pelvic tilt is a subtle move that focuses on your lower back, but also emphasizes your abdominals. This is a good exercise to do if you have a history of lower back problems. The pelvic tilt restores mobility to tight or stiff muscles and it heightens body awareness of the muscles of the lower back. It is also a great warm-up exercise for more strenuous core training.

Getting set

Lie on your back with your knees bent and feet flat on the floor about hip-width apart. Rest your arms wherever they're most comfortable. Start with your pelvis in a level position with the natural curve in your lower spine. See photo A in Figure 11-10.

The exercise

As you exhale, draw your abdominals in toward your spine and gently press your back down, tilting your pelvis backward. Don't tilt your head up and back or hunch your shoulders. As you inhale, return your pelvis to a level position. See photo B in Figure 11-10.

Do's and don'ts

  ✔ DO keep your head, neck, and shoulders relaxed.

  ✔ DON'T lift your lower back off the floor as you tilt your pelvis up.

  ✔ DON'T arch your back off the floor when you lower your hips back down.

Other options

Chair tilt (easier): Lie on your back and place your heels up on the seat of a chair with your knees bent at a right angle and thighs perpendicular to the floor. Then perform the exercise exactly as the basic version.

Bridge (harder): At the top of the pelvic tilt, continue peeling your spine off the floor until only your shoulder blades and shoulders remain on the floor. Work hard to keep your abdominals pulled inward to prevent your back from sagging. Hold a moment and slowly lower your body downward.

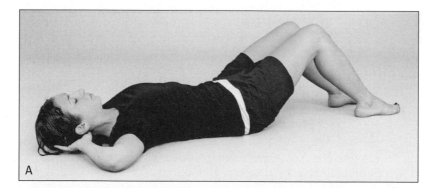

Figure 11-10: Don't lift your upper body as you tilt your pelvis back.

Back extension

The back extension strengthens your lower back muscles. Performing this exercise on a regular basis may help reduce lower back pain.

Use caution if you have a history of back problems or if your lower back is bothering you right now.

Getting set

Lie on your stomach with your forehead on the floor, arms straight out in front of you, palms down, and legs straight out behind you. Pull your abs in, as if you're trying to create a small space between your stomach and the floor.

The exercise

Lift your right arm and left leg a couple of inches off the floor and stretch out as much as you can. Hold this position for five slow counts, lower back down, and then repeat the same move with your left arm and right leg. Continue alternating sides until you've completed the set. See Figure 11-11.

Do's and don'ts

- ✔ DO exhale as you lift and inhale as you lower.

- ✔ DO pretend as if you're trying to touch something with your toes and fingertips that's just out of reach.

- ✔ DO pay special attention to how your lower back feels.

- ✔ DON'T lift up higher than a few inches.

- ✔ DON'T arch your lower back.

Other options

Sequential back extension (easier): If the basic version of the back extension bothers your lower back, lift and lower your right arm, and then lift and lower your left leg.

Kneeling opposite extension (easier): Kneeling on your hands and knees, extend your right arm out in front of you and your left leg out behind you. This version places less stress on the lower back and is an excellent modification for those new to lower back training and those who feel lower back discomfort when doing back extension exercises.

Same-side back extension (harder): Do the same exercise while lifting your right arm and right leg at the same time.

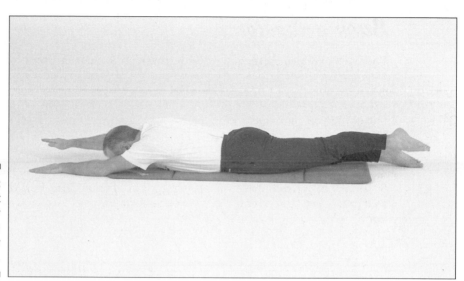

Figure 11-11:
Don't lift your arms or legs more than a few inches.

Chapter 12

Working Your Chest

Many male gym rats make the mistake of overtraining their chests to the point that they create a "gorilla" posture. Their arms hang awkwardly in a rounded horseshoe position and their palms face backward. In contrast, many women avoid chest exercises with the mistaken impression that they belong to the exclusive domain of bench-pressing men.

When it comes to chest exercises, you need to find a happy medium. In this chapter, you realize the importance of chest exercises and why these exercises won't transform you into Pamela Anderson Lee or Arnold Schwarzenegger. Discover tips on choosing the order to perform your chest exercises, and avoid the most common mistakes people make when working their chest muscles.

Understanding Chest Muscle Basics

The technical name for chest muscles is the *pectorals,* but you can shorten the term to *pecs.* You have two pec muscles:

✔ **Pectoralis major:** The pec major is a skeletal muscle that draws the arm inward and rotates it. This muscle enables you to give hugs. Whenever you pledge allegiance, your hand is covering the meat of the pectoralis major.

✔ **Pectoralis minor:** The pec minor moves the scapula forward and down and also raises the ribs. This muscle resides underneath the pec major.

Figure 12-1 shows the location of your pectorals. With the help of other muscles, such as your shoulder muscles and triceps, your pecs are in charge of a variety of pushing and hugging movements.

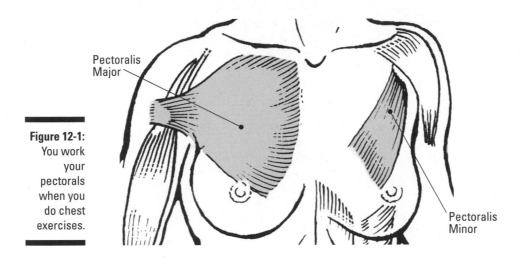

Pectoralis
Major

Pectoralis
Minor

Figure 12-1:
You work
your
pectorals
when you
do chest
exercises.

Enjoying Strong Pecs

This chapter may be the first time you've given your chest muscles any thought, but you've been depending on them your whole life to push things around. Now that you'll be performing chest exercises, you can be pushier than ever. Here's how you profit from training your pecs:

- ✔ **Real-life benefits:** You have more oomph when you push a lawn mower or a full shopping cart with two kids hanging off the end — or when you wrap your arms around Mr. Ted at Thanksgiving after he's eaten an entire pumpkin pie.

- ✔ **Injury prevention:** Your chest muscles attach to your shoulder joint. So with strong pecs, you're less likely to injure your shoulders while rearranging your furniture or pushing your car out of a mudhole.

- ✔ **The feel good factor:** Chest exercises may make a woman's breasts appear perkier, although keep in mind that these exercises won't transform any woman from an AA cup to a DDD cup or vice versa. As for men: Pec training makes your chest fuller. However, both sexes need to maintain realistic expectations about chest exercises.

Getting a Chest Workout

You can change the feel and focus of many chest exercises by adjusting the angle of the bench you use. (See Chapter 4 for descriptions of various benches.) Performing chest exercises on a flat bench emphasizes those fibers in the center of your chest. When you adjust the bench a few degrees to an incline position, you shift the focus of the exercise to the fibers in your upper chest and shoulder muscles. Doing the opposite — adjusting the bench to a decline position — concentrates the work on the lower fibers of the chest. By the way, decline exercises are probably the least important category of chest exercises because they work a relatively small portion of the pecs.

We won't be showing you how to operate one popular chest machine: the *Pec Deck.* You sit with your arms spread apart, each arm bent and placed on a pad. You push the pads toward each other, as if you're clapping in slow motion. We think the Pec Deck should be renamed the *Pec Wreck,* or more accurately, the *Shoulder Wreck.* These machines place an enormous amount of pressure on the shoulder joint and rotator cuff and frequently lead to injury. What's more, they don't actually do much for your pec muscles. A safer and more effective alternative to the Pec Deck is the dumbbell chest fly (shown in this chapter).

Because your chest muscles are among the largest in your upper body, we suggest that you perform more sets of exercises with these muscles than with the smaller muscle groups of your arms. In general, we recommend:

- ✔ **Performing 3 to 12 sets of chest exercises per workout.** True beginners should start with one set.

  By the way, when we say 12 sets, we don't mean a dozen sets of the same exercise; you may want to do 3 or 4 (or more) different exercises. And, if you're like most people who sit during the day, you need to do more sets of back exercises than chest exercises to address any muscle imbalances and prevent slouching and a collapsed chest.

- ✔ **Beginning each exercise with an easy warm-up set.** Even powerlifters who bench-press 500 pounds often warm up with a 45-pound bar.

Which chest exercises should you do first? Experts argue this point, but let personal preference be your guide. Here are our recommendations:

- ✔ Perform free-weight exercises when you're fresh. These exercises require more concentration, strength, and control.

- ✔ Execute flat-bench exercises before incline or decline exercises. Experiment with the order of exercises for a couple of weeks until you come up with a sequence that works for you.

- ✔ Change the sequence from time to time. Changing it up challenges your muscles differently. If you always do the chest fly before the dumbbell chest press, for example, you may never realize your true dumbbell press potential because your chest muscles are always tired by the time you get to that exercise.

- ✔ Perform 8 to 15 reps.

Determining your *one-rep max* — that is, the maximum amount of weight you can lift once — is somewhat of an ancient gym tradition with the bench press. Don't try this until you've been lifting weights for a month or two, and don't attempt to *max out* more often than once a week. In fact, some experts believe that maxing out once a month brings better results. When you do attempt a maximum weight, make sure that you have a *spotter* (see Chapter 5 for tips on how to be spotted). If you're going for your one-rep max, do a few warm-up sets, gradually increasing the weight.

Avoiding Mistakes When Pumping Your Pecs

One morning Liz was working at a gym when a member came up and casually mentioned that another member needed help on the bench press. Liz strolled over to find this man trapped underneath a bar that apparently had been too heavy for his chest muscles to handle. "Caesar," she asked, "how long have you been there?"

"About 20 minutes," he replied.

Why hadn't he yelled for help? He was too embarrassed. The moral of the story: Safety is more important than lifting heavy weights.

In addition to lifting the proper amount of weight, take the following precautions when working your chest:

- ✔ **Don't *lock* your elbows.** In other words, don't straighten your arms to the point that your elbows snap. This arm extension puts too much pressure on the elbow joints and leads to *tendonitis* or inflammation of the elbow joint itself. When you straighten your arms, keep your elbows slightly relaxed.

- ✔ **Don't arch your back.** In an effort to hoist more poundage, some people arch their backs so severely that there's enough room between their back and the bench for a Range Rover to drive through. Sooner or later, this position causes a back injury. Plus, you're doing nothing to strengthen your chest muscles. Instead, you're overstraining your lower back.

- ✔ **Don't flatten your back.** In a sincere effort not to cheat, many people do the exact opposite of overarching their backs — they force their lower backs into the bench. This posture is equally bad for your back. When you lie down, make sure that a slight gap exists between your lower back and the bench, reflecting the natural arch of your lower back.

✔ **Don't lift your shoulder blades off the bench or backrest.** If you do this, your shoulders bear too much weight — without any support from the bench. This error is subtle but one that may be costly for your shoulder joint.

✔ **Don't stretch too far.** When you lie on your back and perform the bench press, you may be tempted to lower the bar all the way to your chest. Similarly, when you perform a push-up, you may want to lower your body all the way to the floor. Don't. Instead, follow the instructions we provide for these and similar chest exercises.

Becoming Skilled at Chest Exercises

If you're following the chest exercises laid out in this chapter, you'll be performing them in order of free weight to machine exercises. Here's a glance at the chest exercises featured in this chapter:

✔ Modified push-up

✔ Bench press

✔ Dumbbell chest press

✔ Incline chest fly

✔ Vertical chest press machine

✔ Cable crossover

✔ Assisted dip

Modified push-up

The modified push-up strengthens your chest muscles, with additional emphasis on your shoulders and triceps.

Be extra careful if you have lower back, shoulder, elbow, or wrist problems.

Getting set

Lie on your stomach, and bend your knees. Bend your elbows and place your palms on the floor a bit to the side and in front of your shoulders. Straighten your arms and lift your body so that you're balanced on your palms and the part of your thighs just above your knees. Tuck your chin a few inches toward your chest so that your forehead faces the floor. Tighten your abdominals. See photo A in Figure 12-2. Don't cross your ankles like in photos C and D of Figure 12-2. Use your inner thigh muscles to keep your legs parallel.

The exercise

Bend your elbows and lower your entire body at once. Instead of trying to touch your chest to the floor, lower only until your upper arms are parallel to the floor. Push back up. See photo B in Figure 12-2.

Do's and don'ts

- ✔ DO keep your abdominal muscles pulled in tight throughout the exercise so that your back doesn't arch like a swaybacked horse; otherwise, you're begging for a lower back injury.

- ✔ DO bring your arms to a full extension.

- ✔ DON'T lock your elbows at the top of the arm extension.

- ✔ DON'T do the dreaded *head bob*. That's when you dip your head toward the floor without moving any other part of your body. Talk about a giant pain in the neck!

Other options

Wall push-up (easier): Stand a few feet away from a wall and place your palms flat on the wall slightly wider than your shoulders. Bend your elbows and lean into the wall. Then press yourself away from the wall by straightening your arms.

Incline push-up: This version is easier than the modified push-up but harder than the wall push-up. Follow the same setup as the basic version of this exercise, but place your hands on top of a step bench that has two or three sets of risers underneath.

Military push-up (harder): Lie facedown with your legs straight out behind you. Bend your elbows and place your palms on the floor a bit to the side and in front of your shoulders. Straighten your arms and lift your body so you're balanced on your palms and the underside of your toes. Tuck your chin a few inches toward your chest so your forehead faces the floor. Tighten your abdominals. Bend your elbows and lower your entire body at once. Instead of trying to touch your chest to the floor, lower only until your upper arms are parallel to the floor. Push back up.

Negative push-up (easier): This version is harder than the modified push-up but easier than the military push-up. Only perform the lowering phase of the military push-up. Slow the movement down and try to lower yourself in five counts. Lower your knees to the ground and follow the modified version when you push yourself up.

Don't cross your feet

Lower your body
in a straight line.

Bench press

The bench press, crowned the king of all chest exercises by bodybuilders,
primarily works your chest muscles, with plenty of emphasis on your shoulders and triceps, too.

You may want to try a modified version of this exercise — or avoid it
altogether — if you have lower back, shoulder, or elbow problems.

Getting set

Lie on the bench with your feet flat on the floor or up on the bench if the
bench is too tall. Grip the bar so your arms are evenly spaced a few inches
wider than shoulder-width apart. Your upper arms should be slightly above
parallel to the floor. Tuck your chin toward your chest and pull your abdominals in tight, but don't force your back into the pad, or overarch it. Lift the
bar off the rack and push it directly up over your shoulders, straightening
your arms without locking your elbows. See photo A in Figure 12-3.

The exercise

Lower the bar until your elbows are slightly below your shoulders. The bar may or may not touch your chest — this depends on how long your arms are and how big your chest is. Press the bar back up. See photo B in Figure 12-3.

Do's and don'ts

- ✔ DO remember to breathe. Exhale as you press the bar up, and inhale as you lower it.

- ✔ DON'T cheat. In other words, if you have to wiggle around or arch your back in order to hoist the bar, you're not doing much for your chest, but you're asking for lower back injuries.

- ✔ DON'T press the bar up too high; keep your elbows relaxed and your shoulder blades on the backrest throughout the exercise.

Other options

Towel chest press (easier): Roll up a large bath towel and place it across your chest. Lower the bar until it touches the towel and then press back up. This variation is good if you have shoulder problems because it reduces the range of motion and lessens the stress on the shoulder joint.

Incline bench press: Incline the bench a few inches and then do the exercise as described above. This version emphasizes the upper fibers of your pecs and shoulders.

Decline bench press: Do this exercise on a decline bench, with your head lower than your feet. This requires a special decline version of the bench press station. Some bench press stations can set flat, incline, or decline, whereas others are fixed permanently in the decline position.

Figure 12-3:
Don't
squirm
or arch
your back
in order
to hoist
the bar.

Don't lower your elbows much below shoulder level.

Dumbbell chest press

The dumbbell chest press closely mimics the bench press. This exercise works your chest muscles, along with your shoulders and triceps.

You may want to modify or avoid this exercise if you have shoulder, elbow, or lower back problems.

Getting set

Lie on the bench with a dumbbell in each hand and your feet flat on the floor (or up on the bench if it's more comfortable). Push the dumbbells up so your arms are directly over your shoulders and your palms face forward. Pull your abdominals in, but don't jam your back into the bench; don't let it arch way up, either. Tilt your chin toward your chest. See photo A in Figure 12-4.

The exercise

Lower the dumbbells down and a little to the side until your elbows are slightly below your shoulders. Push the weights back up, taking care not to lock your elbows or allow your shoulder blades to rise off the bench. See photo B in Figure 12-4.

Do's and don'ts

- ✔ DO allow your lower back to keep its natural arch so you have a slight gap between your lower back and the bench.
- ✔ DON'T contort your body in an effort to lift the weight; lift only as much weight as you can handle while maintaining good form.

Other options

Partial dumbbell press (easier): Lower the weights only about three quarters the distance of the basic version of this exercise. Try this version if you have elbow, shoulder, or rotator cuff problems.

Incline chest press: Perform this exercise on an incline bench, and you use less weight than when you perform a flat-bench press. You'll challenge the upper fibers of the pecs more.

Decline chest press: Do this exercise on a decline bench, with your head lower than your feet. The hardest part of this version is picking up and releasing the weights. Grab the weights while you're sitting up, hold them against your chest, and ease yourself into the decline position. When you're done with the exercise, gently ease the dumbbells off to either side to the floor. (Don't just drop them.) Better yet, ask someone to hand the weights to you at the start of the exercise and take them away when you're done.

Figure 12-4:
Don't lock your elbows at the top of the movement.

Incline chest fly

The incline chest fly primarily works your chest muscles, with lots of emphasis on your shoulder muscles. The exercise also places some emphasis on your triceps, although less than many other chest exercises.

Pay special attention to your form if you've had shoulder (especially rotator cuff), elbow, or lower back injuries.

Getting set

Incline the bench a few inches. Set the incline at 1-5 inches on the bench, depending on the bench. Holding a dumbbell in each hand, lie on the bench with your feet flat on the floor or on the bench, whichever feels more comfortable to you. Press the weights directly above your chest, palms facing each other. Tuck your chin to your chest to align your neck with the rest of your spine and maintain your natural back posture, neither arched nor flattened. See photo A of Figure 12-5.

The exercise

Spreading your arms apart so that your elbows travel down and to the sides, lower the weights until your elbows are just below your shoulders. Maintain a constant bend in your elbows as you lift the dumbbells back up. Imagine that you have a barrel lying on your chest, and you have to keep your arms wide to reach around it. See photo B in Figure 12-5.

Do's and don'ts

- ✔ DO feel a stretch in the outer edges of your chest. Hold a moment in the lowered position to feel it even more.

- ✔ DON'T forget to keep the bend in your elbows as you lower the weights. If your arms are too straight, you place excessive pressure on your elbows and shoulder joints.

- ✔ DON'T move your elbows any lower than specified or you risk damaging your shoulder and rotator cuff muscles.

Other options

Flat chest fly: Do the same exercise on a flat bench. The incline version emphasizes upper chest fibers, while the flat version calls in the middle and lower fibers as well.

Decline chest fly: Do this exercise on a decline bench, with your head lower than your feet. The hardest thing about this version is picking up and releasing the weights. Grab the weights while you're sitting up, hold them against your chest, and ease yourself into the decline position. When you're done with the exercise, gently ease the dumbbells off to either side to the floor. (Don't just drop them.) Better yet, ask someone to hand the weights to you at the start of the exercise and take them away when you're done.

Vertical chest press machine

The vertical chest press machine focuses on your chest muscles, with additional emphasis on your triceps and shoulders. Most vertical chest machines have more than one grip so that you can work your chest muscles in different ways.

Use caution if you have shoulder or elbow problems.

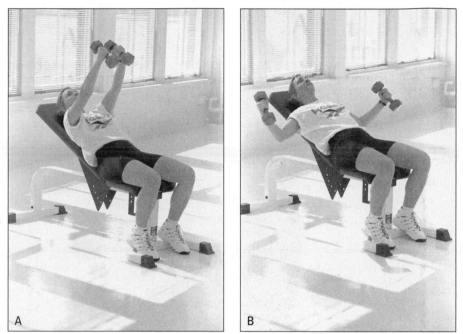

Figure 12-5:
Maintain the bend in your elbows as you lower the weights.

A

B

Getting set

Sit in the machine so the center of your chest lines up with the set of horizontal handlebars. Press down on the foot bar so that the handles move forward. Grip the horizontal handles. Straighten your arms, pushing the handles forward. Keep your abdominals tight so your upper back remains on the pad. See photo A in Figure 12-6.

The exercise

Remove your feet from the foot bar — you'll feel the weight of the stack transfer into your hands. Slowly bend your arms until your hands are just in front of your chest, and then push the handles forward until your arms are straight. When you've completed your set, put your feet back on the foot bar and let go of the handlebars *before* you lower the weight stack all the way down. See photo B in Figure 12-6.

Do's and don'ts

POSTURE PATROL

✔ DO keep your neck against the backrest.

✔ DON'T press so quickly that your elbows snap shut and your shoulders come up off the backrest.

Other options

Different angles: You may find chest machines that position you horizontally and at many angles between horizontal and vertical. Other machines work the left and right sides independently of each other; in other words, the left and right levers of the machine aren't connected to one another, so when you raise the weight, both sides of your body have to fend for themselves. Machines with independent action are a good alternative for those with left-right muscle imbalances or those who want to combine the safety of using a machine with the feel of using free weights. Try them all for variety to challenge your chest muscles differently.

Vertical grip (harder): Use the vertical handle of your chest machine. This grip factors out a lot of the help you get from your shoulders when using the horizontal grip.

Figure 12-6:
Don't press so quickly that your elbows snap shut.

A

B

Cable crossover

The cable crossover strengthens your chest muscles with emphasis on the shoulders as well.

Be careful if you have shoulder, elbow, or lower back problems.

Getting set

Set the pulleys on both towers of a cable machine to the top position. Clip a horseshoe handle (see Chapter 4 for description of all the different cable pulley handles) to each pulley. Stand between the towers with your legs comfortably apart and with one foot slightly in front of the other. Grasp a handle in each hand, palms facing down and slightly forward. Tighten your abdominals, lean slightly forward from your hips, and relax your knees. See photo A in Figure 12-7.

The exercise

Keeping a slight bend in your elbows, pull the handles down so one wrist crosses slightly in front of the other. Then slowly raise your arms up and out to the sides until your hands are level with your shoulders. See photo B in Figure 12-7.

Do's and don'ts

- ✔ DO exhale deeply before bringing your hands together.
- ✔ DO initiate the move from your chest; in other words, keep your shoulders, elbows, and wrists in the same position throughout.
- ✔ DON'T forget that slight forward lean: It takes the pressure off your lower back.

Other options

Flat bench cable fly: Set the cables to the lowest point on the towers, and place a flat bench in the center of the towers. Grasp a handle in each hand and lie on your back. Straighten your arms up directly over your shoulders and then spread your arms down and to the side until your elbows are just below shoulder level. This motion is the same one used in the flat bench dumbbell chest fly.

One-hand crossover: Do the basic cable crossover one arm at a time. Place the unused hand on your hip or hold onto the cable tower.

Assisted dip

The assisted dip primarily works your chest muscles with a lot of emphasis on your shoulders and triceps, too.

Use caution if you have elbow, shoulder, or lower back problems.

Getting set

For this exercise, deciding which plate to put the pin in can be confusing because you follow the exact opposite rule of every other exercise. In this case, you choose more plates if you want the exercise to be *easier* and fewer plates if you want the exercise to be *harder*. The more plates you select, the more your weight is counterbalanced during the exercise. For example, if you weigh 150 pounds and you place the pin in the plate marked 100, you have to lift only 50 pounds of your body weight. But if you put the pin into the plate marked 50, you have to lift 100 pounds.

After you've set your weight, step onto the platform of the assisted dip machine, and then carefully kneel on the kneepad or step on the foot bar as required by the machine at your gym. Grip the lower bars with your palms facing inward and straighten your arms. Pull your abdominals in and keep your body tall. See photo A in Figure 12-8.

The exercise

Lower your body until your upper arms are parallel to the floor and then push back up. See photo B in Figure 12-8.

Do's and don'ts

- ✔ DO relax your shoulders so they don't hunch up by your ears.
- ✔ DO keep your abdominals pulled in so your back doesn't arch.
- ✔ DO keep your neck aligned with the rest of your spine instead of allowing your chin to jut forward.
- ✔ DON'T explode back to the start and snap your elbows.
- ✔ DON'T lower your body farther than the point at which your upper arms are parallel to the floor.

Other options

Traditional dip (harder): Stand facing a dip station, and place your hands on the dip bars. Hop up so your feet are off the floor. Straighten your arms and lift your body upward. Keep your legs straight, or bend your knees slightly and cross one ankle over the other. Remain tall and relaxed with your abdominals pulled inward. Bend your elbows and lower your body only until your upper arms are parallel to the floor. Straighten your arms to lift yourself back up.

Negative-only dip (easier): If you find a traditional dip too difficult, perform only the *negative* phase: Use your muscle power to lower yourself and then jump up to the start after every repetition. However, when you jump up, take it easy on your elbows.

Weighted dip (harder): Do the basic version of the exercise with a special waist belt designed to hold a weight plate on the end of it.

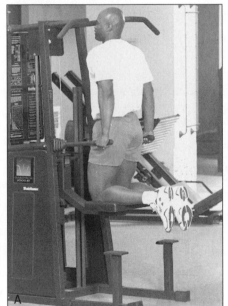 

Figure 12-8:
Don't explode back to the start and snap your elbows.

Chapter 13

Working Your Shoulders

*N*ext time the power goes out in your neighborhood, watch a police offi-cer stand in the middle of a four-way intersection and direct traffic. Or next time you're at the video store, rent *Saturday Night Fever* and watch John Travolta do the Hustle. Either way, you'll get an idea of what the human shoulder muscle can do. When you move your arms in virtually any direction — up, down, backward, forward, sideways, diagonally, in circles — your shoulders are in charge or at least involved. The ingenious design of your shoulder joint makes the shoulders one of the most mobile, versatile muscle groups in your body.

Unfortunately, their amazing capacity for movement also makes the shoul-ders, along with a nearby muscle group called the *rotator cuff,* particularly vulnerable to injury. This chapter shows you how to protect your shoulders by performing a variety of exercises. And if disco ever makes a comeback, you'll be duly prepared.

Understanding Shoulder Muscle Basics

Your shoulder muscles, officially, are called the *deltoids* or *delts*. These muscles rest like a cap on top of the shoulder (the best way to see this is to hold your arm out horizontally). The delts are made up of three sections:

- ✔ **Center:** The top or medial deltoid is on top of the shoulder. When this muscle contracts, you can lift up your arm.

- ✔ **Front:** The front or anterior deltoid lies in front. When it contracts, your arm moves inward toward the center front.

- ✔ **Back:** When the posterior deltoid in the back contracts, your arm moves back to the midline and can even move slightly farther back.

Your shoulder is able to move in so many directions because your shoulder joint is a *ball-and-socket joint:* The round head of your arm bone snaps neatly into your shoulder socket. Your hip is another ball-and-socket joint, but even that joint doesn't have the mobility that your shoulder does.

The *rotator cuff* is a group of four muscles that keep your arm from slipping out of its socket. They lie underneath your delts, performing their job in complete anonymity. Unfortunately, the rotator cuff muscles are so anonymous that many people don't even know that these muscles exist and, therefore, don't bother to train them. The only time they seem to get any recognition is when a professional baseball pitcher is sidelined for the season by a rotator cuff injury. Your rotator cuff muscles stabilize your shoulder joint and enable you to twist your arm while your elbow is straight, such as when you turn your palm to face forward and then backward. They also get into the act during throwing and catching motions and when you raise your arms above your head. Figure 13-1 illustrates the shoulder muscles.

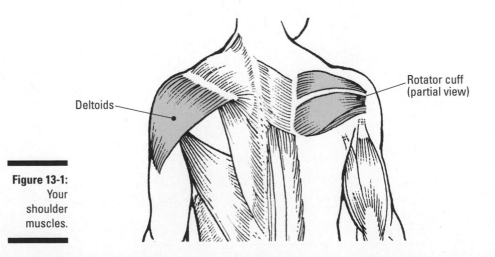

Deltoids

Rotator cuff
(partial view)

Figure 13-1:
Your
shoulder
muscles.

Enjoying Strong Shoulders

Your shoulders do a fair amount of work whenever you perform back and chest exercises, but performing exercises that single out your delts are also important for the following reasons:

✔ **Real-life benefits:** Strong shoulders make most arm movements easier, whether you're beaning your brother with a snowball, passing the potatoes across the table, or lifting your "a little too heavy" suitcase. Virtually every upper body exercise involves your shoulder muscles to some extent, so strengthening your shoulders enables you to lift heavier weights on chest and back exercises.

✔ **Injury prevention:** If your shoulders are weak, they're going to take a beating even if you perform chest and back exercises perfectly. Shoulder exercises also can prevent weekend-warrior type injuries, such as shoulder tears from swinging a sledgehammer, a torn rotator cuff from a softball tournament, or slapping a puck into the garbage can that serves as your hockey goal. If your shoulders are weak, you can even injure yourself while opening a dresser drawer.

✔ **The "Feel Good" factor:** Open up any bodybuilding magazine and you see headlines such as, "Grow Those Big Caps Even Bigger" or "Delts to Die For." Bodybuilders take their shoulder training seriously because they know that these muscles play a big part in their appearance, which, after all, is what bodybuilding is all about. Even if you don't want to build competition-level delts, you can still develop toned, shapely shoulders and reclaim your confidence to wear sleeveless shirts. (Although you should wear sleeveless shirts any time that you please. But a toned shoulder muscle may put a little pep in your sleeveless step.)

Getting a Great Shoulder Workout

You can strengthen your shoulder muscles in through four main types of shoulder movements (although dozen of ways exist). Perform the following exercises in the order that they're listed. In general, you lift the heaviest weights while pressing and the lightest weights while doing back fly movements.

✔ **Press:** Straighten your arms up over your head. Shoulder-press exercises work the entire shoulder muscle.

✔ **Lateral raise:** Raise your arms from your sides out to shoulder level. Lateral raises focus on the top and outside portions of the muscle.

- ✔ **Front raise:** Raise your arms from your sides directly in front of you. Front raises work the front and top of the deltoid.

- ✔ **Back fly:** Bend over from the hips as far as your flexibility permits to align your lift against the pull of gravity. Your chest should be as close to parallel to the ground as possible. Raise your arms out to the sides, working the rear and outside portions of the muscle.

From time to time, vary the order of your exercises to target your weaker muscles first and to provide a variety of stimulation for the muscle group to optimize conditioning. You needn't include all four types of exercises in each shoulder workout, but you should aim to perform each type on a regular basis so you develop evenly balanced shoulder muscles. (Later in this chapter, you find out several variations of each exercise, as well as a few other shoulder movements that don't fall into these categories.)

Perform shoulder exercises with free weights rather than machines. Often, the motion feels unnatural with the machine and places excess strain on the neck. For people of diverse sizes, such as petite women, aligning the machine properly can be hard, especially on a machine that's designed for a larger man's body.

Your rotator cuff muscles are mighty susceptible to injury. Protect these muscles to some degree by

- ✔ **Using stellar weight lifting form.** Follow the form guidelines within this chapter (and all chapters for that matter) for all upper body exercises.

- ✔ **Performing internal and external rotation exercises.** This chapter includes these two exercises that you can do with dumbbells.

- ✔ **Using band exercises.** Rotator cuff exercises that you can do at home or on the road with a rubber exercise band are found in Chapter 24.

Avoiding Mistakes When Training Your Shoulders

For many avid weight lifters, shoulder injuries don't happen overnight. We know countless people who've lifted for years, sometimes ignoring minor shoulder pain, and then — pop! — they're finished. Kaput. But what they perceive as a sudden injury is actually the result of years of overuse and poor form. Avoid the common mistakes to keep your shoulders strong and healthy.

Exaggerating the movement

If the instructions say lift the dumbbell "to shoulder height," don't lift the weight up to the ceiling, because lifting your arm to this unnatural angle adds undue stress to the joint with little advantage for increasing muscle tone. In other words, the risk of injury from lifting higher outweighs any minimal benefit of getting slightly stronger by increasing the size of the movement.

Arching your back

When you perform shoulder exercises while sitting on a vertical bench, make sure that you only have a slight gap between the small of your back and the backrest. Yes, arching your back gives you more leverage to lift heavier weights, but arching also cheats the muscles that you're targeting and puts your lower back in a vulnerable position — causing injury.

Rocking back and forth

When you perform shoulder exercises while standing, relax your knees and maintain a tall posture. Many people lock their knees and lean back, a posture that your lower back muscles don't appreciate. If you're moving any body parts other than your arms, you aren't targeting your shoulder muscles, and you're using too much weight.

Performing behind-the-neck shoulder exercises

You're likely to see lifters press a barbell overhead and then lower it behind the neck rather than in front. Some shoulder machines also involve behind-the-neck movements. Stay away from these exercises! They require a severe backward rotation of your arm, placing your shoulder and rotator cuff muscles in a weakened and precarious position. The movement also compresses the top of your arm bone into your shoulder socket, which tends to grind the bones and place your rotators under a great deal of additional stress. Always keep in mind that the benefit of any exercise should outweigh the risk.

Suzanne, who knows better than to perform these exercises, nevertheless did a set of behind-the-neck shoulder presses while training for a weight lifting competition. The next day she couldn't reach her left arm backward without wincing in agony — nor could she press a measly 5-pound dumbbell overhead without severe pain. Only after *seven* months of rest and rehab exercises did her rotator cuff injury begin to heal. Suzanne learned her lesson the hard way and now cringes when she sees people at her gym performing the very exercise that ruined her workouts for months.

Practicing Shoulder Exercises

Here's a preview of the shoulder exercises coming up:

- Dumbbell shoulder press
- Lateral raise
- Front raise
- Back delt fly
- Internal and external rotation
- Shoulder press machine
- Cable lateral raise

Dumbbell shoulder press

The dumbbell shoulder press targets the top and center of your shoulder muscles. This exercise also works your upper back and triceps.

Use caution if you have lower back, neck, or elbow problems.

Getting set

Hold a dumbbell in each hand and sit on a bench with back support. Plant your feet firmly on the floor about hip-width apart. Bend your elbows and raise your upper arms to shoulder height so the dumbbells are at ear level. Pull your abdominals in so there's a slight gap between the small of your back and the bench. Place the back of your head against the pad. See photo A in Figure 13-2.

The exercise

Push the dumbbells up and in until the ends of the dumbbells are nearly touching directly over your head and then lower the dumbbells back to ear level. See photo B in Figure 13-2.

Do's and don'ts

- ✔ DO keep your elbows relaxed at the top instead of locking them.
- ✔ DO stop lowering the dumbbells when your elbows are at or slightly below shoulder level.
- ✔ DON'T let your back arch a great degree off the back support.
- ✔ DON'T wiggle or squirm around in an effort to press the weights up.

Other options

Palms-in dumbbell press (easier): Do this exercise with your palms facing each other. This position allows your wrists and biceps muscles to help execute the movement.

Figure 13-2:
Don't lock your elbows at the top of the movement.

A   B

Lateral raise

The lateral raise works the center of your shoulder muscles. Make sure that you use stellar technique if you have neck or lower back problems.

Getting set

Hold a dumbbell in each hand and stand up tall with your feet as wide as your hips. Bend your elbows a little, turn your palms toward each other, and bring the dumbbells together in front of the tops of your thighs. Pull your abdominals in. See photo A in Figure 13-3.

The exercise

Lift your arms up and out to the side until the dumbbells are just below shoulder height. Slowly lower the weights back down. It may help to imagine that you're pouring two pitchers of lemonade on the floor in front of you. See photo B in Figure 13-3.

Do's and don'ts

✔ DO lift from the shoulders; in other words, keep your elbows stationary.

✔ DON'T arch your back, lean backward, or rock back and forth to lift the weights.

✔ DON'T raise the weights above shoulder height.

Other options

Bent-arm lateral raise (easier): Start with your arms bent at a 90-degree angle, palms facing each other, and the dumbbells in front of your body. Keeping your elbows bent at 90 degrees throughout the motion, lift the weights until your elbows are at shoulder height.

The bent-arm lateral raise exercise doesn't give your shoulders quite as good a workout as the basic version, but if you have weak shoulders or a history of shoulder problems, you can do this modified version of the lateral raise exercise.

Seated lateral raise: For a change of pace, perform the lateral raise exercise sitting on a bench, starting with your arms hanging straight down at your sides, elbows slightly bent.

Thumbs-up lateral raise (easier): Do this movement with your palms facing forward and your thumbs pointing upward. This version places the least stress on your rotator cuff muscles and is often used in physical therapy.

Keep your elbows slightly bent.

Figure 13-3:
Don't raise
the weights
above
shoulder
height.

A

B

Front raise

The front raise isolates the front portion of your shoulder muscles. Use caution if you have a history of lower back or neck discomfort.

Getting set

Hold a dumbbell in each hand and stand up tall with your feet as wide as your hips. Let your arms hang down at your sides — elbows relaxed and palms facing back. Stand up tall, pull your abdominals in, and relax your knees. See photo A in Figure 13-4.

The exercise

Raise your right arm up to shoulder height and then lower it back down. Then do the same with your left arm. Continue alternating until you complete the set. Or, for more of a challenge, do all your reps with one arm and then the other. See photo B in Figure 13-4.

Do's and don'ts

- ✔ DO keep your elbows slightly bent as you perform the exercise.
- ✔ DON'T arch, lean back, or wiggle around in an effort to lift the weight.
- ✔ DON'T lift your arm above shoulder height.

Other options

Palms-up front raise: Turn your palm up and do the exercise exactly as it's described in the basic front raise. Try this version if you're prone to shoulder or rotator cuff injuries.

Diagonal front raise (harder): When the dumbbell is at shoulder height, move your arm a few inches in until the weight is in front of the top of your chest. Skip this version if you have chronic shoulder problems.

Seated front raise (harder): Perform the front raise sitting on a bench with a back support; this position removes *any* possibility of cheating!

Lying front raise (harder): Lie on your stomach on a bench holding a dumbbell in each hand, arms straight in front of you (or slightly out to the side), palms facing in and thumbs up. Raise the dumbbells as high as you comfortably can but no higher than shoulder level. You'll have to use a much lighter weight for this version of the exercise. You can also incline the bench and do the same exercise.

Figure 13-4:
Don't lift your arm above shoulder height.

A

B

Back delt fly

The back delt fly is an excellent move for strengthening the back of the shoulders and upper back and for improving your posture.

Getting set

Hold a dumbbell in each hand and sit on the edge of a bench. Lean forward from your hips so your upper back is flat and above parallel to the floor (if you can, support your chest against your knees). Let your arms hang down so your palms are facing each other with the weights behind your calves and directly under your knees. Pull your chin back and in and draw your abdominals inward. See photo A in Figure 13-5.

The exercise

Raise your arms up and out to the sides, bending your elbows a few inches as you go until your elbows are level with your shoulders. Squeeze your shoulder blades together as you lift. Slowly lower your arms back down. See photo B in Figure 13-5.

Do's and don'ts

- ✔ DO keep your chin tilted slightly toward your chest throughout the motion so your head and neck don't drop forward.

- ✔ DO lean forward from your hips instead of rounding your back.

- ✔ DON'T allow the rest of your body to move as you do the exercise.

Other options

Back delt row: Use the same starting position except orient your palms backward. As you lift the weights, you need to bend your elbows more than in the basic version.

Cable back delt fly: If you have a history of neck pain, try the cable back delt fly version. Set the cable on the setting closest to the floor; hook up a horseshoe handle. Kneel alongside the cable tower and grasp the handle in the hand that's farthest away from the tower. (The cable passes underneath your body.) Squeeze your shoulder blade and lift your arm up to the side, as in the basic version. Do the same number of reps with each arm.

Standing back delt fly: Do the same exercise while standing with your feet placed as wide as your hips. Lean forward so that your torso forms a 45-degree angle with the floor. Keep your abs pulled in to protect your lower back and resist any rocking movement.

Figure 13-5:
Keep the
rest of your
body still
as you
perform the
exercise.

External rotation

External rotation focuses on your rotator cuff muscles, but these exercises also work your shoulder muscles.

If these movements bother your neck, try resting your head on your outstretched arm.

Getting set

Holding a dumbbell in your right hand, lie on the floor on your left side. Bend your right elbow to a 90-degree angle and tuck it firmly against your side so your palm faces downward. Pull your abdominals in. Bend your left elbow and rest the side of your head in your left hand or lie on your outstretched left arm.

The exercise

Keeping your right elbow glued to your side, raise your right hand as far as you comfortably can (the distance depends on your flexibility). Slowly lower the weight back toward the floor. Complete an equal number of repetitions with each arm. Figure 13-6 shows the external rotation.

Do's and don'ts

- ✔ DO imagine that your shoulder is the hinge of a door that's opening and closing.
- ✔ DO perform the exercise gently and smoothly.
- ✔ DON'T tighten up your neck and face.
- ✔ DON'T throw the weight up.
- ✔ DON'T force the weight farther than your natural flexibility allows.

Other options

Band external rotation: See Chapter 24 for a version of this exercise that you can do with exercise bands.

Traffic cop (harder): Hold a weight in both hands and stand with your feet as wide as your hips. Bend your elbows and raise your arms up to shoulder height (in the classic stick-em-up position). Keeping your elbows still, rotate your forearms down until your palms are facing behind you and then rotate back up to the start.

Internal rotation

Internal rotation also targets your rotator cuff muscles and works your shoulder muscles.

Again, if these movements bother your neck, try resting your head on your outstretched arm.

Getting set

For internal rotation repetitions, switch the weight to your left hand and lie on your back. Bend your elbow so your forearm is perpendicular to the floor and your palm is facing inward.

The exercise

Lower your hand down to the floor as much as your flexibility permits, and then lift back up. Complete an equal number of repetitions with each arm. Figure 13-7 illustrates the internal rotation.

Do's and don'ts

✔ DO imagine that your shoulder is the hinge of a door that's opening and closing.

✔ DO perform the exercise gently and smoothly.

✔ DON'T tighten up your neck and face.

✔ DON'T throw the weight up.

✔ DON'T force the weight farther than your natural flexibility allows.

Other options

Band internal rotation: See Chapter 24 for a version of this exercise that you can do with exercise bands.

Traffic cop (harder): Hold a weight in both hands and stand with your feet as wide as your hips. Bend your elbows and raise your arms up to shoulder height (in the classic stick-em-up position). Keeping your elbows still, rotate your forearms down until your palms are facing behind you and then rotate back up to the start.

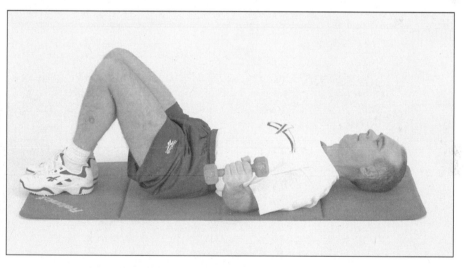

Figure 13-7: Internal rotation. Perform this exercise gently, without throwing the weight up.

Shoulder press machine

The shoulder press machine is a good overall shoulder exercise because it challenges all of your shoulder muscles. It also works your triceps and upper back.

Take extra caution if you're prone to neck, elbow, or lower back problems.

Getting set

Set your seat height so the machine's pulley is even with the middle of your shoulder. Hold on to each of the front handles. (Your palms face each other.)

Pull your abdominals in tight but leave a slight, natural gap between the small of your back and the seat pad. See photo A of Figure 13-8.

The exercise

Press the handles up without locking your elbows. Lower your arms until your elbows are slightly lower than your shoulders. See photo B in Figure 10-8.

Do's and don'ts

- ✔ DO relax your shoulders and keep them well below your ears, especially while your arms are straightened fully.
- ✔ DON'T arch your back or wiggle around in an effort to lift the weight.
- ✔ DON'T thrust upward with more force than necessary; this strain puts a lot of stress on your elbows.

Other options

Many shoulder machines have arms that work "independently" of each other. That is, the left and right sides aren't connected, so each arm handles its own share of the load. If your gym has this option, we recommend that you give it a try. You'll get the structure and support that a machine has to offer but also develop balance and uniform strength as you would with free weights.

Figure 13-8: Don't arch your back or wiggle around in an effort to lift the weight.

Chapter 14

Working Your Arms

· ·

In This Chapter

▶ Studying your biceps, triceps, and wrist muscles

▶ Enjoying strong arms

▶ Getting a great arm workout

▶ Avoiding mistakes when training your arms

· ·

*T*rue story: Liz once met a woman from New York City who decided to join a gym because of her new hairstyle. She explained that her "personal hair manager" had changed her blow-drying method to one that required more bending and straightening of the arms. "I couldn't believe how weak my arms were," she told Liz. "I had to start lifting weights so my hair would look good." Even if your hairstyle doesn't depend on your arm strength, plenty of other aspects of your life do. This chapter tells you how you can develop strong, firm arms.

Understanding Arm Muscle Basics

Your *biceps* muscle spans the front of your upper arm. Hang out in any gym and you'll see people flexing these muscles in the mirror, usually when they think that nobody's watching. The main job of your biceps (nicknamed your *bis* or your *guns*) is to bend your arm; in gymspeak, this motion is called *curling* or *flexing*.

Your *triceps,* located directly opposite your biceps, spans the rear of your upper arm. The biceps and triceps, like many muscle groups, work together in pairs. When you squeeze your biceps, your triceps relaxes and your arm bends, and when you squeeze your triceps, your biceps relaxes and your arm straightens. Maintaining a good balance of strength in the relationship between the two muscles is important so that one muscle doesn't dominate the other. That's why you need to train both.

Another group of arm muscles allows your wrists to move in a variety of ways. To spare you some jargon, we're going to refer to these as your *wrist muscles.* These muscles let you bend your wrist up, arch it down, twirl it in a circle, tilt it left and right, and turn your palm up or down. One of the most important jobs of the wrist muscles is to keep the wrist stable and the wrist joint flat or neutral. If your wrists are weak, the wrist muscles can bend at inopportune times (like when you're holding a 100-pound barbell over your chest). Weak wrists also mean that you can't get a grip — on a baseball bat, a stubborn weed, or a can of mushroom soup — and leave you prone to conditions like *carpal tunnel syndrome,* an inflammation of your wrist nerves.

Figure 14-1 helps you locate all of your arm muscles.

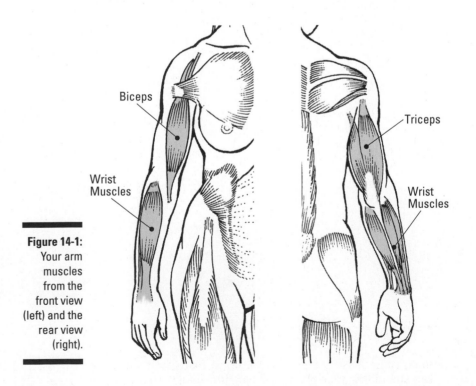

Biceps

Triceps

Wrist Muscles

Wrist Muscles

Figure 14-1: Your arm muscles from the front view (left) and the rear view (right).

Enjoying Strong Arms

Because we use our arms so often in daily life, we tend to take our arm muscles for granted. However, giving these muscles extra attention in the weight room really does pay off.

- ✔ **Attaining real-life benefits:** Your arms are the link between your upper body and the rest of the world. If your arms are weak, your larger, upper body muscles can't work to full capacity. You're only as strong as your weakest link. For example, the lat pulldown, a back exercise described in Chapter 11, mainly requires back strength, but weak biceps limit your ability to do this exercise. With stronger triceps, you can more effectively challenge your chest muscles in exercises such as the push-up or the bench press. Strong wrists are crucial for many weight lifting exercises and for activities outside of the gym: gripping a golf club, shelling peanuts, shuffling cards, or working at your computer keyboard without pain.

- ✔ **Preventing injury:** Strong arms help protect your elbows from harm. Carry around a heavy briefcase with a straight arm long enough and eventually your elbow starts to ache. With stronger arm muscles, you can haul that briefcase around longer without pain, and you're less likely to get *tennis elbow,* which is inflammation of the elbow joint. Powerful arms also minimize your chances of soreness or injuries when you perform weight lifting exercises or when you lift a dumbbell, barbell, or weight plate off of a rack. Strong wrists, in particular, help you avoid carpal tunnel syndrome. Repetitive movements such as typing, scanning items at the grocery checkout, or operating the mouse of your computer can cause this painful and sometimes debilitating condition.

- ✔ **The confidence factor:** The feel-good factor: We tend to equate toned biceps with masculine strength. Popeye's biceps are almost the size of his head. In women, the jury is still out. Popular opinion can't come to a consensus on whether it prefers women with toned arms or weak arms. The bottom line is that strong arms help you to enjoy life better and toned muscles look healthy. Society's judgment about whether men and women should have big or small muscles is likely to change with the winds of fashion, but being healthy and strong and feeling great are always positive.

Getting a Great Arm Workout

Your arm muscles are smaller than your chest, back, and shoulder muscles, so you can spend less time training them and still get great results. If your goal is to increase your arm strength and develop some tone, one to three sets per arm muscle will suffice. You need to do five to eight sets per arm muscle if you want to develop maximum strength and significant size.

Give your biceps and triceps equal time. If one of these muscle groups is disproportionately stronger than the other, you're more prone to elbow injuries. Chances are, you'll enjoy training one of these muscle groups better than the other.

- Liz and Suzanne picks:

   - **Biceps:** Both women tend to get bored training their biceps. No matter how you slice 'em, these exercises involve bending and then straightening your arms.

   - **Triceps:** Liz and Suzanne have a lot of fun training their triceps. Of course, this is kind of odd, considering that working your triceps involves a movement that, on paper, is no more thrilling: straightening and then bending.

- Shirley's favorites:

   - **Biceps:** She enjoys training biceps, particularly with the reverse curl because it strengthens the wrist and forearms and the concentration curl because you focus on the targeted muscle and feel the mind-body connection.

   - **Triceps:** When it comes to triceps, Shirley loves training them as well. Because triceps are typically so weak, Shirley believes that after you develop a certain level of triceps strength, you never want to lose it. And, that desire not to have to go through that beginning stage again is enough to motivate her and many of her clients to love training them.

Oh well, the psychology of weight training can't always be explained. If you do prefer training one of these muscle groups over the other, work your least favorite group first so you're not tempted to blow it off. If you do some of the split routines described in Chapter 21, you can work these muscle groups on different days.

Always work your arm muscles last in your upper body workouts. Otherwise, they may be too tired to help out when you do the big-money exercises for your much larger chest and back muscles. Your wrists should be the last upper body muscle you work before hitting the showers.

Avoiding Mistakes When Training Your Arms

Some people use such herky-jerky form when they perform arm exercises that they look like people dancing under a strobe light. Keep the following tips in mind when training your arms:

✔ **Don't cheat.** If you contort your whole body to lift the weight, you work your whole body, not your arms. Rocking back and forth is also a great way to throw out your lower back. Think about how you'll feel explaining to your friends that you wrenched your back while exercising your arms.

✔ **Don't skip your wrists.** Few people pine away for forearms the size of Popeye's. However, as explained in the "Enjoying Strong Arms" section of this chapter, you'll go far in life with well-developed wrist muscles.

✔ **Go easy on the elbows.** Exercise captions throughout this chapter tell you to straighten your arms. This, however, doesn't mean snapping your elbows into a fully straightened position.

✔ **Keep your elbows still.** When your elbows veer out to the side during many biceps and triceps exercises, you're able to lift more weight. However, this is only because you have more leverage; your arms aren't getting any stronger. When you're doing biceps exercises such as the dumbbell reverse biceps curl (covered later in this chapter), you may also have a tendency to pull your arms and elbows forward to lift the weight. You can't avoid this extra movement completely, but keep it to a minimum.

Practicing Arm Exercises

Here's a list of the exercises for strengthening your arms:

✔ **Biceps exercises:** Barbell biceps curl, dumbbell reverse biceps curl, concentration curl, and arm curl machine

✔ **Triceps exercises:** Triceps pushdown, triceps kickback, bench dip, and triceps dip machine

✔ **Wrist exercises:** Wrist curl and reverse wrist curl

Barbell biceps curl

The barbell biceps curl targets your biceps.

Be especially careful if you have elbow problems. Whenever you add weight and bend a joint, it increases the stress to that joint. Therefore, if you have a weakened joint, you need to exercise extreme care not to overdo it and cause an injury. If you have lower back problems, you may want to choose a seated biceps exercise instead.

Getting set

Hold a barbell with an underhand grip and your hands about shoulder-width apart. Stand with your feet as wide as your hips, and let your arms hang down so the bar is in front of your thighs (see photo A of Figure 14-2). Stand up tall with your abdominals pulled in and knees relaxed.

The exercise

Bend your arms to curl the bar almost up to your shoulders (see photo B of Figure 14-2), and then slowly lower the bar *almost* to the starting position.

Do's and don'ts

- ✔ DO keep your knees relaxed. This protects your lower back.

- ✔ DON'T rock back and forth or lean way back to lift the weight. If you need to do that, you should be arrested for using too much weight.

- ✔ DON'T just straighten your arms and let the bar drop down to your thighs like a sack of rocks. Instead, lower the bar slowly to get the most muscle power from the exercise and to protect your elbows. And don't lower the bar all the way back down because you lose tension on the muscle.

Figure 14-2: Don't rock back and forth to lift the weight.

Don't curl all the way to your shoulders.

Other options

Reverse-grip biceps curl (harder): Do the basic version of the barbell biceps curl holding the bar with an overhand grip. You feel this exercise more in your wrists. (Hint: Use a lighter weight for this version.)

Cable biceps curl: Place the cable on the setting closest to the floor and attach a short or long straight bar. Hold the bar with an underhand grip and stand about a foot away from the cable tower. Curl the weight up and down exactly as in the basic version of the barbell biceps curl.

Double biceps curl: Hold a dumbbell in each hand with your palms facing up, elbows resting lightly against your sides, and arms hanging down. Curl the dumbbells up and down together as if they were a barbell.

Dumbbell reverse biceps curl

The dumbbell reverse biceps curl focuses on your biceps.

Use caution if you have lower back or elbow problems.

Getting set

Hold a dumbbell in each hand with an overhand grip, and stand with your feet as wide as your hips. Let your arms hang down at your sides with your palms facing toward the back. See photo A of Figure 14-3. Pull your abdominals in, stand tall, and keep your knees relaxed.

The exercise

Curl your right arm close to your shoulder so your arm faces out away from your shoulder at the top of the movement. Slowly lower the dumbbell back down, and then repeat with your left arm. Continue alternating until you've completed the set. See photo B of Figure 14-3.

Do's and don'ts

- ✔ DO keep your knees relaxed and your posture tall. This prevents you from swinging your body forward and back to help move the weight.

- ✔ DON'T swing your elbows out wide as you bend your arm to raise the weight. Keep your elbows close to your body *without* supporting them on the sides of your stomach for leverage.

- ✔ DON'T just let the weight fall back to the starting position. Lower it slowly and with control.

Figure 14-3:
Keep your elbows close to your body throughout the exercise.

A

B

Other options

Hammer curl: Instead of beginning with palms facing back, start with palms facing in and keep your palms facing in throughout the motion. Imagine that you're pounding nails into a board with two large hammers. This version of the exercise puts more emphasis on your forearm muscles, as well as some of the muscles that reside underneath the biceps.

Zottman curl (harder): Instead of beginning with palms facing back, begin with palms facing front with an underhand grip. As you curl your arm upward, rotate your palm in toward your body and bring it up and across to the opposite shoulder. This version of the dumbbell curl is slightly harder than the basic version.

Seated biceps curl: If you find yourself cheating too much even with light weights, try sitting on a bench or a chair.

Concentration curl

The concentration curl is especially good for targeting your biceps and excluding all other muscles.

Be careful if you've had elbow injuries or are prone to lower back discomfort.

Getting set

Hold a dumbbell in your right hand, and sit on the edge of a bench or a chair with your feet a few inches wider than your hips. Lean forward from your hips, and place your right elbow against the inside of your right thigh, just behind your knee. The weight should hang down near the inside of your ankle. Place your left palm on top of your left thigh. See photo A of Figure 14-4.

The exercise

Bend your arm and curl the dumbbell almost up to your shoulder (see photo B of Figure 14-4), and then straighten your arm to lower the weight back down.

Do's and don'ts

> ✔ DO bend forward from your hips instead of rounding your lower back to lean forward.

> ✔ DON'T lean away from your arm as you lift the weight up to help get better leverage. (Hey, that's cheating!)

Figure 14-4: Bend forward from your hips instead of rounding your lower back.

Other options

Slant biceps curl: Sit on a bench with the back inclined a few inches. Lean back and curl the weight up. You can do this one hand at a time or with both hands together and with a twist as you curl upward or without a twist.

Standing concentration curl: Hold a dumbbell in one hand. Stand alongside a flat bench, lean over, and place your other hand on top of bench. Let the arm holding the weight hang straight down to the floor. Bend your elbow so the weight moves up and in toward your armpit, and then slowly lower it back down.

Arm curl machine

The arm curl machine focuses on your biceps.

Be careful if you've had elbow injuries.

Getting set

Adjust the seat so when you sit down and extend your arms straight out, your arms are level with your shoulders and your elbows are lined up with the moving hinge or pulley of the machine. Sit down and grasp a handle in each hand with an underhand grip. See photo A in Figure 14-5.

Figure 14-5: Don't hunch your shoulders as you pull the machine handles.

The exercise

Bend your elbows and pull the handles until they're just above your shoulders (see photo B of Figure 14-5), and then slowly lower the handles back down.

Do's and don'ts

✔ DO make sure that you set the seat height correctly. If you set the seat too low, you'll have trouble bending your arms and may place too much strain on your elbows.

✔ DO sit up tall and make an effort to pull exclusively with your arms as opposed to hunching up your shoulders or leaning back.

✔ DON'T use a chest pad to help haul the weight. If there's a pad, use it for light support only.

Other options

Some gyms have arm curl machines that do a fair job of mimicking dumbbell work: The two sides aren't connected so each arm has to do the work of lifting the weight. This type of machine is a good substitute or supplement for free weight work.

Triceps pushdown

The triceps pushdown targets your triceps.

Pay special attention to your form if you have elbow problems. Standing up straight with your abdominal muscles pulled in helps you avoid lower back problems.

Getting set

Set the pulley of the cable at the topmost setting and attach a straight or U-shaped bar. Grasp the bar with your palms facing down and your hands about a thumb's distance from the center of the bar. You can stand either with your feet parallel or with one foot slightly in front of the other. Bend your elbows so your forearms are parallel to the floor and your elbows are alongside your waist (see photo A of Figure 14-6). You can lean *slightly* forward at the hips, but keep your abdominals pulled in and your knees relaxed. See photo B of Figure 14-6.

The exercise

Push the bar straight down, keeping your elbows close to your sides (see photo B of Figure 14-6). Then bend your arms to allow the bar to rise slowly until your arms are slightly above parallel to the ground.

Figure 14-6:
Don't let
your elbows
splay out to
the sides as
you push
down.

Keep your knees relaxed.

Do's and don'ts

- ✔ DO push down smoothly, exerting the same amount of pressure with both hands so both sides of the bar travel down evenly.

- ✔ DON'T lean too far forward or too heavily on the bar.

- ✔ DON'T allow your elbows to splay out to the sides, especially as you push down.

- ✔ DON'T let your arms fly back up as you return the bar to the starting position. Concentrate on controlling the bar.

Other options

Reverse grip pushdown (easier): Turn your hands around and use an underhanded grip. Because this version allows your biceps to assist your triceps a great deal, it's less challenging than the basic version.

One-hand triceps pushdown: Attach the horseshoe, and grasp it with one hand in an underhand grip. (You can also use an overhand grip, although it's tougher.) Place your other hand on your hip. Straighten your arm, pushing the handle until it's alongside your hip. Then slowly raise the handle back up.

Rope attachment (harder): Use the rope attachment, and move your hands a few inches apart as you press the rope down. You may need to use less weight with the rope than you do with a bar.

Triceps kickback

The triceps kickback works your triceps.

Use caution if you have elbow or lower back problems.

Getting set

Hold a dumbbell in your right hand, and stand next to the long side of your bench. Lean forward at the hips until your upper body is at a 45-degree angle to the floor, and place your free hand on top of the bench for support. Bend your right elbow so your upper arm is parallel to the floor, your forearm is perpendicular to the floor, and your palm faces in (see photo A of Figure 14-7). Keep your elbow close to your waist. Pull your abdominals in and relax your knees.

The exercise

Keeping your upper arm still, straighten your arm behind you until the end of the dumbbell is pointing down (see photo B of Figure 14-7). Slowly bend your arm to lower the weight. When you've completed the set, repeat the exercise with your left arm.

Do's and don'ts

- ✔ DO keep your abdominals pulled in and your knees relaxed to protect your lower back.

- ✔ DON'T lock your elbow at the top of the movement; do straighten your arm but keep your elbow relaxed.

- ✔ DON'T allow your upper arm to move or your shoulder to drop below waist level.

Other options

Cable triceps kickback: Put the pulley on the topmost setting and attach a horseshoe handle. Grasping the handle in one hand, position yourself in the same way described in the basic kickback, and perform the same exercise. You may have to step a foot or two away from the cable tower to prevent the cable from going slack.

Triceps kickback with a twist (harder): As you straighten your arm, twist it so that at the top of the movement, your palm faces up.

Figure 14-7:
Don't let
your upper
arm move
or your
shoulder
drop below
waist level.

A   B

Bench dip

The bench dip is one of the few triceps exercises that strengthens other muscles, too — in this case, the shoulders and chest.

Be careful if you have wrist, elbow, or shoulder problems.

Getting set

Sit on the edge of a bench with your legs together and straight in front of you, pointing your toes upward. Keeping your elbows relaxed, straighten your arms, place your hands so you can grip the underside of the bench on either side of your hips and slide your butt just off the front of the bench so your upper body is pointing straight down (see photo A of Figure 14-8). Keep your abdominals pulled in and your head centered between your shoulders.

The exercise

Bend your elbows and lower your body in a straight line. When your upper arms are parallel to the floor, push yourself back up. See photo B of Figure 14-8.

Figure 14-8:
Don't lower yourself past the point at which your upper arms are parallel to the floor.

Do's and don'ts

- ✔ DO try to keep your wrists straight rather than bent backwards.
- ✔ DO keep hips and back (as you lower) as close to the bench throughout the motion.
- ✔ DON'T simply thrust your hips up and down, a common mistake among beginners. Make sure that your elbows are moving.
- ✔ DON'T lower yourself past the point at which your upper arms are parallel to the floor.

Other options

Bent-leg bench dip (easier): Instead of extending your legs out in front of you, bend your knees at a right angle so you're positioned as if you're sitting in a chair.

Feet-up bench dip (harder): Place your feet on another chair of equal height. Or, for an even tougher version, place a weight plate or dumbbell on your lap.

Triceps dip machine

The triceps dip machine targets your triceps and, to some extent, your shoulder and chest muscles.

Take special care if you have shoulder, elbow, or neck problems.

Getting set

Set the seat height so that when your arms are fully bent, your elbows are at or below chest level. Sit in the seat with your feet flat on the floor. If the machine has a seat belt, wear it to prevent you from popping up out of the seat while you do the exercise. Grasp a handle in each hand so your elbows are bent and your palms are facing in. Pull your abdominals in and sit with your back, buttocks, and shoulder blades against the back support. See photo A of Figure 14-9.

Figure 14-9: Don't slam your arms or lock your elbows.

The exercise

Press the handles down until your arms are straight but your elbows remain relaxed (see photo B of Figure 14-9). Slowly bend your arms until your elbows are up near chest height.

Do's and don'ts

- DO keep your shoulders relaxed instead of hunching them up near your ears.
- DO keep your wrists in line with your forearm instead of bending them outward.
- DON'T slam your arms or lock your elbows.

Other options

Different grips: Most triceps dip machines have the option of a narrow or a wide grip. Start with the wide grip because you're more likely to use correct form. However, when you become more proficient with this machine, the inside grip does an excellent job of isolating the triceps muscles.

Modified triceps dip machine: You can raise the seat higher to restrict the distance your arms travel. This variation is an excellent option for those with neck and shoulder problems because the raised seat keeps you from raising your arms as high and ensures that the neck and shoulders won't be hunched and tight.

Triceps extension machine: Some gyms have a triceps extension machine rather than a triceps dip machine. The extension machine works the muscles the same way except that you start with your arms at shoulder height with your elbows resting on a pad; then you press the handles, straightening your arms out in front of you instead of downward.

Wrist curl and reverse wrist curl

The wrist curl and reverse wrist curl are great for strengthening your wrist muscles.

Be careful if you've had wrist or elbow problems.

Wrist curl

Hold a weight in your right hand with an underhand grip, and sit on the edge of your bench with your knees as wide as your hips. Lean slightly forward, and place your entire forearm on top of your thigh so your hand hangs over the edge of your knee. Clasp your left palm over your wrist to hold it steady (see photo A of Figure 14-10). Curl your wrist up so the dumbbell moves toward your forearm, and then lower the weight back down.

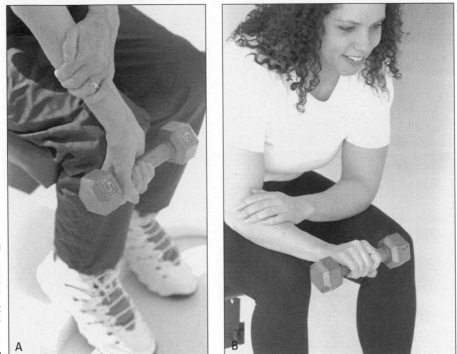

Figure 14-10:
Don't let
your
forearm lift
off your
thigh.

A

B

Reverse wrist curl

Turn your palm down, and, again, secure your wrist in place with your other hand. Bend your wrist up to raise the dumbbell to thigh height (see photo B of Figure 14-10), and then lower the weight back down. (Hint: You may need slightly less weight to do the reverse wrist curl.)

Do's and don'ts

✔ DO curl straight up; try to avoid moving the weight to the side.

✔ DON'T let your forearm lift off your thigh.

Other options

Modified wrist curl: If you have weak wrists and find this exercise difficult, simply move the weight up and down a shorter distance.

Wrist-and-finger curl (harder): At the bottom of the wrist curl, roll the weight down to the tips of your fingers and then roll it back before curling the weight up. This exercise is excellent for typists or others who use their hands a lot because it strengthens the forearms and prevents carpal tunnel syndrome.

Chapter 15

Working Your Abdominals

*W*e were happy a few years back when the market for abdominal gizmos went flabby. After spending more than a half billion dollars on the AbFlex, AbTrainer, and their two dozen inbred cousins, the public finally seemed to tire of these devices (although, remarkably, a few new ones are on the market). This decline in gizmos was great news — the public finally saw through misleading slogans like, "Go from flab to abs!" and "Get a flat stomach before you know it!"

But it seems we're wrong — but only slightly. America may have stopped buying these products like crazy, but many people still buy into the notion that abdominal exercises melt fat off your midsection. Suzanne writes *Shape* magazine's "Weight Loss Q&A" column, and every month she receives a dozen or so letters from readers who won't let go of this idea. "I've been doing 100 abdominal crunches a day for two months, and my belly isn't dropping any inches," one reader wrote. Another reader wrote: "Help! My lower abdomen pooches out and no amount of crunching seems to slim down this area."

In this chapter, you start to understand why abdominal exercises — with or without machinery — *aren't* an effective way to shrink your midsection. You also realize why it's still important for you to train your abdominal muscles.

Introducing Abdominal Muscle Basics

At this point, every household in America probably knows that the abdominal muscles are collectively referred to as the abs. Keep in mind that your abs aren't just in front of your body but wrap around your body. This fact is important in training because many people only seem to be concerned with training what they see — the front and center — but your abs cover much more of your body.

You have four abdominal muscles:

✔ *Rectus abdominis:* This is the largest abdominal muscle and runs from your breastbone to your pubic bone, a few inches below your belly button. The rectus abdominis

   • Curls your spine forward when performing crunches (or when you double over with laughter from watching *Desperate Housewives*).

   • Keeps your spine still when you move other parts of your body, such as when you lift a heavy box off the floor.

✔ *Obliques, internal and external:* These muscles run diagonally up and down your sides. Your obliques

   • Help your rectus abdominis curl your spine forward.

   • Enable you to twist and bend to the side.

   • Provide lower back support.

✔ *Transversus abdominis:* The transversus abdominis sits directly beneath the rectus abdominis and is the deepest of all your abdominal muscles. This muscle

   • Is continuously working when you're sitting and standing.

   • Helps support your lower back and keep good posture.

This chapter features exercises that emphasize the rectus abdominis and the obliques. To tone the transversus abdominis while doing these exercises, breathe deeply and pull your abdominals inward as you exhale. Figure 15-1 gives you a view of your abdominal muscles. To understand more about the importance of the transversus abdominis muscle, check out Chapter 17.

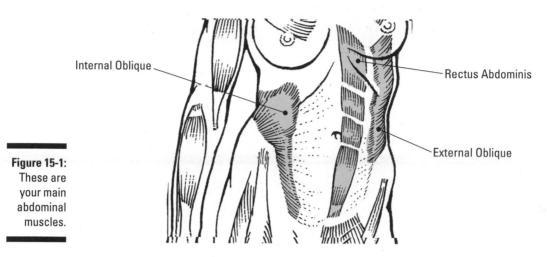

Internal Oblique

Rectus Abdominis

External Oblique

Figure 15-1:
These are
your main
abdominal
muscles.

Enjoying Strong Abdominals

Abdominal exercises won't eliminate fat around your midsection, but abdominal exercises serve you in many other important ways.

- ✔ **Real-life benefits:** Your abs play a crucial behind-the-scenes role in your daily life, supporting your spine in all of your movements. For instance, as you're sitting here reading this book, you probably think your abs have very little to do. In fact, they're the reason you sit up reasonably straight in your chair, as opposed to oozing off the edge like a blob of Jell-O. Your abs are even more important when you perform more complicated movements. Strong abs enable you to stand in line or shovel dirt in your garden for a lot longer without getting a backache.

- ✔ **Injury prevention:** Most back pain can be reduced — perhaps even eliminated — by strengthening the abdominal muscles along with the lower back muscles and the buttocks. All of your abdominals work together to support and move your spine. The most common way people injure their back is when they combine bending with rotation, especially during lifting. Strong muscles and proper movement habits prevent this and other injuries.

- ✔ **The "Feel Good" factor:** The notion of washboard abs creates a great deal of anxiety and insecurity among many individuals. Unless you have the genetics to not store fat above your rectus abdominus muscle, the tone of your abdominals, no matter how fit you are, will not show directly under your skin. Models and celebrities often have this fat vacuumed out through liposuction to reveal the muscularity underneath or they have airbrush contour tans sprayed on to give the appearance of 'cut' abs. Feel good about yourself from simply knowing that you have strong abdominal muscles, regardless of whether the world can see them or not.

Getting Past the Myths of Abdominal Workouts

To design an effective abdominal program, you need to separate the hype from the truth. Forget everything you may have found out from TV infomercials. Here we debunk the remarkably persistent myths about abdominal training.

Myth #1: Abdominal exercises get rid of the blubber around your middle

Reality: Ab exercises can't help you "go from flab to abs," as many infomercials claim, because flab and abs are separate entities. Abdominal exercises strengthen and tone your muscles, but these muscles lie underneath the layer of fat on top. Spot reducing through toning exercise is a fantasy. The only way to lose your belly fat is to eat less and exercise more — a strategy that reduces your overall body fat. However, even then you have no guarantee that you will lose the fat from your middle.

Myth #2: Everyone can develop washboard abs if they try hard enough

Reality: Even if you make it your life's mission to eat a low-fat diet, spend hours a day on the StairMaster, and perform abdominal exercises to utter perfection, you still may not develop that rippled look unless your body is genetically programmed to carry almost no fat in the abdominal area. And very few of us are built that way.

Myth #3: For best results, you should do several hundred repetitions of abdominal exercises

Reality: Treat your abs like any other muscle group; in other words, perform 8 to 15 repetitions per set to fatigue for optimal strength and endurance conditioning. To focus on endurance training for the abs, do more reps — up to 24 — to fatigue. If you can do more than this, you're either doing the exercise incorrectly or you're performing an exercise that's too easy for you. Either way, you're not doing your abs much good.

Myth #4: You need to work your abs every day

Reality: Again, your abdominals are like every other muscle group. They respond best to hard work followed by a day of rest. Overtraining your abs simply invites neck and lower back problems, not to mention boredom. Strength training for your abs, however, is different from endurance training for the core. Core training is covered in Chapter 17.

Myth #5: The front of your stomach has two separate muscles: The upper abs and lower abs

Reality: The rectus abdominis is one long, flat, continuous sheet of muscle. Any abdominal crunch exercise works the entire muscle, although lifting your upper body off the floor emphasizes the upper portion of the rectus, and lifting your hips off the floor emphasizes the lower portion. When you do ab exercises slowly and with perfect form, you feel the entire muscle working no matter what exercise you do.

Myth #6: You need a gadget to train your abs

Reality: Although ab roller-type contraptions help novices understand the crunch movement, the floor works as well as or better than any device, and last time we checked, the floor was free. Besides, exercises such as the ones shown in this chapter are more challenging and versatile than those performed with a gadget. We're not fond of health club abdominal machines, either. Most of them strengthen your back and hips more than they do your abs.

Myth #7: Sit-ups are better than crunches

Reality: With any sit-up-type movement, your abdominals are involved only in the first part of the motion. After your shoulders clear the floor, your hip flexor and lower back muscles take over. So there's no point in sitting all the way up to your knees.

Avoiding Mistakes When Training Your Abdominals

Mistakes are so common with abdominal exercises that the crunch has the dubious honor of qualifying for a spot in Chapter 9 as one of the exercises most often performed incorrectly.

Here's a close look at abdominal training no-nos:

✔ **Avoid doing neck-ups.** In other words, lift from your abs, not your neck; otherwise, you're asking for neck pain. Your head and neck shouldn't be involved in abdominal exercises at all — they're just along for the ride. Place your hands behind your head without lacing your fingers together, slide your shoulders down, and tilt your chin slightly so there's about a fist's worth of space between your chin and your chest. Your head and neck need to stay in this position throughout the exercise.

✔ **Don't move your elbows.** Your elbows have nothing to do with abdominal exercises. After you position your elbows out and slightly rounded inward, leave them there. If you pull your elbows up and in, you'll end up pulling on your neck.

✔ **Don't arch or flatten your back.** We frequently remind you to pull your abs in, but always keep a slight gap, the width of a finger or two, between the small of your back and the floor. Avoid squeezing your buttocks and jamming your lower back into the floor.

✔ **After the lift, don't forget the curl.** The crunch involves more than simply lifting your head, neck, and shoulder blades off the floor; you also need to curl forward, as if you're doubling over. Imagine how you'd move if you were lying on the floor and someone dropped a weight on your stomach. That's the movement you're aiming for here.

Discovering Exercises in This Chapter

Here's a list of the abdominal exercises in this chapter:

✔ Basic abdominal crunch

✔ Reverse crunch

✔ Oblique crunch

✔ Bent knee side crunch

✔ Roll down negative curl

Basic abdominal crunch

The basic abdominal crunch is the fundamental abdominal exercise that works all of your abdominal muscles.

Pay special attention to your form if you have lower back or neck problems.

Getting set

Lie on your back with your knees bent and feet flat on the floor hip-width apart. Place your hands at your sides. Keep your head upright and don't press it into your chest. Gently pull your abdominals inward. See photo A of Figure 15-2.

The exercise

Curl up and forward so your head, neck, and shoulder blades lift off the floor. Hold for a moment at the top of the movement and then lower slowly back down. See photo B of Figure 15-2.

Figure 15-2: Gently pull your abdominals inward

Curl up and forward.

Do's and don'ts

- ✔ DO keep your abdominals pulled in so you feel more tension in your abs and so you don't overarch your lower back.

- ✔ DO curl as well as lift. For an explanation of curling, refer to the introduction to this chapter and to Chapter 9, in which you ascertain common crunch mistakes.

- ✔ DON'T pull on your legs with your hands.

Other options

Cross-arm crunch (easier): Fold your arms across your chest, palms down, and tuck your chin so it rests on your hands. This position saves you the effort of having to lift the weight of your arms.

Legs-up crunch: Keeping your knees bent, pick your legs off the floor, and cross your ankles.

Weighted crunch (harder): Hold a *lightweight* plate on your chest, or for an even greater challenge, hold a weight on top of or behind your head. Just don't press the plate down too hard.

Reverse crunch

The reverse crunch emphasizes the lower portion of your main abdominal muscles (the rectus abdominis).

Use caution if you're prone to lower back discomfort.

Getting set

Lie on your back with your legs up, knees slightly bent, and feet in air. Rest your arms on the floor and place your fingertips behind your head. Rest your head on your hands, relax your shoulders, and pull in your abdominals.

The exercise

Lift your butt one or two inches off the floor so your legs lift up and a few inches backward. Hold the position for a moment, and then lower slowly. See photo A of Figure 15-3.

Do's and don'ts

- ✔ DO keep your shoulders relaxed and down.

- ✔ DO keep the crunch movement small and precise; you don't have to lift very high to feel this exercise working.

✔ DO use a minimum of leg movement.

✔ DON'T thrust or jerk your hips.

✔ DON'T involve your upper body at all.

✔ DON'T cross your feet at the ankles (see photo B in Figure 15-3).

✔ DON'T roll your hips so your buttocks and back come way off the floor. This type of movement involves your front hip muscles more than your abdominals.

Other options

Modified reverse crunch (easier): Hold onto the back edges of an exercise mat or stable object such as the underside of a couch or stuffed chair to help stabilize your upper body. Perform the reverse crunch.

One-leg reverse crunch (easier): Lift one leg at a time. Bend your other knee so your foot is flat on the floor. Avoid pushing on your foot. Use your abs to lift your hips.

Incline reverse crunch (harder): Place three risers underneath one end of a step bench and one riser underneath the other end. Lie on the step with your head at the higher end of it. Stretch your arms out behind you and hold on to the undercling of the step directly behind your head. Perform a reverse crunch by lifting your hips up. This version of the reverse crunch is more difficult because you're working against gravity.

Figure 15-3:
Lift your butt
one or two
inches off
the floor.
Don't cross
your ankles!

A

B

Oblique crunch

The oblique crunch works all your abdominal muscles with an emphasis on your obliques.

Pay special attention to form if you have a history of lower back or neck discomfort.

Getting set

Lie on your back with your knees bent and your feet hip-width apart and flat on the floor. Place your left hand behind your head so your thumb is behind your left ear. Place your right arm along the floor beside you. Bring your elbow out to the side and round it slightly inward. Tilt your chin so your chin and your chest are a few inches apart. Pull your abdominals in. See photo A of Figure 15-4.

The exercise

As you curl your head, neck, and shoulder blades off the floor, twist your torso to the right, bringing your left shoulder toward your right knee. (Your elbow won't actually touch your knee.) Lower back down. Do all the repetitions on one side and then switch to the other side. See photo B of Figure 15-4.

Do's and don'ts

- ✔ DO concentrate on rotating from your middle instead of simply moving your elbows toward your knees.
- ✔ DO keep both hips squarely on the ground as you twist to protect your lower back.

Other options

Legs-up crunch with a twist (harder): Lift your bent knees off the floor and cross one ankle over the other.

Straight-arm crunch with a twist (harder): Reach for your opposite knee with your arm straight rather than your elbow bent. Reach past the outside edge of your knee.

Bent knee side crunch

The bent knee side crunch challenges your obliques to work together with all of your abdominal muscles.

Figure 15-4:
Lift your
shoulder
toward your
knee.

Twist from your middle; don't pull from your elbow.

Getting set

Lie on your back with your knees bent and your feet hip-width apart and flat on the floor. Drop both of your knees to one side and keep your legs stacked together. Place both hands behind your head without lacing your fingers. Place thumbs at base of skull. See photo A of Figure 15-5.

The exercise

Curl straight upward keeping your legs together and drawing your ribs toward your hips. Lower back down. Do all the repetitions on one side and then switch to the other side. See photo B of Figure 15-5.

Do's and don'ts

✔ DO keep torso rotated at the waist and legs together.

✔ DO keep your head, neck, and shoulders relaxed.

✔ DO move slowly and take the time to feel your abs working.

✔ DON'T pull on your neck or touch your elbow to your knee.

Other options

Weighted bent knee side crunch (harder): Hold a *lightweight* plate or dumbbell on your chest, or for an even greater challenge, hold a weight on top of or behind your head. Just don't press the plate down too hard.

Roll down negative curl

The roll down negative curl focuses on the hardest part of the crunch — the lowering phase.

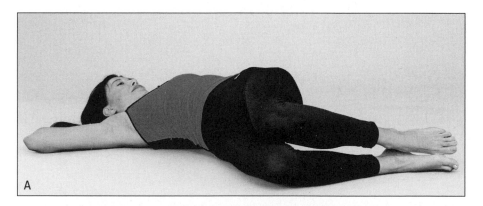

Figure 15-5:
Do keep your legs together.

Pay special attention to your form if you have lower back or neck problems.

Getting set

Sit with your knees bent and feet flat on the floor hip-width apart. Reach forward and place your hands on the outside of your thighs. Slide your shoulders down and tilt your chin slightly so there's a few inches of space between your chin and your chest. Gently pull your abdominals inward. See photo A of Figure 15-6.

The exercise

Tuck your pelvis and slowly lower back as far as you can go and keep your feet on the ground. Hold for a moment and then curl slowly back up. See photo B of Figure 15-6.

Figure 15-6:
Curl back
with feet on
the ground.

Do's and don'ts

✔ DO keep your abdominals pulled in so that you feel more tension in your abs.

✔ DO curl as well as lift. For an explanation of curling, refer to the introduction to this chapter and to Chapter 9, in which you find out common crunch mistakes.

✔ DON'T hunch or collapse your shoulders.

Other options

Hands on chest negative curl (harder): Fold your arms across your chest, palms down and tuck your chin in slightly. This position increases the weight of your upper body.

Hands behind head negative curl (harder): Place your hands behind your head without lacing your fingers. This version further increases the weight of your upper body.

Chapter 16

Working Your Butt and Legs

*Y*our butt and legs are home to the largest muscle groups in your body, and these muscles carry you everywhere you go, whenever you rely on your own locomotion. Having strong lower body muscles is key to living independently into old age. Being able to stand up from chairs, pick yourself up off the floor, climb stairs, step out of cars, and even get off the toilet are key factors to enjoying life on your own. Your lower body muscles, therefore, deserve plenty of attention. If you give them their proper due in your strength training routine, they'll carry you even farther and faster. This chapter introduces you to terms such as *glutes* and *quads,* and explains how best to strengthen and tone these and other lower body muscles.

Understanding Butt and Leg Muscle Basics

You have several muscles that make up the lower portion of your body. Each muscle serves a purpose and works with the other muscles in your lower body to help you move around. Take a look at the breakdown of the muscles below your waist:

✔ *Gluteus maximus (glutes):* The glutes is the granddaddy of all muscles in your body and covers your entire butt — both cheeks. The gluteus maximus straightens your legs from your hips when you stand up and propels you forward when you walk or run.

✔ *Hip flexors:* The muscles opposite your gluteus maximus, located at the front of your hips. Your hip flexor muscles help you lift your leg up high so you can march in a parade or step up onto a ladder. You don't need to spend much time working your hip flexors; they tend to be relatively stronger than the glutes in most people.

When the hip flexors become disproportionately strong and tight compared to other muscles, they pull your pelvis forward and throw your hip and lower spine into an excessively arched position. This strength imbalance may contribute to poor posture and lower back pain. Keep in mind that balanced muscle development is as important as strong muscles.

✔ *Abductors:* The sides, or meat, of your hips: your outer thighs. Your outer hips move your leg away from your body, like when you push off while ice-skating. The main outer hip muscle is called the *gluteus medius*.

✔ *Adductors:* The muscles that span the inside of your upper leg or inner thighs. They pull your leg in toward the center of your body or, when they're feeling ambitious, they sweep one leg in front of and past the other, like when you kick a soccer ball off to the side.

✔ *Quadriceps (quads):* The quads are located at the front of your thighs. Together these four muscles have one purpose: to straighten your leg from the knee.

✔ *Hamstrings (hams):* These muscles reside directly behind your thighbone. They bend your knee, bringing your heel toward your buttocks, and help the glutes do their thing.

✔ *Gastrocnemius (gastroc):* The gastroc is shaped like a diamond. The gastroc allows you to rise up on your tiptoes to see over your neighbor's fence. Check out the calves of any competitive bicyclist, and you'll see precisely what this muscle looks like.

✔ *Soleus:* Your soleus lies directly underneath the gastroc and helps out the gastroc when your knee is bent and you need to raise your heels up, like when you're sitting at the movies and you realize that you just stepped in gum.

✔ *Tibialis anterior:* The partner to your calf muscles is your shin muscle, covering the front of your lower leg. Whenever you're listening to music that makes you feel like tapping your toes, you can thank this muscle for allowing you to literally make this movement happen.

Check out Figures 16-1 and 16-2 for a look at all the muscles you'll be working on when you do the exercises in this chapter.

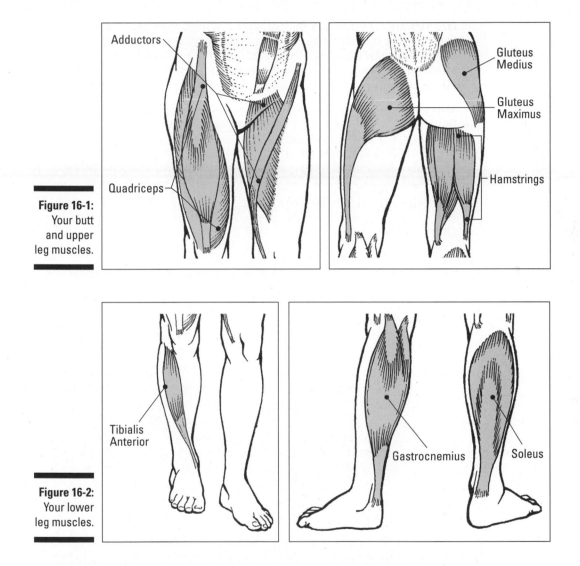

Figure 16-1: Your butt and upper leg muscles.

Figure 16-2: Your lower leg muscles.

Enjoying a Strong Lower Body

According to research, the key predictor of whether you'll need to live in an assisted living facility when you're elderly is your leg strength. Here's why you need to work on those glutes, quads, hams, and calves:

✔ **Real-life benefits:** When you take the time to strengthen your legs, you have more stamina for waiting in line at the post office, racing through the grocery store to catch a small child, climbing office stairs when the elevator is broken, and standing on tiptoe to paint the corner of your ceiling.

✔ **Injury prevention:** Strengthening your lower body muscles is a good way to preserve your hip, knee, and ankle joints — three joints that put in a lot of overtime and are particularly susceptible to injury. It's true that many joint injuries result from torn ligaments or tendons (the connective tissue that holds your bones in place), but many of these injuries won't occur in the first place if you have a strong army of muscles surrounding and protecting your joints. Often, lower body injuries result from a lifetime of repetitive motions such as walking up and down stairs. Weak muscles allow the bones to grind down the protective cartilage more rapidly and can't support the proper alignment that is necessary for healthy joint function.

By strengthening the muscles that surround the joints, you give them the support they need to do their job day after day. With strong lower body muscles you're less likely to sprain your ankle by stepping off a curb because your joints have the strength to hold up even when they're wrenched into positions they'd prefer to avoid. If you're already at the point where you have bad knees or a "trick ankle," it's not too late to pump some iron with your lower body muscles.

✔ **The "Feel Good" factor:** When your lower body is strong, you feel confident because you know that you can lift that heavy item, you can walk up those stairs, and you can take care of yourself. Leg strength is the leading indicator of who will end up living in nursing homes. Be strong and feel good about you.

Getting a leg up on the competition

If you're on an aerobic mission like training for a 10K or a bike-a-thon, strong legs are even more essential. Many runners and cyclists are afraid to lift weights, figuring that they'll develop bulky legs that'll slow them down. But the reality, according to mounds of research, is that leg and butt exercises help you go farther and faster. The key is in maintaining a good balance between strength and endurance training.

One guy we know couldn't break the four-hour barrier in the marathon until he started doing lower body weight training exercises. His hips used to tire out at around mile 16, so he wasn't able to stretch his legs out to their full stride, and he'd shuffle through the last 10 miles. At age 49, thanks to a regular leg routine, he was finally able to cruise through the finish line in 3 hours and 50 minutes. Even if your athletic goals aren't as ambitious as running 26.2 miles, leg workouts are important. Say you simply want to ride your stationary bike for 30 minutes three times a week. Stronger legs help you pedal faster and harder so that you can burn more calories during that half hour.

Getting a Great Lower Body Workout

In general, work your large muscles before moving on to your small ones. So perform your lower body workouts in the following order:

1. Glutes

2. Quads

3. Hamstrings

4. Inner and outer thighs

5. Calves

6. Shins

The only exception to this rule is if you specifically want to target a smaller muscle that's lagging far behind in its strength and is creating a too noticeable weak link. If that's the case, it's a good idea to switch your exercise order around so you target the weakest muscle when it's fresh.

Do at least four or five lower body exercises on a regular basis for balanced muscle development and visible training results. Your workouts need to include two types of exercises:

✔ *Compound exercises,* which involve several muscle groups at once

✔ *Isolation exercises,* which hone in on a single muscle group

If you're starting out with bad knees or hips, you may want to take a few weeks to simply focus on the muscles surrounding those joints. If your knees are the problem, for example, start with exercises that isolate your quads (the thigh squeeze and the leg extension machine) and your hams (the leg curl machine) and wait a few weeks before graduating to compound exercises (the squat and the lunge).

Here are some tips for working specific lower body muscle groups:

✔ **Glutes:** It's tough to isolate your butt muscles because nearly every butt exercise also involves the front and/or rear thigh muscles. However, you can maximize the emphasis on your maximus with a few simple technique tricks. For instance, when you're doing the leg press or the squat, keep your toes pointed straight ahead as much as possible and your weight shifted slightly back onto your heels, especially as you press back up into the straight-leg position. The more weight you shift onto your toes, the more your quadriceps become involved. Also, when you stand up, squeeze your cheeks to make sure your glutes are really working and aren't just going along for the ride.

✔ **Quadriceps:** The leg extension — an exercise in which you straighten your legs from a bent position — may give you a twinge of pain in your kneecap as you near the fully extended position. In this case, stop just before your legs are straight. Many leg extension machines have a device that stops the lever of the machine from going past the point you set. The machine may also let you start from a higher position than normal if you feel pain when you're initiating the movement.

✔ **Hamstrings:** The most popular way to work the hamstrings is with a leg curl machine; you start with your legs straight and curl your heels toward your butt. You typically find this machine in three varieties: lying, seated, and standing. In this chapter we show you how to use the lying leg curl because it's the one you see most often and the one we generally like best (although our opinions vary from brand to brand). With some leg curl machines, you lie flat on your stomach; others have a severe bend in the support pad. Our favorite variety has you lying at an angle with your hips above your head. Try all the hamstring machines available to you, and use any of the machines that feel comfortable.

✔ **Calves:** When you perform the standing calf raise, experiment with the angle of your toes to find the position that's most comfortable. But don't angle your toes too much outward or inward or you'll place too much stress on your knees and ankles. And perform calf exercises slowly. Bouncing your heels up and down causes your calf muscles to tighten and uses momentum to power the movement instead of maximally challenging your muscles.

Expect to feel sore and walk a little stiffly for a day or two after your first few lower body workouts. Of course, any muscle that's new to weight training is likely to be sore after the first few sessions, but leg muscles seem particularly prone to this phenomenon. Start out with just your own body weight or light weights; otherwise, you may find yourself walking like Herman Munster or wincing in agony when you get up from the breakfast table.

Avoiding Mistakes When Working Your Lower Body

Here are the most common pitfalls to watch out for when training your butt and legs:

✔ **Don't play favorites.** In other words, don't work your butt muscles and neglect your thighs just because you want to fill out the back of your jeans. Strive for balance. If one lower body muscle group is monstrously strong compared to the others, it pulls your posture out of alignment and you may end up with an injury.

✔ **Don't put your knees in jeopardy.** Avoid locking your knees when you're lifting a weight, and don't allow your knees to shoot out past your toes in the squat, lunge, or leg press. If you feel knee pain during an exercise, stop immediately. Try another exercise and return to the one that gave you trouble after you've been training for a few weeks. Or perform a simpler version of the exercise, restricting the distance you move the weight.

✔ **Don't perform more than 15 repetitions for any leg exercise for strength training.** Some people, afraid of developing bulky legs, use extremely light weights and perform 40 repetitions. You're not going to build much strength this way, and you'll probably fall asleep in the middle of a set. You also increase your chance of injury from placing too much repetitive stress on your joints.

Learning Lower Body Exercises

Here's a preview of the exercises we show you in this chapter:

✔ **Butt and leg exercises:** squat, lunge, leg press, and kneeling butt blaster

✔ **Quadriceps (front thigh) exercises:** quad press and leg extension machine

✔ **Hamstring (rear thigh) exercises:** kneeling leg curl and leg curl machine

✔ **Inner and outer thigh exercises:** inner and outer thigh machine, side-lying leg lift, and inner thigh lift

✔ **Calf and shin exercises:** standing calf raise and toe lift

Squat

In addition to strengthening your butt muscles, the squat also does a good job of working your quadriceps and hamstrings.

If you have hip, knee, or lower back problems, you may want to try the modified version.

Getting set

Hold a dumbbell in each hand or place your hands on your hips or on the tops of your thighs, or allow them to hang comfortably down at your sides. Stand with your feet as wide as your hips and with your weight slightly back on your heels. Pull your abdominals in and stand up tall with square shoulders. See photo A of Figure 16-3.

The exercise

Sit back and down, as if you're sitting into a chair. Lower as far as you can without leaning your upper body more than a few inches forward. Don't lower any farther than the point at which your thighs are parallel to the floor, and don't allow your knees to shoot out in front of your toes. When you feel your upper body fold forward over your thighs, straighten your legs and stand back up. Take care not to lock your knees at the top of the movement. See photo B of Figure 16-3.

Do's and don'ts

- ✔ DON'T allow your knees to travel beyond your toes. We know we said this before, but it bears repeating.

- ✔ DON'T look down. Your body tends to follow your eyes. So if you're staring at the ground, you're more likely to fall forward. Instead, keep your head up and your eyes focused on an object directly in front of you.

- ✔ DON'T shift your body weight forward so your heels lift up off the floor. When you push back up to the standing position, concentrate on pushing through your heels.

- ✔ DON'T arch your back as you stand back up.

Other options

Weightless squat (easier): If you have trouble balancing or completing at least eight repetitions of the squat with good form, skip the weights. Instead place your hands on your hips or the tops of your thighs as you do the exercise.

Bench squat (easier): Place the end of a bench behind you and allow your buttocks to lightly touch the top of it as you sit downward. This placement helps you guide your movement and perfect your form.

Plié squat: To add emphasis to the inner and outer thighs, place your feet out a little wider apart and angle your toes outward. Most people lower farther in this position because they feel more stable. Still, don't travel any lower than the point at which your thighs are parallel to the floor, and don't let your knees shoot out past your toes.

Barbell squat (harder): When you've mastered the squat, progress to the barbell squat for even greater challenges. Place a weighted bar in a power cage so when you stand underneath it, the bar rests gently across the top of your shoulders. Stand with your feet as wide as your hips, weight shifted slightly back on your heels, and hold on to either side of the bar with your hands wider than shoulder-width apart. Pull your abdominals in and stand up tall with square shoulders.

Figure 16-3:
Don't shift your body weight forward so that your heels lift up off the floor.

Sit back and down, as if you're sitting into a chair. Lower as far as you can without leaning your upper body more than a few inches forward. Don't lower any farther than the point at which your thighs are parallel to the floor, and don't allow your knees to shoot out in front of your toes. When you feel your upper body fold forward over your thighs, straighten your legs and stand back up.

Lunge

The lunge is a great overall lower body exercise: It strengthens your butt, quadriceps, hamstrings, and calves.

If you feel pain in your hips, knees, or lower back when you do this exercise, try the split lunge version described in the "Other options" section.

Getting set

Stand with your feet as wide as your hips and your weight back a little on your heels, and place your hands on your hips. Pull your abdominals in and stand up tall with square shoulders. See photo A of Figure 16-4.

The exercise

Lift your right toe slightly and, leading with your heel, step your right foot forward an elongated stride's length, as if you're trying to step over a crack on the sidewalk. As your foot touches the floor, bend both knees until your right thigh is parallel to the floor and your left thigh is perpendicular to it. Your left heel will lift off the floor. Press off the ball of your foot and step back to the standing position. See photo B of Figure 16-4.

Do's and don'ts

- ✔ DO keep your eyes focused ahead; when you look down, you have a tendency to fall forward.
- ✔ DON'T step too far forward or you'll have trouble balancing.
- ✔ DON'T lean forward or allow your front knee to travel past your toes.

Other options

Split lunge (easier): Start with one leg a stride's length in front of the other. Bend both knees, and lower your body so your ending position is the same as in the basic lunge. You may want to lightly grasp the back of an upright bench or a chair for support.

Lunge with weights (harder): Hold a dumbbell in each hand with your arms down at your sides, or place a barbell behind your neck and across your shoulders. You also can do the split lunge while holding a dumbbell in each hand or by using the Smith Machine.

Backward lunge (harder): Step your right leg back about a stride's length behind you, and bend both knees until your left thigh is parallel to the floor and your right thigh is perpendicular to it. You'll feel this version a bit more in your hamstrings.

Traveling lunge (harder): Perform the basic lunge, alternating legs so you travel forward with each repetition. You need a good 10 yards of space to do this. Bend your arms to 90 degrees and swing them purposefully. This variation is great for skiers, hikers, and climbers as it mimics the moves that are used in those activities.

Leg press machine

The leg press machine covers a lot of ground, strengthening your butt, quadriceps, and hamstrings. It's a good alternative if the squat or lunge bothers your lower back.

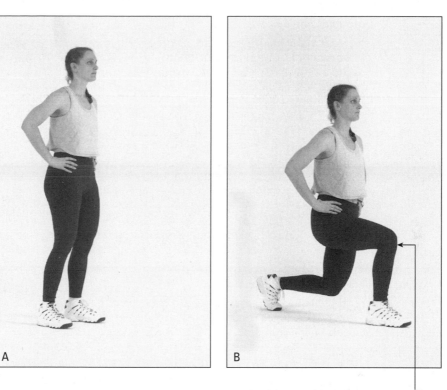

Figure 16-4:
Keep your
eyes
focused
ahead.

Don't let your knee shoot past your toes.

You may want to try the modified version if you experience pain in your hips or knees.

Getting set

Set the machine so that when you lie on your back with your knees bent and feet flat on the foot plate, your shoulders fit snugly under the shoulder pads and your knees are bent to an inch or so below parallel to the foot plate. Place your feet as wide as your hips with your toes pointing forward and your heels directly behind your toes. Grasp the handles. Pull your abdominals in and keep your head and neck on the back pad. See photo A of Figure 16-5.

The exercise

Pressing through your heels, push against the platform until your legs are straight. Then bend your knees until your thighs are parallel with the platform and the weight plates you're lifting are hovering just above the weight stack. See photo B of Figure 16-5.

Do's and don'ts

- ✔ DO press your heels into the foot plate instead of allowing them to lift up.
- ✔ DON'T lower your thighs past parallel with the foot plate or allow your knees to shoot in front of your toes.
- ✔ DON'T arch your back off the pad to help move the weight.
- ✔ DON'T lock your knees when your legs are straight.

Other options

Different types of machines: You may run across several types of leg press machines. One has you sitting in an upright position, pressing your legs out straight. Another is called a 45-degree leg press: You lie in a reclining position and press up and out diagonally. Yet another version has you lie on your back and press your legs straight up. All these variations are acceptable. Just remember: Don't bend your legs so far that your thighs are smooshed against your chest and your knees are hanging out there in Never-Never Land. Keep in mind that your foot position changes the emphasis of the exercise. The higher you place your feet on the foot platform, the more you emphasize your butt muscles.

Modified leg press (easier): If you have chronic knee problems, you can still do this exercise. Set the seat height so your thighs are a few inches above parallel — this position limits the distance you can bend your knees. However, this version focuses more on your front thigh muscles and less on your butt.

One-leg leg press (harder): Use the same form as with the basic version of this exercise with one foot lifted up and off the foot plate. After you complete your reps, switch legs.

Kneeling butt blaster

The kneeling butt blaster works your butt with some emphasis on your hamstrings, too.

Make sure that you keep your abdominals pulled in on this exercise, especially if you're prone to lower back discomfort.

Getting set

Kneel on your elbows and knees on top of a thick towel, with your knees directly under your hips and your elbows under your shoulders. Clasp your hands together or turn your palms toward the floor. Flex your right foot so it's perpendicular to the floor. Tilt your chin slightly toward your chest, and pull your abdominals in so your back doesn't sag toward the floor. See photo A of Figure 16-6.

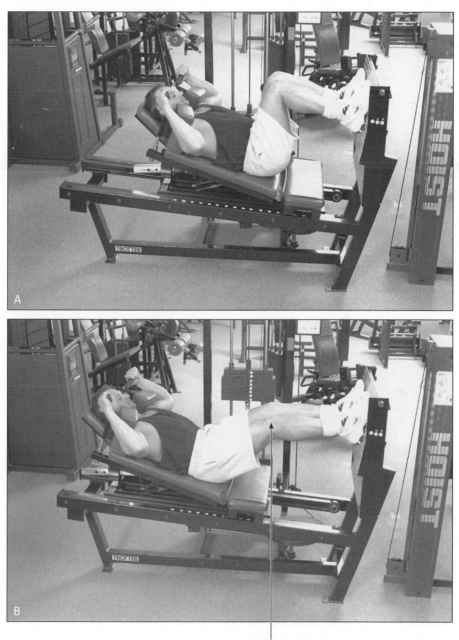

Figure 16-5:
Don't lower
your thighs
past parallel
with the
foot plate.

Don't lock your knees.

Figure 16-6:
Don't arch
your back
as you lift
your leg.

Raise your knee to hip.

The exercise

Keeping your knee bent, lift your right leg and raise your knee to hip level. Then slowly lower your leg back down. Between repetitions, your knee almost, but not quite, touches the floor. Complete all the repetitions with one leg before switching sides. See photo B of Figure 16-6.

Do's and don'ts

- ✔ DO keep your neck still and your shoulders relaxed.
- ✔ DO move slowly.
- ✔ DON'T throw your leg up in the air.
- ✔ DON'T raise your knee above hip height.
- ✔ DON'T arch your back as you lift your leg.

Other options

Kneeling butt blaster with weight (harder): Add an ankle weight to this exercise or squeeze a small dumbbell in the well of your knee. We love this last option because your muscles have to work even harder to hold the weight in place.

Butt blaster machine: This machine mimics the kneeling butt blaster. You kneel with one knee on a platform, place your other foot onto a foot plate, and then press back and up. This machine is fine as long as you remember to keep your abdominals pulled in and resist arching your lower back.

Quad press

The quad press is a particularly good quadriceps exercise for people who feel pain when they bend and straighten their knees.

Getting set

Roll up a bath towel. Sit on the floor and lean against a wall with your legs straight out in front of you. (Or bend the nonworking knee into your chest if that's more comfortable.) Place the towel underneath the well of your right knee. See photo A of Figure 16-7.

The exercise

Squeeze your quadriceps tightly and press down on the towel. Hold for five slow counts, relax, and repeat until you complete the set. Then switch legs. See photo B of Figure 16-7.

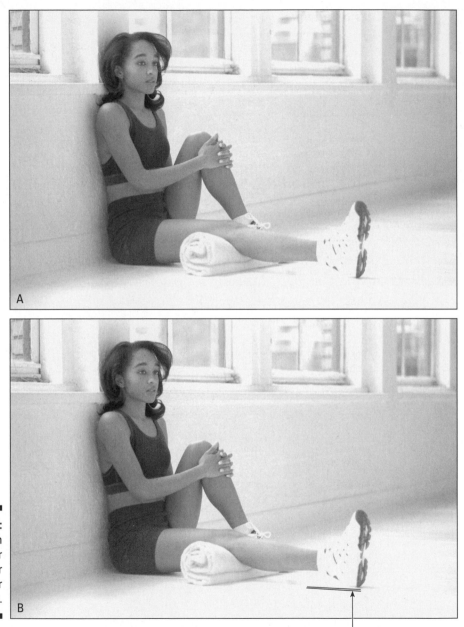

Figure 16-7:
Don't hunch
your
shoulders or
round your
back.

When you squeeze your quadriceps, your heel will lift slightly off the floor.

Do's and don'ts

✔ DO bend your nonworking knee into your chest if that makes the exercise more comfortable.

✔ DON'T tighten your face, hunch your shoulders, or round your back.

Other options

Modified quad press (easier): If you experience pain in your knee when you do this exercise, try squeezing your muscle for a shorter period of time. Start with one second and build up. Also try squeezing without the towel underneath your knee. Or to make the exercise tougher, replace the towel with a firmer object such as a tennis ball or filled water bottle. This replacement allows you to squeeze harder.

Straight leg raise (harder): Sit in the same position, but instead of pressing your thigh downward, lift your entire leg up and off the floor a few inches. Hold a moment and slowly lower to the start. You can also do this version of the exercise with an ankle weight wrapped around your ankle or draped across your thigh.

Leg extension machine

The leg extension machine zeroes in on your quadriceps muscles.

If this exercise bothers your knees, try the modified version or choose a different exercise.

Getting set

Set the machine so your back sits comfortably against the backrest, the center of your knee is lined up with the machine's pulley, and your shins are flush against the ankle pads. (On most machines you can move the backrest forward and back and the ankle pads up and down.) Sit down and swing your legs around so your knees are bent and the tops of your shins are resting against the underside of the ankle pads. Hold on to the handles. Sit up tall and pull your abdominals in. See photo A of Figure 16-8.

The exercise

Straighten your legs to lift the ankle bar until your knees are straight. Hold for a second at the top position, and then slowly bend your knees. See photo B of Figure 16-8.

Figure 16-8:
Don't arch your back in an effort to help you lift the weight.

A   B

Do's and don'ts

✔ DO make sure that you take the time to set the machine properly.

✔ DO move slowly.

✔ DON'T ram your knees at the top of the movement.

✔ DON'T arch your back in an effort to help you lift the weight.

Other options

Modified leg extension (easier): If one leg is noticeably stronger than the other, slide one leg out of the way and do this exercise one leg at a time. You probably will need less than half the weight you use when lifting both legs together.

Single-leg extension: Many leg extension machines have a mechanism you set to limit the distance that you bend and straighten your legs. Use this device if your knees give you trouble at any point of the exercise.

Ball squeeze leg extension (harder): Place a soccer ball, weighted ball, or rolled towel between your knees. As you extend your leg, concentrate on squeezing the ball so it doesn't slip out of place. This version of the exercise forces your quads to work harder in order to hold onto the ball.

Kneeling leg curl

The kneeling leg curl targets your hamstring muscles.

Pay extra attention to good form if you have lower back or knee troubles.

Getting set

Kneel on your elbows and knees on a mat or thick towel, with your knees directly under your hips and your elbows directly under your shoulders. Clasp your hands together or turn your palms toward the floor. Flex your right foot so it's perpendicular to the floor. Keeping your knee bent, lift your right leg and raise your knee up to hip level. Tilt your chin slightly toward your chest and pull your abdominals in so your back doesn't sag. See photo A of Figure 16-9.

The exercise

Straighten your leg and then bend your knee. Complete all the repetitions with one leg before switching sides. See photo B of Figure 16-9.

Do's and don'ts

- ✔ DO keep your neck still and your shoulders relaxed.
- ✔ DO move slowly so you feel the tension in the back of your thigh.
- ✔ DON'T use an ankle weight for this exercise: It places too much pressure on your knee.
- ✔ DON'T just throw your leg out straight and snap it back again.
- ✔ DON'T raise your leg above hip height.
- ✔ DON'T arch your back as you curl and uncurl your leg.

Other options

Variations (easier): To make this exercise easier, lie on the floor with your forehead resting on your forearms. Lift your thigh slightly off the floor, and then curl and uncurl. Or do this exercise while standing and holding onto the back of a chair or the back of an upright bench with your hands.

Weighted leg curl (harder): Add weight to this exercise by wrapping an ankle weight around your ankle or thigh. Or do a kneeling or standing version of the exercise with the low pulley of a cable machine that has a padded ankle strap.

Keep your neck in line with the rest of your spine.

Figure 16-9:
Don't arch
your back
as you curl
and uncurl
your leg.

Leg curl machine

The leg curl machine does a great job of strengthening your hamstring
muscles.

Use caution if you have a history of lower back discomfort.

Getting set

Set the ankle pads of the machine so that when you lie on your stomach, the underside of the pads are flush with the tops of your heels. Lie down, rest the side of your face on the support pad, and grasp the handles. Gently flex your feet. Pull your abdominals in and tuck your hips down so your hipbones press into the pad. See photo A of Figure 16-10.

The exercise

Bend your knees to lift the ankle bar until your calves are perpendicular to the floor. Then slowly straighten your legs. See photo B of Figure 16-10.

Do's and don'ts

- ✔ DO keep your hipbones pressed against the machine and your abdominals pulled in. You may want to lift your thighs just a hair upward before you bend your knees.

- ✔ DO lower your legs back down slowly so the weights you're lifting don't slam down against the rest of the stack.

- ✔ DON'T — and this is a *big* don't — allow your butt to pop off the pad. This puts stress on your lower back and minimizes the work being done by your hamstrings.

- ✔ DON'T kick your heels all the way to your butt.

Other options

Other curl machines: Some machines work your hamstrings from a standing or seated position. Others have independent left and right sides so that each leg has to carry its own share of the weight. Still others have a "range limiting" device that allows you to cut off the movement at the top or bottom — a good variation if you're experiencing any pain while doing this exercise.

Single-leg curl: Lift with both legs, straighten one out of the way, and lower the weight down with one leg only.

Inner/outer thigh machine

The inner/outer thigh machine sets to strengthen either your inner thigh muscles or your outer thigh muscles. Skaters, skiers, and basketball players — anyone involved in side-to-side movements — can help prevent injury by using this machine.

Figure 16-10:
Don't let
your butt
pop off
the pad.

Don't let your hips pop up.

Getting set

Set the machine so the leg mechanisms are together and the knee and ankle pads are rotated to the outside. Sit up tall in the seat, and bend your knees so they rest against the thigh pads and the outside of your ankles rest against the ankle pads. If there's a seat belt, wear it to help keep you from popping out of the machine. Pull your abdominals in and sit up tall. See photo A of Figure 16-11.

The exercise

Press your knees outward until you feel tension in your outer thighs. Hold the position for a moment, and then slowly allow your legs to move back together. This is the outer thigh, or *abduction*, exercise. To set the machine for the inner thigh, or *adduction,* exercise, shift the leg mechanisms so they're comfortably spread apart, and turn the knee and ankle pads toward the inside. Position your legs so that the inside of your knees rest against the thigh pads, and the inside of your ankles rest against the ankle pads. Pull your legs together, and then slowly move them back out to a point at which you feel a comfortable stretch through your inner thighs. See photo B of Figure 16-11.

Figure 16-11: Control the movement in both directions.

Do's and don'ts

✔ DO control the movement in both directions. If you hear the weight stack come crashing down, slow down.

✔ DO change the weight between exercises if you need to. Most people use approximately the same weight for both inner and outer thigh exercises, but don't take that for granted.

✔ DON'T arch your back or wiggle around in the seat in an effort to assist your legs.

Other options

Vary seat position: Some machines allow you to decline the seat back a few degrees or even all the way down so you can lie flat. Experiment with different back positions to see what's most comfortable for you and to give the exercise a different feel.

Side-lying leg lift

The side-lying leg lift strengthens your outer thigh muscles.

Pay attention to the instructions marked by the Posture Patrol icon, particularly if you have a history of lower back pain.

Getting set

Lie on the floor on your left side with your legs a few inches in front of you, knees bent slightly, and head resting on your outstretched arm. Bend your right arm and place your palm on the floor in front of your chest for support. Align your right hip directly over your left hip and pull your abdominals in so your back isn't arched. See photo A of Figure 16-12.

The exercise

Keeping your knee slightly bent, raise your right leg until your foot reaches shoulder height. Then slowly lower your leg back down. Switch sides and do the same number of repetitions with your left leg. See photo B of Figure 16-12.

Do's and don'ts

✔ DO keep your top hip stacked directly over your bottom hip; don't roll backward.

✔ DO keep your head down and your neck and shoulders relaxed.

✔ DO keep your abdominals pulled in to help your body remain still so you work only your outer thigh.

✔ DON'T raise your foot any higher than shoulder height.

Other options

Modified leg lift (easier): Bend your top knee even more when performing the side-lying leg lift.

Leg lift with rotation (harder): When you reach the top of the movement, rotate your thigh outward by turning your knee up to the ceiling; then rotate back to the original position and lower your leg back down.

Leg lift with a weight (harder): Place an ankle weight on your ankle or, if you have knee problems, on top of your thigh.

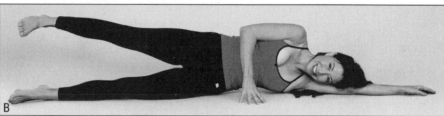

Figure 16-12: Keep your top hip stacked directly over your bottom hip; don't roll backward.

Inner thigh lift

The inner thigh lift strengthens your inner thigh muscles.

Use caution if you have lower back problems.

Getting set

Roll up a bath towel (or use a step aerobics platform). Lie on your right side with your head resting on your outstretched arm. Bend your left leg and rest your knee on top of the rolled towel so that your knee is level with your hip and your top hip is directly over your bottom hip. Place your left hand on the floor in front of your chest for support. Pull your abdominals in. See photo A of Figure 16-13.

The exercise

Lift your bottom (right) leg a few inches off the floor. Pause briefly at the top of the movement, and slowly lower your leg back down. Switch sides and do the same number of repetitions with your left leg. See photo B of Figure 16-13.

Do's and don'ts

- ✔ DON'T lift your leg more than a few inches. Stop when you feel tension in your inner thigh. How high you need to lift depends on your flexibility, your strength, and your build.

- ✔ DON'T arch your back as you lift your leg.

Other options

Modified inner thigh lift (easier): Instead of placing your top knee on the towel, bend your knee and place your foot behind your bottom leg.

Inner thigh lift with a weight (harder): Wear an ankle weight while performing the inner thigh lift. If you have bad knees, drape the weight on top of your inner thigh.

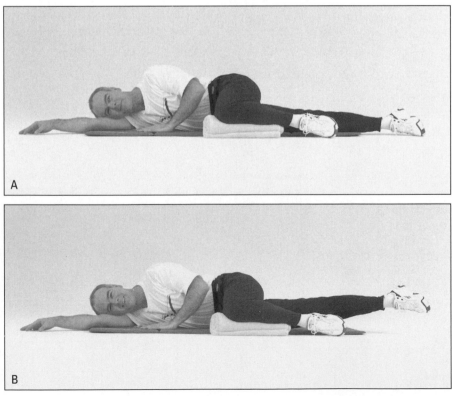

Figure 16-13:
Don't lift your leg more than a few inches.

Standing calf raise

The standing calf raise hones in on your calf muscles.

Getting set

Stand on the edge of a step. (Or, if you have a step aerobics platform, place two sets of risers underneath the platform.) Stand tall with the balls of your feet firmly planted on the step and your heels hanging over the edge. Rest your hands against a wall or a sturdy object for balance. Stand tall with your abdominals pulled in. See photo A of Figure 16-14.

The exercise

Raise your heels a few inches above the edge of the step so you're on your tiptoes. Hold the position for a moment, and then lower your heels back down. Lower your heels below the platform in order to stretch your calf muscles. See photo B of Figure 16-14.

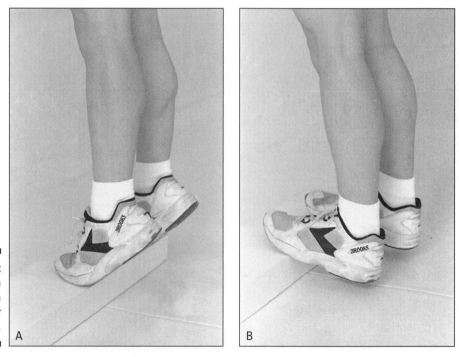

Figure 16-14: Lift as high as you can onto your toes.

A

B

Do's and don'ts

- ✔ DO lift as high as you can on your toes.
- ✔ DO lower your heels down as much as your ankle flexibility allows.

Other options

Standing calf machine: Stand with your shoulders snugly underneath two pads and your heels handing off the edge of a platform. The standing calf machine isolates the gastrocnemius. If you want to get your soleus into the act (and you do if you do a lot of activities that involve walking, running, or jumping), look for a seated calf machine. Your knees fit underneath a platform and your heels again hang off the edge.

Add a dumbbell (harder): Holding a dumbbell in one hand adds resistance to this exercise and also forces you to balance more because you won't be able to hold onto something with both hands.

One-leg calf raise (harder): To work one calf at a time, bend one knee behind you and raise the heel of your other foot up and down. Do the same number of repetitions with each leg.

Toe lift

If you're prone to shin splints and ankle problems, adding the toe lift to your repertoire is a must.

Getting set

Stand with your feet as wide as your hips and your legs straight but not locked. You may hold onto a sturdy object for support. See photo A of Figure 16-15.

The exercise

Keeping your heels firmly planted into the floor, lift your toes as high as you can. Feel the tightening through the lower part of your shins. Lower your toes. See photo B of Figure 16-15.

Do's and don'ts

- ✔ DO lift only the part of your foot that's in front of the ball of your foot.
- ✔ DON'T rock back onto your heels.

Other options

Seated toe lift (easier): Do the toe lift while seated with your knees bent.

Exercise sequence (harder): Do the toe lift immediately following calf raises.

Band toe lift (harder): Do the toe lift while seated, but wrap a band around the back edges of your toes. You'll feel resistance both when lifting your toes and when lowering them. (Don't use the band to help lift though.)

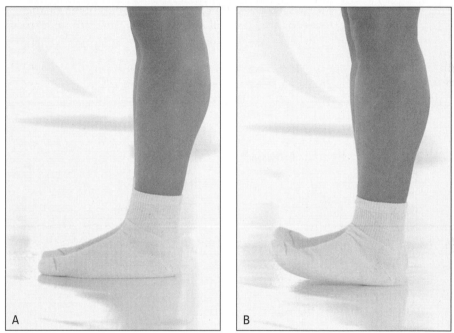

Figure 16-15: Don't rock back onto your heels.

Chapter 17

Working Your Core

Core training, core strength, and core programs are popular exercise buzzwords these days. On health club group exercise class schedules, sessions are devoted to training the core and so much more.

Many exercisers mistakenly think that core training simply is another name for working more abdominals. This idea is wrong. Core training is about training your body's center and building a strong foundation. Core stabilization exercises challenge your body to remain solid and centered. This training builds great posture and prevents injury. In fact, simply by standing with good posture, you look taller and slimmer, as if you've lost 5 pounds. Many of Shirley's training clients gain up to an inch in height, lose inches around the waist, and eliminate back pain after doing core exercises regularly. This news is remarkable when you consider that most people get shorter as they age.

In this chapter, you discover the meaning of *core*. You also understand why having a strong and stable core is important to feel and look your best.

Introducing Core Stabilizer Muscle Basics

Core refers to the anatomic center of the body. You can also use the terms trunk or torso interchangeably with the word core. Stabilizer muscles hold your joints together properly to improve movement efficiency, prevent injury, and promote stability. When athletic trainers typically think of core training, they refer to muscles that stabilize the hips and lower back. For peak sports performance, athletes need to be able to transfer the strength and power of their legs and hips through the trunk. Think of a great tennis or basketball player and how this player uses his core muscles to add power to the game.

To improve everyday living, it's a good idea to take a broader view of the core and include muscles that support the spine, shoulders, and hips. These muscle groups all work together to create good posture and provide balance and control. In Chapters 11, 13, 15, and 16, we discuss training your back, shoulders, abs, butt and legs from the perspective of training your *mover* muscles. In this chapter, we discuss training your *stabilizer* muscles.

Core stabilizer muscles include the following muscles:

✔ Trunk stabilizers

- *Transversus abdominis*
- *Internal obliques*
- *Multifidus*
- *Quadratus lumborum*

✔ Shoulder stabilizers

- *Trapezius*
- *Rhomboids*
- *Levator scapulae*
- *Serratos anterior*
- *Pectoralis minor*

✔ Pelvic stabilizers

- *External rotators*
- *Hip abductors* (includes the *gluteus medius* and *minimus* [glutes] and *tensor fascia latae*)
- *Pelvic floor* and *diaphragm* (some researchers believe)

Many of these muscle names may be familiar to you from other chapters in this book. The difference when it comes to core training is that instead of strengthening these muscles as movers, the focus in core training is on improving the endurance of these muscles as stabilizers.

Your stabilizer muscles work whenever you're awake and standing, sitting, or otherwise moving. Strong core stabilizers

✔ Enable you to sit upright on a bench with no backrest for long hours to watch your kid's soccer game.

✔ Ensure that your shoulders and hips work properly.

✔ Help you avoid injury or the need for joint replacement surgery.

✔ Keep your balance when you stand on one leg.

✔ Help prevent falls.

Enjoying a Strong Core

Core stabilization exercises aren't sexy, but they're critically important to enjoying everyday living.

✔ **Real-life benefits:** A strong core supports good posture and proper joint alignment. Good posture not only makes you look and feel better but also prevents back pain. A strong core allows you to stand for long periods of time without pain or survive sitting at your desk and working at your computer for long hours.

✔ **Injury prevention:** Good posture places the least amount of stress on your joints. Strong stabilizers keep your neck, shoulders, hips, and knees properly aligned to minimize wear and tear on your body. Strong stabilizers also let you use the strength in your arms and legs. For example, if you don't have a stable shoulder joint, regardless of how strong your arms and back are, lifting items like a suitcase without hurting your shoulder may be tough.

✔ **The "Feel Good" factor:** Nothing boosts your confidence like great posture and moving from the center of your being. Standing up tall; facing life straight on. That's what it's all about.

Getting a Core Workout

To get a great core stabilization workout, you need to focus on keeping your torso solid. Because the objective of core training is to improve muscle endurance, instead of sheer strength, isometrically held exercises such as the plank (described later in this chapter) are effective training methods.

In addition, core exercises train your body's stabilizer muscles to work together. For example, preventing low back pain isn't simply about strengthening your abs. To provide optimal support for your spine, your abs, back, pelvic floor, and hip muscles all need to work together. Unlike other exercises that isolate and target a specific muscle or muscle group, core stabilization exercises challenge your whole body to work together. Form is critically important. Always stop doing an exercise when you can no longer execute it with perfect form.

Unlike the mover muscles that are closer to the surface of your body, your deep stabilizer muscles are made up of almost 100 percent slow twitch fibers. In other words, these muscles aren't designed for short bursts of strength and power. Instead, these muscles are meant to be working at all times that you're in motion. Therefore, unlike strength training exercises that require you to push yourself to fatigue and then rest for at least 48 hours, you can do core stabilization exercises daily. In fact, daily core stabilization exercises remind you to use your postural muscles as you sit, drive, stand, run your errands, or work at the office.

Last, but certainly not least, core exercises improve your sex life. As you tone up your pelvic floor and your deep abdominals, regain mobility in your spine, and improve control over your pelvis, your sex life gets a great boost. Shirley, as a health and wellness educator, assures you that research evidence shows that a healthy sex life is definitely good for your overall well-being. As if we need studies to tell us that.

Avoiding Mistakes When Training Your Core

Most of us are weak in the core, so we need to pay particular attention to form and quality of movement.

Keep these tips in mind to get the most out of each of your core exercises:

- ✔ **Avoid looking like an old donkey.** When you forget to tighten your abdominal muscles, particularly the deepest layer (the *transversus abdominis*), your back sags in the middle. When Shirley was guest teaching at a resort in Jamaica, she saw an old donkey — the perfect example of this curved posture. Now, when she teaches core exercises, she always reminds her students not to look like old donkeys.

  To avoid donkey posture, draw your abdominals in toward your spine as you exhale and keep your abdominals contracted for the duration of the exercise.

- ✔ **Don't pop out your rib cage.** Another good way to check whether your deep abdominal muscles are active is to look at the position of your rib cage. Draw your lower ribs in snug toward your spine. If your ribs flare up and out, your deep trunk stabilizers aren't active. Tighten them up.

- ✔ **Don't stick your butt up in the air.** When you're training your abs and back in positions like the plank or a push-up, you need to rely on the strength of your core muscles and not your legs. You can always tell that you are cheating by relying on your leg strength if your butt is sticking up in the air. Make sure that it is no higher than your shoulders.

✔ **When you exhale, always lift your pelvic floor up and pull your abdominals in toward your spine.** The best way to activate your deep abdominals and pelvic floor muscles is by exhaling actively as you lift your muscles up and in. Exaggerate your exhalation as you do your core stabilization exercises to make sure that you're using these muscles.

Performing Exercises in This Chapter

Here's a list of the core stabilization exercises presented in this chapter:

✔ Plank

✔ Side plank

✔ All fours spinal stabilization

✔ Reverse plank

✔ Leg slide

Plank

The plank is a basic core stabilization exercise that works your abs, back, glutes, and shoulder stabilizer muscles.

Do the easiest version if you have any shoulder discomfort.

Getting set

Lie facedown with your knees bent. Place your elbows under your shoulders. Slide your shoulders down and lengthen the back of your neck so your ears are in line with your shoulders. Gently pull your abdominals inward. See photo A of Figure 17-1.

The exercise

As you exhale, curl your toes under and push up onto the balls of your feet. Avoid arching your upper or lower back. Work up to a 30-second hold. See photo B of Figure 17-1.

Figure 17-1:
Gently pull your abdominals inward.

Do's and don'ts

✔ DO keep your abdominals pulled in so you feel more tension in your abs and so you don't overarch your lower back or pop out your ribs.

✔ DO keep your shoulders down and your neck lengthened. Avoid hunching your shoulders.

✔ DON'T lift your butt in the air and rest your weight on your legs.

Other options

Plank on knees (easier): Lift up on your knees, keeping your abs and glutes tight and your spine lengthened. Supporting a shorter length is easier for the core stabilizers.

One-legged plank (harder): Keep your torso parallel to the ground. Lift one leg. Work up to a 30-second hold. To make it even more difficult, pick up and extend the opposite arm as you also hold up one leg.

Side plank

The side plank conditions core stabilizers, especially the muscles that support the shoulder girdle and lower back.

Use caution if you're prone to shoulder discomfort.

Getting set

Recline on your left side, left hand palm down under your shoulder. Place your top right hand in front of your body. Keep your torso perpendicular to the ground, relax your shoulders, and pull in your abdominals. See photo A of Figure 17-2.

The exercise

Push into your left hand and lift your hips up into a side plank position. Work up to a 30-second hold. See photo B of Figure 17-2.

Do's and don'ts

- ✔ DO keep your shoulders down and neck lengthened. Don't hunch or collapse into your shoulder.
- ✔ DO continue to breathe normally as you hold the position. Avoid holding your breath.
- ✔ DO move smoothly and with control.
- ✔ DON'T collapse your chest forward or lean backward. Keep your torso perpendicular to the floor.

Other options

Modified side plank (easier): Start with your right elbow under your shoulder and with your lower leg bent at a right angle at the knee. Keep the top leg long and straight.

Side plank lifts: Instead of holding the elevated position for 30 seconds, lift and lower your hips and work up to 12 repetitions.

One-legged side plank (harder): When you reach the elevated position, pick your top leg off the floor and hold it straight at hip height.

Figure 17-2:
Don't hunch
or collapse
into your
shoulder as
you lift.

All fours spinal stabilization

All fours spinal stabilization is an excellent exercise to condition postural muscles and to prevent lower back pain.

If you have wrist pain when you put your palms on the ground, try doing the exercise on your closed fists.

Getting set

Kneel on all fours in a tabletop position with your hands under your shoulders and knees under your hips. Slide your shoulders down. Pull your abdominals in. See photo A of Figure 17-3.

The exercise

Lift and extend opposite arm and leg out straight. Keep your chest and hips parallel to the ground. Lower your arm and leg back to start. Repeat with other arm and leg. See photo B of Figure 17-3.

Do's and don'ts

   ✔ DO concentrate on keeping your torso parallel to the ground.

   ✔ DON'T hunch your shoulders or arch your back.

Other options

Spinal stabilization arms only or legs only (easier): Instead of simultaneously lifting the opposite arm and leg, only lift alternating arms. Repeat, only lifting alternating legs.

Spinal stabilization same side arm and leg (harder): Instead of lifting your opposite arm and leg, lift the arm and leg on the same side.

Figure 17-3: Keep your torso parallel to the ground.

Reverse plank

The reverse tabletop plank is an all-around excellent core stabilizer, working abs, back, glutes, and shoulder stabilizer muscles. This exercise excels because it works so many muscles simultaneously, which is the way that we challenge our bodies in real life.

Getting set

Lie on your back with your knees bent and palms under your shoulders, and then lift yourself into a tabletop position. See photo A of Figure 17-4. Point your fingers in whatever direction is most comfortable for your shoulders. Slide your shoulders down. Pull your abdominals inward.

The exercise

As you exhale, squeeze your buttocks and push up onto your heels. Avoid arching your upper or lower back. Hold your head in the most comfortable position for your neck — either upright and looking down your torso or lowered gently toward the back. Work up to a 30-second hold.

Do's and don'ts

- ✔ DO keep your abdominals pulled in so you don't arch your lower back or pop out your ribs.
- ✔ DO keep your shoulders down. Avoid hunching or collapsing into your shoulders.
- ✔ DON'T let your bottom sag down.

Figure 17-4:
A reverse tabletop plank (A), and a variation with straight legs (B).

Other options

Reverse plank (easier): Lie on your back with your legs straight and palms under your shoulders, and then lift yourself onto your hands. See photo B of Figure 17-4. Lift your hips, keeping your knees over your ankles, your abs and gluts tight and your spine lengthened. Supporting a shorter length is easier for your core stabilizers.

Reverse plank with leg lift (harder): Keep your torso parallel to the ground as in photo A in Figure 17-4. Alternate lifting and lowering one leg at a time as high as you can without lowering your hips.

The slide

The slide is the perfect abdominal exercise for people prone to lower back or neck pain. Performing the slide is a good way to get your abs in shape for more challenging abdominal exercises.

Getting set

Remove your shoes. Lie on your back with your knees bent comfortably, feet hip-width apart, toes up, and heels digging into the floor. Rest your arms at your sides. Pull your abdominals in and gently push — but don't force — your back into the floor so, to some extent, you flatten out the natural curve of the small of your back. See photo A of Figure 17-5.

The exercise

Slowly slide your heels forward as you gradually straighten your legs; don't allow your abs to push upward or your back to pop up off the floor, even a little. Continue straightening your legs until you can't keep your abs tight or your back on the floor or until your legs fully extend. Then slowly slide your heels back to the starting position, again taking care not to relax your middle muscles. See photo B of Figure 17-5.

Do's and don'ts

✔ DO slide your legs out only as far as you can while keeping your back in contact with the floor. As you get stronger, you'll be able to straighten your legs all the way while keeping your abs pulled in and your back flat.

✔ DO keep your head, neck, and shoulders relaxed.

✔ DO move slowly and take the time to feel your abs working.

Other options

Single-leg slide (easier): Slide out one heel at a time. Do an equal number of reps with each leg.

Figure 17-5:
Don't allow
your lower
back to
pop up.

Slide with paper plates (harder): Place your heels on two paper plates or in plastic bags. You have to work even harder to slide slowly and with control.

Short slide (harder): Slide your heels out to the point where you need to work the hardest to maintain your back placement on the floor. Slide your heels a few inches back and forth several times so you're constantly working.

Part IV
Setting Up Your Workout Programs

The 5th Wave   By Rich Tennant

OK-TIME FOR AEROBICS!!

WEIGHT ROOM

In this part . . .

Part IV shows you how to start designing your workout program — whether you lift weights twice or five times a week, whether you have 20 minutes or 2 hours, or whether your goal is to build strong bones or biceps the diameter of a watermelon.

In this part, you discover a variety of training routines from the very basic beginners' workout to advanced routines. You'll also gather plenty of training techniques to give your workouts extra pizazz. We reveal strategies for training your core, preventing back pain and injury, and improving your balance. We also show you how to modify your training to meet the needs of the stages of life — from kids to older adults. And, you'll start to understand how Yoga and Pilates can contribute to your workout program.

Chapter 18

Basic Workouts to Get Started

● ●

In This Chapter

▶ Designing your own routines

▶ Reviewing the essential elements of every routine

▶ Trying sample routines that strengthen your whole body

● ●

*I*n Part III, we describe more than 170 exercises. Certainly you're not expected to do all these moves in one workout — your workouts would last longer than the Academy Awards. So how do you choose?

In this chapter, you begin by discovering how to create a routine based on your own goals, preferences, time schedule, and available equipment. You quickly review your program variables — the ingredients essential to all weight training routines covered in Chapter 2. Then you figure out how to select the right weight for each exercise. You're ready to begin lifting!

A number of sample beginner routines are included to get you started. All the workouts in this chapter strengthen the entire body. In Chapters 19, 20, 21, and 22, we include a variety of routines that suit every time situation, that provide more challenging workouts, and that meet special needs.

Custom-designing a Routine

You've probably read magazine articles that reveal an athlete or actor's weight training routine. Often, the stories imply that if you follow the routine to the letter, you too can become a sculpted celebrity — or at least look like one. Don't buy into this notion. Everyone has a unique genetic makeup — and a unique set of preferences and priorities. In other words, you may not be able to dedicate three hours daily to training, hire a personal trainer to work with you daily, and hire a chef to manage all your meals. You certainly can pick up good ideas from reading about other peoples' workouts, but you're better off designing your own routines by considering the following factors.

Identifying why you want to train

Too many people blindly go through the motions of a weight training program without stopping to ask themselves, "What the heck am I trying to accomplish?" So give this question some serious thought. Are you planning to scale the Grand Tetons, or do you just want to strengthen your back to add oomph to your golf swing? Remember the principle of specificity.

Here's a rundown of some common goals and how you can reach each of them. You may want to consult a trainer or medical doctor for advice that's even more specific to your needs.

- ✔ **Improve your health.** If you aspire to increase your strength, keep your bones strong, and avoid common injuries, you need not spend half of your waking hours with hunks of steel in your hands. You can get by with one exercise for every major muscle group in your body. Simply perform one set of 8 to 15 repetitions for each of the following muscle groups:

    - Butt (glutes)

    - Front thighs (quadriceps)

    - Rear thighs (hamstrings)

    - Calves

    - Chest (pecs)

    - Back

    - Abdominals (abs)

    - Shoulders (delts)

    - Front of upper arm (biceps)

    - Rear of upper arm (triceps)

    The American College of Sports Medicine (ACSM) recommends doing two or three workouts a week.

- ✔ **Alter your looks.** Weight training can be a powerful tool for changing your appearance by toning up your muscles, adding definition to your body's shape, and adding size if desired and your genetics permit. If you're large boned and muscular, however, weight training can't make you lean and flexible — and vice versa. You need to work within your body's parameters.

Significantly overhauling your body's appearance requires more of a time commitment than simply improving your health. (And keep in mind that your diet, lifestyle, and cardiovascular workouts play a large role, too.) Instead of training your entire body in 25 minutes, you may need to spend 20 minutes simply on your upper body. To develop a noticeably firmer body, we suggest performing at least three sets per muscle group. To build some serious bulk, you may need to perform even more sets and use some of the advanced techniques described in Chapter 21.

✔ **Train for an athletic event.** Preparing for an athletic challenge at any level takes time and dedication (and weight training, of course, is just one aspect of your training). For best results, you need to tailor your weight routine precisely to the event. For example, if you're working toward a hilly 10K walk or run, you need to give extra attention to your leg and butt muscles. And your workout will be completely different if you want to simply complete a 10K run rather than win it. Serious competitors should expect to spend a lot of serious time in the weight room at certain times of the year (primarily the off-season). And, you should consult a trainer or coach who specializes in working with athletes for a comprehensive, periodized program.

When you've identified the reason why you want to train, use the S.M.A.R.T. goal system explained in Chapter 3 to set short-term goals that ensure your long-term success. Your short-term goals should focus on the behaviors, in other words the things that you need to do or not do, to achieve your long-term objective. Your training program design should reflect your specific training objectives.

Your equipment

Naturally, the exercises you choose are limited to the equipment that's available to you. If you belong to a health club the size of Wal-Mart, you may be able to try every exercise in this book — and probably a few thousand more. One four-story club in New York City devotes an entire *floor* to leg machines.

If you work out at a smaller club or at home, your choices are more limited, but even with rudimentary equipment, you can get your body into great shape. In Part III, for example, we describe dozens of exercises that you can do at home with nothing more than dumbbells and a bench. If you're short on equipment, you may want to consult a trainer to find out how to make the most of the gizmos you have access to or to help you decide which key pieces of equipment you should own to achieve your particular goals.

Reality check: Plastic or perfect?

By the way, take a big reality check: Don't expect to look like the sculpted, fat-free people who sell weight training products on TV infomercials or magazine ads. Many of these models have unusual genetics, have taken drugs, and/or have undergone liposuction and added implants to achieve their looks (in addition to being digitally enhanced by professional film producers). In fact, among men, chest or pec and calf implants are popular, while more and more women are getting butt implants. Mentioning this phenomenon is *not* to advocate plastic surgery. This is simply to let you know that most people who have bodies that look a little too perfect are likely to have achieved that look through unnatural means. So don't set yourself up for failure before you begin by trying to look like a TV or magazine model by using natural methods. It's impossible. Simply aim to be your best you.

Your exercise preferences

When you first take up weight training, you may be overwhelmed by the challenge of knowing the basics of each exercise — how to stand, where to grab the weight, how to adjust the machines, when to inhale and exhale. But you soon develop strong preferences for certain exercises and equipment. Before you know it, you'll be saying things like, "I love the incline chest fly, but I'd much rather do the dumbbell chest press on a flat bench." Pay attention to which exercises feel good to you and which equipment you enjoy using, and design your workout accordingly. Keep in mind, however, that it's natural to prefer the exercises that you're better at doing. Sometimes, you may need to push yourself to do exercises that you don't love to balance out your conditioning. Keep an open mind. You may even surprise yourself when you grow to love the push-ups that you used to hate.

Your lifestyle

Ask yourself (and answer honestly): "How many times can I work out each week? How many hours can I spend at the gym, including time in the shower and the locker room?" If you're a busy parent who also works full time, chances are you have less time to work out than a college student or retired person.

Be realistic. Don't vow to do six sets per muscle group if the only time you're able to lift weights is during your 30-minute lunch break on Tuesdays and Thursdays. Otherwise, you fall into that *why-bother?* trap. You're better off doing a 20-minute routine than skipping that 2-hour workout you planned but somehow never got around to.

Your current level of fitness

If you haven't lifted weights since high school 20 years ago, don't start with the routine your old football coach gave you. Otherwise, you can expect a lot of muscle soreness — and maybe an injury or two — in your immediate future. Don't let your enthusiasm, your flexible schedule, or your access to fancy equipment cloud your judgment as you design your routine. Remember, the best goals are those that are achievable, and to be achievable, your plans need to be realistic.

Reviewing Your Program Variables

There are six basic program variables that you need to keep in mind when designing your training programs.

- ✔ Exercise selection
- ✔ Training frequency
- ✔ Exercise order
- ✔ Amount of weight and number of reps
- ✔ Number of sets
- ✔ Rest periods

Doing exercises in the right order

In general, follow the rule of doing your upper and lower body exercises in the order of your larger muscles first, and then your smaller muscles. Lastly, exercise your middle body, your lower back and abdominals, as they serve to stabilize your body as you do all the prior exercises.

Upper body

1. Chest and back (It doesn't matter which comes first.)
2. Shoulders
3. Biceps and triceps (It doesn't matter which comes first.)
4. Wrists

Lower body

1. Butt

2. Thighs

3. Calves and shins (It doesn't matter which comes first although we prefer to work our calves before our shins.)

Middle body

Perform your abdominal and lower back muscle exercises in any order you want. Mix up your core stabilization exercises with those that target the *mover* muscles, or do your mover exercises first, followed by your stabilizer exercises or vice versa. Researchers haven't yet determined whether an ideal order exists for training the muscles of this part of the body.

Choosing the right weight

The right weight level depends on what you want to achieve from your training, because it relates to the number of reps that you perform. To develop strength, you want to do one to six reps. To increase muscle size, do between 6 to 12 reps. And, to improve endurance, do between 12 and 20 reps. A one-rep max equals the total amount of weight you can lift with one repetition and means you're giving a 100 percent effort. More reps represent what are referred to as sub-maximal loads. See the bullet points below for reference.

- 1 rep = 100 percent
- 2-3 reps = 95 percent
- 4-5 reps = 90 percent
- 6-7 reps = 85 percent
- 8-9 reps = 80 percent
- 10-11 reps = 75 percent
- 12-13 reps = 70 percent
- 14-15 reps = 65 percent
- 16-20 reps = 60 percent

As you can see, a moderate intensity workout of lifting 70 to 80 percent of your one rep max is in the 8 to 13 rep range. Performing fewer reps — and using ultra-heavy weights — carries a greater risk of injury. And doing more than 12 reps is generally not effective for building strength, but doing up to 20 to 25 reps does improve muscular endurance.

To keep yourself motivated and your muscles challenged, you may want to vary the number of reps you perform. You can use a periodized program as explained in Chapter 3 that first emphasizes muscular strength and then later emphasizes muscular endurance. For example, you can do 6 to 8 repetitions one month and then 12 to 15 the next. Finding the right weight for each exercise requires some trial and error. Don't be afraid to add or subtract weight after you start a set. We've seen people contort their bodies to finish a set just because they overestimated what they could lift but who were too embarrassed, too stubborn, or simply not aware of the huge risk of injury to drop down a plate.

Using the rest period

How long you rest in-between sets is also a part of your routine. If you want to increase maximal strength, you need a long rest period of up to four minutes. If you're looking to improve muscular endurance, 30 seconds or even less rest is fine. And, if you want to increase size, your rest period should be about 30 seconds to one-and-a-half minutes. If you are a beginner, and that lasts for at least the first three consecutive months of training, take as long as you need. You're considered a beginner until you have completed three consecutive months of consistent training at least two to three days a week.

Trying Sample Beginner Routines

You can combine exercises in countless ways to create an effective weight routine. All the routines in this section include one or two exercises per muscle group.

Doing circuits at the gym

Many gyms have a dozen or so machines arranged in a circle or row called a *circuit.* They're placed in a logical order (from larger to smaller muscles) so you can move from machine to machine without having to use any brainpower to decide which exercise to do next. For reasons we explain in Chapter 15, we suggest skipping the abdominal machines and doing the basic abdominal crunch (or other ab floor exercises) at the end of your circuit instead.

Some fitness facilities, such as Curves®, revolve entirely around circuit training. Many facilities also offer cardio-resistance circuits where in-between strength training stations, they have cardio stations. For example, you may jog or march in place, do jumping jacks, or jump on a trampoline in-between lifting weights. The concept behind these workouts is keeping your heart rate at the low end of an aerobic training zone so you also receive some aerobic conditioning benefits as well. Because this workout represents a compromise, you're not getting an optimum cardio or strength workout. Instead, you're trying to hit two goals at once, which is of course, better than hitting only one or no goals, especially if you're time crunched.

After reviewing weight training principles, you may understand why circuits are a good place for beginners to start training. Typically, you'll do one set at each machine and have about a 30-second rest interval between stations. This is the lower intensity side of the spectrum and has a reduced risk of injury. See Table 18-1.

Table 18-1	Sample Weight Machine Circuit
Butt and legs	Leg press machine, leg extension machine, leg curl machine
Back	Lat pulldown
Chest	Vertical chest press machine
Shoulders	Shoulder press machine
Biceps	Arm curl machine
Triceps	Triceps dip machine
Abdominals	Basic abdominal crunch

Doing circuits at home

If you like the idea of doing circuits, design your own home circuit. You may choose to stick with one circuit for a few weeks and then switch to another circuit. Or you may integrate circuit training on a rotating schedule for a lower intensity workout that you incorporate into a plan that also includes a high-intensity strength workout component and a bulk-building segment. See Table 18-2.

Table 18-2	Sample Home Equipment Circuit
Butt and legs	Squat, lunge
Back	Band lat pulldown, one-arm dumbbell row
Chest	Push-up
Shoulders	Dumbbell shoulder press, lateral raise

Biceps	Dumbbell reverse curl
Triceps	Triceps kickback
Abdominals	Basic abdominal crunch, bicycle, plank

Dumbbells-and-a-bench routine for the gym or home

For this routine, you need several sets of dumbbells and a bench with an adjustable back rest. This workout is typical for someone who works out at home, but many gym-goers like it, too. See Table 18-3.

Table 18-3	Sample Dumbbells-and-a-Bench Routine
Butt and legs	Squat, lunge, standing calf raise
Back	One-arm row, back extension chest, incline chest fly
Shoulders	Lateral raise
Arms	Dumbbell biceps curl, triceps kickback
Abdominals	Abdominal crunch with a twist

The mix 'n' match routine at the gym

Most experienced weight lifters use a combination of machines and free weights. Over time you develop certain preferences — some exercises feel better with free weights, others are more fun with machines. We encourage you to try all the equipment at your disposal at least a few times. See Tables 18-4, 18-5, and 18-6.

Table 18-4	Liz's Favorite Mix 'n' Match Routine
Butt and legs	Lunge, leg press, inner/outer thigh machine, standing calf raise
Back	Cable row
Chest	Push-up

(continued)

Table 18-4 *(continued)*

Shoulders	Cable lateral raise
Arms	Dumbbell biceps curl, triceps pushdown, wrist curl
Abdominals	Abdominal crunch

Table 18-5 **Shirley's Favorite Mix 'n' Match Routine**

Butt and legs	Squat, lunge, inner/outer thigh machine, leg curl machine
Back	Lat pulldown, machine row
Chest	Incline chest fly, push-up
Shoulders	Dumbbell lateral raise and shoulder press
Arms	Dumbbell reverse curl, triceps kickback
Abdominals	Reverse crunch, bent knee side crunch, bicycle

Table 18-6 **Suzanne's Favorite Mix 'n' Match Routine**

Butt and legs	Squat, seated leg curl, standing calf raise
Back	Pull-up
Chest	Bench press
Shoulders	Dumbbell shoulder press
Arms	Barbell biceps curl, triceps kickback
Abdominals	Reverse crunch

Chapter 19

Quickie Workouts for Busy Days

*F*or best results, you want to train your entire body at least two to three times a week. Three times a week gives you faster results but takes more of your personal time. Studies show that you get 75 percent of your results from training two days a week, compared to training three days a week. Life happens. You can't always stick to an ideal training schedule. For those days and weeks that are simply too busy, shorter workouts are better than no workouts. Or you can split up training your body into short increments daily so you hit at least each section of your body at least two times a week. Your training program needs to fit your life.

In this chapter, you get a variety of quickie workouts to use for those busy periods when you can't follow an ideal training schedule. The quickies are organized in 10 and 15 minute segments and are appropriate for either the gym or the home. As a personal trainer and international presenter who's trained thousands of people worldwide, Shirley recommends that you try to find at least 15 minutes each day in your schedule for a workout so that exercising becomes part of your daily routine — like brushing your teeth. These routines give you plenty of choices for what to do in those 15-minute increments. Chapter 17 describes core programs and includes quickie core workouts.

Making the Most of Quickie Training

Organize these quickies in whatever way works best for you. The following suggestions give you several ideas on how to fit quickie workouts into your lifestyle.

- ✔ **Emergency total body conditioning:** Normally, you do a 25-minute weight training workout 3 days a week. Imagine a time when your schedule is overloaded and you can't possibly follow your normal workout routine. Instead of doing nothing, use one of the total body workouts to keep your muscles stimulated.

- ✔ **Add on to your cardio workout:** Let's say you weight train two days a week and hit the gym for cardio on three days a week. When you can't make it for your dedicated weight training sessions, add on a 15- or 10-minute quickie workout on the weight machines, after you finish your cardio-training.

- ✔ **Divide your workout throughout the day:** Sometimes it's simply impossible to find more than a few spare minutes. Instead of giving up on strength training entirely, fit in a quickie workout in the morning and in the afternoon. You might even want to add on another session at night. Three 10- or 15-minute workouts easily add up to 30 or 45 minutes of training.

- ✔ **Do a daily quickie:** Maybe all you ever have time for during the week is a quickie workout. Until your life settles down and you find more time, schedule a daily quickie workout. Each day target either the upper or lower body and the core. Take Friday off. On Saturday, fit in one thorough total body workout and rest on Sunday.

Putting Together Your Quickie Routine

Even when you're doing quickie programs, you need to keep in mind the basic weight training principles explained in Chapter 2. Observe the following points each time that you train.

- ✔ **Always warm up.** Even for a quick workout, you need to prepare your body for more rigorous work. Walk briskly for five minutes before you exercise. This warm-up includes walking quickly around the house, the yard, or in the parking lot at the office.

✔ **Work all major muscle groups.** Be sure to do exercises for your upper body, your lower body, and your core a minimum of twice a week.

✔ **Apply program variables.** Even for short workouts, training frequency, exercise selection, order, amount of weight, number of reps, number of sets, and your rest periods are all still important components. Just because you're doing a quickie workout does not mean that you can throw all the weight training principles out the window. All the rules still apply.

✔ **Train in one minute sets.** In general, one set of a particular exercise takes approximately one minute. If each rep requires two seconds up, a brief pause, and two seconds down, plan on five to six seconds per rep. Therefore, a set of 10-12 reps takes roughly one minute.

✔ **Alternate upper and lower body exercises.** When you want to reduce the waiting time during rest periods, switch between upper and lower body exercises so that one part of your body rests while the other works. Save your core exercises for last.

✔ **Mix in stretching exercises.** To be even more efficient, use your rest periods for stretches that target the muscle that you just worked. You can stretch your body all throughout the workout, and you won't need extra time for a stretching segment at the end.

Doing 15-minute Workouts

Perform these 15-minute workouts in any of the suggested manners. You may even think of more ways to use these quickie suggestions. The important thing is to do exactly that — use these workouts and get and stay toned and firm.

15-minute gym total body workouts

The workouts shown in Tables 19-1 through 19-3 are the absolute bare minimum and are for emergency situations only — they're by no means complete routines. But these workouts tide you over for a few sessions until you get back on track for a more thorough total body workout. Take five minutes to warm up before you start lifting by doing some form of aerobic movement: walking, marching, jumping rope, cycling, rowing, and so on.

Table 19-1	15-minute Machine Routine
Butt and legs	Leg press machine
Back	Machine row
Chest	Vertical chest press machine
Shoulders	Shoulder press machine
Abdominals	Basic abdominal crunch, bicycle

Table 19-2	15-minute Mix 'n Match Routine
Butt and legs	Squat
Back	Machine row
Chest	Push-up
Shoulders	Shoulder press machine
Abdominals	Basic abdominal crunch, bicycle

Table 19-3	15-minute Mix 'n Match Routine
Butt and legs	Leg press machine
Back	One-arm dumbbell row
Chest	Vertical chest press machine
Shoulders	Dumbbell shoulder press
Abdominals	Basic abdominal crunch, bicycle

15-minute at home total body workouts

When you're really pressed for time, sometimes the best thing to do is plan your workout for home — either first or last on your day's schedule. This way, you'll always be sure to complete your workout, no matter what happens. Use Tables 19-4 through 19-7 as your guides.

Table 19-4	15-minute Dumbbell Routine
Butt and legs	Squat
Back	One-arm dumbbell row
Chest	Dumbbell chest press
Shoulders	Dumbbell shoulder press
Abdominals	Basic abdominal crunch, bicycle

Table 19-5	15-minute Band Routine
Butt and legs	Band squat
Back	Band lat pulldown
Chest	Band push-up
Shoulders	Band one-arm shoulder press
Abdominals	Basic abdominal crunch, bicycle

Table 19-6	15-minute Ball Routine
Butt and legs	Ball bridge, ball march
Back	Ball extension
Chest and shoulders	Ball push-up
Abdominals	Ball crunch, ball oblique crunch, ball plank

Table 19-7	15-minute Body Weight Routine
Butt and legs	Squat, lunge
Back	Pelvic tilt, back extension
Chest	Push-up
Arms	Bench dip
Abdominals	Basic abdominal crunch, bicycle
Core	Side plank, reverse plank, plank

Doing 15-minute upper or lower body workouts

If you decide to organize your 15-minute workouts into split routines focusing on either the upper or the lower body, use the following suggestions, or create your own workouts modeled after the ideas in Tables 19-8 through 19-11.

Table 19-8	15-minute Upper Body Dumbbell Routine
Chest	Push-up
Back	One-arm dumbbell row
Shoulders	Dumbbell shoulder press
Front upper arm	Concentration curl
Rear upper arm	Triceps kickback
Abdominals	Basic abdominal crunch
Core	Plank

Table 19-9	15-minute Upper Body Band Routine
Back	Band lat pulldown
Chest	Band push-up
Shoulders	Band one-arm shoulder press
Front upper arm	Band biceps curl
Rear upper arm	Band triceps extension
Abdominals	Basic abdominal crunch
Core	All fours spinal stabilization

Table 19-10	15-minute Lower Body Dumbbell Routine
Butt	Squat
Front thighs	Lunge

Rear thighs	Kneeling leg curl
Inner thighs	Inner thigh lift
Outer thighs	Side-lying leg lift
Calves	Standing calf raise

Table 19-11	15-minute Lower Plank Core Body Band Routine
Butt	Band butt blaster
Rear thighs	Band squat
Inner thighs	Band inner thigh lift
Outer thighs	Band outer thigh lift
Calves	Band calf press
Core	All fours spinal stabilization

Exercising with the Ten-Minute Routines

On some days you may not even have 15 minutes to lift weights. Instead of skipping your workout altogether, try plan B: the absolute bare minimum. The workouts listed in Tables 19-12 and 19-13 are for emergency situations only — they are by no means complete routines. But a ten-minute workout tides you over for a few sessions until you get back on track.

Shorter workouts are better than no workouts, but don't get the impression that it's the best or only way to train. The exercises in this chapter are supposed to be the exception rather than the rule. Some marketers make the claim that this is "all" one needs to do, and yes, these quickies can contribute to improve health, but don't get the impression that someone can get very "fit" exercising this way. That's not realistic or truthful.

Table 19-12	Ten-minute Machine Routine
Butt and legs	Leg press machine
Back	Machine row
Chest	Vertical chest press machine

Table 19-13	Ten-minute Dumbbell Routine
Butt and legs	Squat
Back	One-arm dumbbell row
Chest	Dumbbell chest press

Home gym ten-minute mix 'n' match routines

You can do a quickie mix 'n' match routine with whatever type of equipment you've chosen for home use. Tables 19-14 through 19-16 show some fun combination workouts.

Table 19-14	Dumbbells and Band Mix 'n' Match Routine
Butt and legs	Band butt blaster
Back	Band lat pulldown
Chest	Dumbbell chest press
Shoulders	Band one-arm shoulder press
Abdominals	Abdominal crunch

Table 19-15	Dumbbells and Ball Mix 'n' Match Routine
Butt and legs	Squat
Back	Ball extension
Chest	Ball push-up
Shoulders	Dumbbell shoulder press
Abdominals	Ball crunch

Table 19-16	Band and Ball Mix 'n' Match Routine
Butt and legs	Band squat
Back	Band lat pulldown
Chest	Ball push-up
Shoulders	Band one-arm shoulder press
Abdominals	Ball plank

Doing ten-minute upper or lower body workouts

Tables 19-17 through 19-20 list ten-minute workouts organized as split routines focusing on either the upper or the lower body. Use the following suggestions, or get creative and design your own quickie split workouts.

Table 19-17	Ten-minute Upper Body Dumbbell Routine
Back	One-arm dumbbell row
Chest	Dumbbell chest press
Shoulders	Dumbbell shoulder press
Abdominals	Basic abdominal crunch

Table 19-18	Ten-minute Upper Body Band Routine
Back	Band lat pulldown
Chest	Band push-up
Shoulders	Band one-arm shoulder press
Abdominals	Bicycle

Table 19-19	Ten-minute Lower Body Dumbbell Routine
Butt and legs	Squat
Inner thighs	Inner thigh lift
Outer thighs	Side-lying leg lift
Calves	Standing calf raise

Table 19-20	Ten-minute Lower Body Band Routine
Butt and legs	Band squat
Inner thighs	Band inner thigh lift
Outer thighs	Band outer thigh lift
Calves	Band calf press

Enjoying a ten-minute stretch workout

Stretching feels great at the end of a workout. Stretching restores length to muscles that may feel tighter after being contracted during exercise. Stretching also releases muscular tension from your body, leaving you feeling more relaxed in general. You can also do the stretch sequence in Table 19-21 as an early morning wake-up routine or as an end-of-day relaxation session. Breathe deeply and hold each stretch three breath cycles. One breath cycle equals one inhalation and one exhalation. As time permits, repeat each stretch three to five times.

Table 19-21	Ten-minute Stretch Routine
Butt and legs	Pretzel stretch, hamstrings stretch, quadriceps stretch
Back	Cat stretch, reach-up stretch
Chest and shoulders	Hand-clasp stretch

How to set up your home gym for quickies

If you think you'll need quickie workouts from time to time to keep up your conditioning; then streamlining your home gym is essential. If you only have ten minutes to exercise, you don't want to spend six of those minutes trying to find where you put your exercise bands. Management of your home gym space is critical for successful quickies. See Chapter 6 for a thorough discussion of what you need to set up your home gym. The following tips help ensure that your home exercise space is ideal for quickies.

✔ **Consistent space:** If space permits, the ideal situation is to have a dedicated space that's only used for your exercise sessions. In many homes, however, space is at a premium. If you can't allocate a spot only for exercise, at a minimum choose a place that you use consistently and that's large enough for your movement needs.

✔ **Storage containers for equipment:** You must have proper storage for your equipment in order to find it quickly and to avoid accidents. Storage is particularly important when it comes to dumbbells because other family members or you may trip over randomly placed equipment. For every type of equipment that you purchase — dumbbells, bands, tubing, stretch straps, mats — you need to have a place for it to belong. Store dumbbells on racks and use baskets or crates for bands, tubing, and stretch straps.

✔ **Workout plans or log:** You want to be able to do your routine immediately. If you haven't memorized it, you need to reference it quickly and easily. If you keep a workout log, keep it with all of your equipment. All of your workout design resources (such as *this* book) should also be easily available.

✔ **Clock or timer:** If you know that time is always going to be an issue, keep a clock visible either in or near your workout area. As an alternative, keep a timer and set it for 10 or 15 minutes or whatever you've allocated, so you'll stay within your time budget and be sure to complete your planned exercises.

Chapter 20

Core Programs for Good Balance and a Healthy Back

More than 80 percent of adults in North America suffer from back pain at some point in their adult life. That statistic is staggering. In the United States, back pain is the leading cause of disability from work. One major American corporation spent $75 million in only one year to pay healthcare providers who treated employees with low back pain.

Back pain is often related to poor posture and lack of stability in the spine, due to weak core muscles. In addition, poor postural stability over the years eventually leads to balance problems in later years. Increasingly, older adults are suffering from falls or from the fear of falling. The same contributing factors that present as a pain in the back when you're younger, can lead to a broken hip or permanent use of a walker when you're older. One out of every three people over age 65 falls at least once a year. Twenty five percent of people over the age of 50 who break a hip die from a fall within the first year after the accident. About 50 percent of those who break their hips never regain full walking ability. That should get your attention. The loss of balance and postural control doesn't happen overnight, but occurs slowly over the years, as the muscles that support good posture grow weaker.

Just as you need to take preventive measures against osteoporosis and muscle wasting, you need to act now to preserve your sense of equilibrium for the future. Better balance also serves you well in dozens of sports, from mountain biking to rock climbing to in-line skating. You'll catch on to these activities more quickly and avoid injuries that would befall those with a shakier sense of balance.

More and more health clubs are adding classes onto their schedules that incorporate core training and balance exercises and use balance training equipment. In Chapter 17, you discover your core muscles and some basic exercises. In this chapter, we cover specific balance exercises, training tools, and routines to train your core and improve your balance. You're provided a number of sample routines that you can use depending on how much time you can give.

Saying Goodbye to Back Pain

Regular exercise is one of the best ways you can prevent back pain. Good body mechanics, or moving properly, as you sit, stand, bend over, pick things up, and push and pull furniture are also important. Repetitive motions, if performed incorrectly over time, can cause joint strain and injury.

You aren't helpless against back pain. What you do daily makes a powerful difference. Small changes can go a long way to preventing debilitating pain. Observe the following basic tips for a lifetime of back health.

- **Exercise regularly:** Following a consistent, balanced exercise program will go a long way toward keeping you fit and strong.

- **Use good posture:** You can practice good posture every waking moment and improve your posture. Naturally, you aren't going to remember every minute, but the more times that you catch yourself slouching, the more often you can correct yourself and use your core stabilizers.

- **Move properly:** The most common way people injure their backs is when they bend over, pick something up, and turn their body as they stand. Practice good movement mechanics whenever you lift, bend, or pick up and carry anything. Even if you pick up a pencil, use good movement habits. That way when you pick up something that is heavier, you're much more likely to do it properly.

- **Check your desk setup:** Make sure your desk at the office and at home is set up according to good ergonomic principles. Make sure that your chair fits your body and that your computer and monitor are positioned so that as you work, you use good posture.

✔ **Use a headset:** Many people spend a lot of time talking on the phone and bending their necks into awkward positions. Your head weighs anywhere from 8 to 12 pounds. If you hold it improperly, you can affect your overall posture. Use headsets whenever possible, especially for extended conversations.

✔ **Use a backpack:** People often carry heavy and unbalanced loads on their shoulders. Balance the weight by using a good quality backpack and avoid carrying things that are too heavy.

✔ **Buy furniture that offers support:** Every chair or couch that you sit on affects your posture, particularly if it's a piece of furniture that you use often. A good bed is also important, because you spend one-third of your life sleeping, and if you're not getting good support, it will affect your posture. Make sure the furniture in your life is also supporting a healthy back and good posture.

Evaluating Your Posture

An easy and quick way to assess your posture is to look at yourself from a side profile. The following five points should align vertically:

✔ Ear

✔ Shoulder

✔ Hip

✔ Knee

✔ Ankle

Your posture should reflect the natural S-shaped curve of the spine. These curves help reduce impact forces on your body by allowing it to be more resilient. Imbalances in your body usually contribute to poor posture. These imbalances may result from any of the following:

✔ **Muscle imbalances:** Muscles create movement by working in combination with other muscles. In a well-balanced body, muscles co-exist in balance with each other. For example, weak shins usually co-exist with tight calves and contribute to tighter muscles along the back of the legs.

✔ **Tight muscles:** Tight muscles, often a result of muscle imbalances, also create stress on joints, and result in less flexibility and less ROM.

✔ **Past injuries:** Accidents from your youth such as broken bones and torn ligaments can permanently alter your posture. A broken leg can lead to one leg being shorter than another. A shoulder injury that tore ligaments can lead to lingering stiffness and a reduced ROM on one side of your body when compared to the other side.

✔ **Genetics:** Certain postural deviations can be part of your family heritage. For example, scoliosis, a curvature of the spine is often an inherited condition. Another congenital condition that affects posture is flat feet.

After you've identified the causes of your postural imbalances, start addressing them. If the reasons are muscular, use an exercise program to improve your posture. Following one of the suggested core routines would be a great start, because these routines are beginning workouts that are suitable for people at all levels of ability. If the reasons are due to injury or genetics, your healthcare provider can help you find appropriate support such as heel lifts or orthotics for your shoes. Whatever your condition, you can always improve and if you have ideal posture, then you can work to keep up your great shape to stay that way.

Wearing high-heeled shoes daily contributes to poor posture. If worn regularly, high heels cause tightening and shortening of the calves, tightness in the lower back, and knee pain. Your best bet is to vary your heel heights and not wear the same shoes two days in a row. Reserve your high-heeled fashion shoes for times when you don't need to walk long distances. Also, buy your shoes a half size larger and invest in some comfortable insoles, or for fashion shoes, get the less noticeable narrow versions.

Benefiting from Good Posture

Improving your posture literally changes your life. Not only will you look taller, appear slimmer, and feel better, but also you'll have fewer daily aches and pains. Regardless of your age and current level of fitness, improving your posture with the exercise programs listed later in this chapter benefit you. Everyone needs good posture, because it is important to musculoskeletal health and injury prevention. Older adults can dramatically reduce the odds of falling and maintain a good quality of life. Athletes can improve their performance on the playing field.

You'll gain a few benefits from posture training.

✔ Prevent or reduce the likelihood of low back pain

✔ Reduce injuries

✔ Enhance joint efficiency

✔ Increase range of motion

✔ Improve flexibility

✔ More energy

Keeping Your Balance

Special receptor cells located in your skin, muscles, joints, and tendons — the fancy term for these cells is *proprioceptors* — process information about your body's orientation as it moves through space. For instance, when you walk across a lawn, your proprioceptors tell you things like "Okay, I'm putting my feet here now. The ground is spongy because it's grass. It has a little give and isn't completely uniform."

The majority of these special receptor cells that are responsible for your postural stability are located in your *multifidus*, deep muscles located in your lower back. Your deep abdominals and deep back muscles are primarily responsible for your ability to maintain your balance. Unless you continue to challenge your core stabilizer muscles and your sense of balance, you lose your abilities. This process is explained by the popular saying, "Use it or lose it," which is an accurate description.

As you age and allow these muscles to weaken, these proprioceptors become less sensitive, giving your brain less information and feedback to work with. Now when you walk across a lawn, you don't get quite so much input about the texture or give of the surface, and you're more likely to stumble on little inconsistencies of terrain. Slower reflexes and decreased muscular strength, combined with deteriorating eyesight and depth perception, also contribute to a diminished sense of equilibrium.

A fear of falling may be another reason that older people experience a loss of balance. Ironically, this fear may increase the risk of falling. When people worry about taking a tumble, they try to compensate by standing with their feet farther apart and walking with smaller steps. However, these adjustments actually prevent you from judging subtle cues from the environment, like the firmness of the ground and small changes in height of the surface you're walking on.

What's more, poor balance results in a shaky, unsteady gait. It becomes harder to go up or down stairs or negotiate high curbs and other obstacles that you may not otherwise give a second thought. You may find it more difficult to reach for objects on overhead shelves or to stand in tight spots on trains, in line, and in crowds with your feet close together.

Fortunately, you can reduce or reverse some of these problems and, as a result, you can become less accident prone. One study looked at 110 men and women with an average age of 80. After three months of performing balance exercises regularly, most of the subjects had the body control of people three to ten years younger.

Practicing Yoga, Tai Chi, or Qigong

The ancient practices of hatha yoga, tai chi, and qigong that come to us from India and China are rooted in cultural traditions that included these exercises as a way of maintaining physical, mental, and spiritual well-being and balance. Numerous modern studies of these practices substantiate these benefits after putting them to the test with rigorous scientific analyses.

All these practices are suitable for people of all ages, young and old, and are particularly attractive to older adults because they can be pursued on a gentle basis. While many American practitioners of yoga enjoy more vigorous styles, these exercises can be easily adapted to suit a variety of levels as shown in the accompanying photographs. See Figure 20-1 A, B, and C for examples of posture.

Figure 20-1:
The Yoga Tree posture, level 1 (A), level 2 (B), and level 3 (C).

A   B   C

Balance-specific Exercises

While you can improve balance by practicing ancient East Asian movement arts, you can also do balance-specific exercises. Whatever approach you choose to improve your balance is appropriate. The key is to select the exercises that appeal to you and motivate you to do them regularly.

We think that balance-specific exercises like the ones listed below are taught best one-on-one or in small groups supervised by a trainer or physical therapist with a practiced eye and in-depth knowledge of anatomy and body alignment. However, you can also do a number of excellent drills on your own.

Keep in mind that balance exercises are about quality not quantity. Focus hard when you perform the following moves, and don't get frustrated if you're not graceful at first. For example, walking across a low wooden beam, or pretending you are, (see Figure 20-2) requires a constant correction of knee, hip, and head alignment. All of your muscles from head to toe must work in synch in order for you to glide across the beam without extending your arms in the air or wandering off the edge. This can be tough at first, but with practice, you can master this move in just a few sessions. After a while, balance exercises awaken reflexes and add to body awareness and control on a subconscious level. This can translate into lasting improvements in posture and overall quality of movement.

Do these exercises two or three times a week at the end of your regular weight training sessions. Start with one set of each exercise and gradually work up to three sets. If you feel that you need more work, try an additional session or two each week. This type of training is deceptively challenging and can leave you feeling exhausted and sore if you overdo it at first. Even if you know other balance exercises, don't do more than four moves in a session.

- ✔ **Balance beam walk:** Walk slowly across a low wooden beam, while maintaining a tall posture, keeping your knees forward and your hands relaxed at your sides. If you don't have a balance beam, draw or tape a straight line 6 to 12 feet long on the floor. Place one foot directly in front of the other and stay as steady as possible. If you fall off the beam or wander off your line, simply get back on and continue from that point. See Figure 20-2.

  Focus your eyes on the end of the beam to help you keep your balance.

  Easier version: Extend your arms out to the side, but only as much as is necessary. Aim to make three back-and-forth trips.

  Harder version: Walk backwards.

✓ **Fulcrum:** With your arms relaxed at your sides, stand on one foot with your other leg extended behind you and a few inches off the floor. Lean a few inches forward and maintain your balance for up to one minute. Then slowly bring your foot back to the floor, and repeat with your other leg. Do three to five repetitions with each leg.

Easier version: Rest your fingertips lightly against a wall, chair, or other sturdy object.

Harder version: Lean forward a few inches more. When you get good at this, lean forward until your torso is perpendicular to the floor. See Figure 20-3.

✓ **Ostrich:** With your arms relaxed at your sides, stand on one foot with your opposite knee bent and your opposite foot a few inches off the floor directly in front of you. Hold this position for up to a minute, slowly return your foot to the floor, and then repeat with the other foot. Do three to five repetitions with each leg.

Easier version: Rest your fingertips lightly against a wall, chair, or some other sturdy object.

Harder version: Do the exercise with your eyes closed.

Figure 20-2:
Place one foot directly in front of the other and stay as steady as possible.

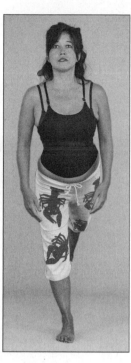

Figure 20-3:
Try to maintain your balance for up to one minute.

Previewing Balance Gadgets

In addition to balance-specific exercises, you can find some helpful gadgets for training balance at equipment specialty stores. Three catalogs, Fitness Wholesale (800-537-5512), SPRI® (800-222-7774), and Power Systems® (800-321-6975), all sell these gadgets through their catalogs and through their online Web sites. Many of these training tools come with helpful manuals that demonstrate exercises.

One of Liz and Suzanne's favorite tools is a balance board, a round board balanced on a knob or a ball. You stand on this and balance in a variety of one- and two-legged positions. With her background as a yoga and Pilates trainer, Shirley loves stability balls, foam rollers, and the BOSU®. Available worldwide, the BOSU is a dome-shaped training product that can be used right side up or upside down. That is why its name comes from "both sides up." The BOSU comes with great workout routines.

Putting Together Back Health and Balance Routines

Core training has a different emphasis than training for strength. Follow these tips to maximize the effectiveness of your workout routines.

- **Always warm up:** Because these are shorter workouts, you can do your warm-up as part of your workout with core specific and balance exercises. Active exercises that warm up your muscles and challenge your core stabilizers include lunges or squats, particularly one-legged squats. You can even use push-ups. Don't work at an all-out level, but instead work at a level that is appropriate for a warm-up.

- **Focus on endurance:** To improve core stabilization, your focus is on increasing muscular endurance. Do anywhere from 12 to 20 reps depending on the specific exercise. Do two to three sets as time permits.

- **Thirty-second rest periods:** Your rest periods should be shorter because you're focusing on improving endurance.

- **Use good form:** Don't continue to perform an exercise past the point where you can execute it with good form. Because these exercises are also for the purpose of improving your movement efficiency, it's critical that you use good quality movement in every repetition.

- **Listen to your body:** You want to be particularly careful to avoid any strain to your lower back or to your neck. Listen to your body. If any exercise causes you pain, don't do it. If you have specific back issues, follow the instructions of your healthcare provider.

- **Always stretch:** To be more efficient, you can incorporate stretches either directly after particular exercises to use the time during the rest period, or you can do a series of stretches at the end of your workout. For best results, always include stretches to enhance balanced muscle development and promote flexibility and ease of movement.

Sampling Healthy Back and Balance Routines

The following are just a few ways you can improve your posture, prevent low back pain, and maintain your sense of balance over a lifetime.

20-minute routine

For this routine, you need a mat, ball, and a band. If you don't have ball, then you can do the ball exercises on the mat. Follow the routines outlined in Tables 20-1 and 20-2.

Table 20-1	Mat, Ball, and Band Routine
Warm-up	Squat, lunge
Balance specific	Ostrich
Back	Band lat pulldown

Table 20-2	Chest Push-up
Lower back	Pelvic tilt, ball back extension
Abdominals	Ball crunch
Core stabilizers	Plank, all fours spinal stabilization
Stretches	Cat, hamstrings, pretzel stretch, quadriceps, reach up, hand clasp

15-minute routine

If you took 15 minutes to focus on your core stabilizers at least 3 days a week, it would go along way toward improving your posture and balance. Don't think that you must devote hours to your training. Sometimes a little bit goes a long way. Follow the routine given in Table 20-3.

Table 20-3	Mat and Ball Routine
Warm-up	Pelvic tilt, leg slide, ball march, ball push-up
Back	Ball extension
Abdominals	Ball crunch, ball oblique crunch
Core stabilizers	Ball plank
Stretches	Cat, hamstrings, pretzel stretch, quadriceps, reach up, hand clasp

Ten-minute routine

It's better to do something rather than nothing. You can do this ten-minute routine daily. In fact, it may be a good habit to do it first thing in the morning or last thing at night before you go to bed. A good routine to follow is given in Table 20-4.

Table 20-4	Mini-Back Care Routine
Warm-up	Pelvic tilt, leg slide
Core stabilizers	Plank, side plank, reverse plank
Stretches	Cat, hamstrings, pretzel stretch, quadriceps, reach up, hand clasp

Chapter 21

Tackling More Advanced Programs

*Y*ou may come to a point in your weight training career when moving through the same 12 weight machines or performing the same old dumbbell exercises isn't enough — not enough to keep you interested and not enough to keep giving you results. Out of boredom or disappointment, you may start skipping your workouts. This is a warning sign that it's time to start progressing your program.

In this chapter, we show you how to go beyond the basics to create a more sophisticated, stimulating weight training program. The strategies we present fall into three basic categories: designing your weekly schedule, arranging your exercises during a particular workout, and structuring an individual set.

You can experiment with one of the strategies we discuss in this chapter, or you can use every one. Just don't try them all at once. You'll feel less overwhelmed if you incorporate change gradually. Plus, you can pinpoint more precisely which strategies work for you and which don't. Beginners certainly can benefit from the techniques we discuss here and should read this chapter. But you'll find the strategies here more valuable if you've been lifting weights for at least a month.

Understanding Progression

Progressing your program or increasing intensity over time requires skill and patience. You don't want to progress too quickly or you risk injury; but, if you don't progress your program, it will become stale. After you've mastered 15 reps to fatigue at a particular weight, you're ready to progress to two sets. After you've mastered two sets of 15 reps to fatigue, you can add an additional set or you can progress to a heavier weight level in the 8 to 12 rep range. Increase your weight by up to 5 percent. For example, let's say you've been lifting 40 pounds for 15 reps for two sets. To progress, you would increase by 2 pounds and lift 42 pounds for 8 to 12 reps for one set.

The challenge with lower weight ranges is that it is difficult to find small weights to add the incremental poundage. If you're working on machines, look for the small 5-pound bars that you can rest on top of the stack. If you're working with dumbbells with narrow handles, you can hold more than one in your hand.

Another way to progress your program is to add variety by performing more exercises for each muscle group. This continues to stimulate the muscle by working the muscles through different movement patterns and by requiring more muscle fibers to work.

Split Routines

Regardless of your goals, you need to hit each muscle group at least twice a week. The simplest way to accomplish this is to perform two *total-body* workouts per week; in other words, twice a week perform a routine that works every major muscle group.

Total-body workouts are great if you're doing only one or two exercises per muscle group. But when you get serious about weight training — adding exercises and sets — a total-body workout can become tedious. If your schedule permits you to lift weights at least 4 days a week (the sessions can be as short as 15 minutes), consider doing a *split routine.* You split a total-body routine into two or three shorter routines. For example, you can train your upper body on one day and your lower body the next. You can even split your upper body muscles into three different workouts. (We discuss these options in detail later in this section.)

Split routines are ideal for people who have the time to work out several days a week but may not have much time for each workout session. Split routines also work well for people who have a short attention span for weight training or who want to give each muscle group an extra-hard workout. Brief, focused workouts help you stay motivated. If you walk into the gym knowing that all you have to do today is work your back and biceps, you're more likely to give those muscle group exercises an all-out effort.

When designing a split routine, you need to follow two basic rules: Hit each muscle group at least twice a week, and don't work the same muscle group on consecutive days. This second rule is a bit more complicated than it sounds. For example, you may think that it's okay to work your triceps and thighs on Monday and then your chest and butt on Tuesday. Actually, it's not. You see, most chest exercises *also* work the triceps, and most butt exercises *also* work the thighs. So, if you work your triceps on Monday, they won't have recovered sufficiently by Tuesday to help out on your chest exercises. These rules may sound confusing, but within a few weeks, they'll become second nature. Until then, here's a list of muscle pairs that you shouldn't work on back-to-back days:

- Chest and triceps
- Back and biceps
- Butt and thighs

The split routines that we describe in the following sections heed the preceding two basic rules.

The upper body/lower body split

The upper body/lower body split is perhaps the simplest split, a good one for beginners to try. You don't have much to remember: It's pretty obvious which exercises work the muscles above the belt and which work your muscles down south. When you work your upper body one day and your lower body the next, each zone of your body gets more of a complete rest than for any other way you do your split.

People who do the upper/lower split generally train their abdominals with their lower body, but this isn't a hard-and-fast rule. Don't make the mistake of working your abs every workout. Remember, the abs are like any other muscle group: They need time to recover. Two or three abdominal workouts a week will suffice. Table 21-1 shows two sample weekly schedules based on the upper/lower split.

Table 21-1	Sample Weekly Schedules for Split Routines
Day of the Week	*Body Area or Rest Period*
Sample Upper/lower split #1	
Monday	Upper body
Tuesday	Lower body and abdominals
Wednesday	Rest
Thursday	Upper body
Friday	Lower body and abdominals
Saturday	Rest
Sunday	Rest
Sample Upper/lower split #2	
Monday	Upper body and abdominals
Tuesday	Rest
Wednesday	Lower body and abdominals
Thursday	Rest
Friday	Upper body and abdominals
Saturday	Rest
Sunday	Lower body

Tables 21-2 and 21-3 are two examples of the exercises you can include in your upper body/lower body split routine — one routine is for beginners and one is for more experienced lifters.

Table 21-2	Sample Exercises for Basic Upper Body/Lower Body Split Routine
Body Part	*Exercises*
Upper body	
Back	Lat pulldown, machine row, pelvic tilt
Chest	Dumbbell chest press, incline chest fly

Body Part	Exercises
Shoulders	Dumbbell shoulder press, lateral raise
Biceps	Hammer curl, concentration curl
Triceps	Triceps pushdown, triceps kickback
Lower body	
Butt and legs	Squat, lunge, leg extension machine, leg curl machine, inner and outer thigh machines, standing calf raise machine
Abdominals	Slide, basic abdominal crunch

Table 21-3	Sample Exercises for Advanced Upper Body/Lower Body Split Routine
Body Part	**Exercises**
Upper body	
Back	Chin-up, lat pulldown with triangle grip, seated cable row, back extension, machine pullover
Chest	Bench press, incline dumbbell press, assisted dip, decline fly
Shoulders	Military press, lateral raise, back delt fly, internal and external rotation
Biceps	Barbell biceps curl, preacher curl, alternating dumbbell biceps curl
Triceps	Triceps pushdown, french press, bench dip
Lower body	
Legs	Barbell squat, backward lunge, stiff-legged deadlift, leg extension machine, leg curl machine, inner/outer thigh machine, single-leg calf raise
Abdominals	Hanging abs, reverse crunch, abdominal crunch with a twist

Push/pull split routine

This type of split separates your upper body *pushing* muscles (the chest and triceps) from the upper body muscles involved in *pulling* (your back and biceps). You can do your lower body and abdominal exercises on either day or on a separate day altogether. Or you can include your legs with your pushing muscles and your abdominals with your pulling muscles.

Savvy readers will notice that we haven't mentioned where your shoulders fit into the push/pull split. There's no simple answer because shoulders don't fit neatly into either the push or the pull category; the shoulders are partially involved in both movements. Where you work in your shoulders is a matter of personal preference. Some people like to work their shoulders right after their chest muscles. Others like to do shoulder exercises after their back exercises. Still others prefer to divide their body into three workouts: back and biceps; chest and triceps; shoulders, leg, and abs.

Push/pull split routines are popular among experienced exercisers who want to go to town with each muscle group. You may see people spend two hours just working their back and biceps. However, other people feel unbalanced after one of these routines because they worked only one side of their torso. Table 21-4 shows sample push/pull split routine schedules.

Table 21-4	Sample Push/Pull Split Routine Schedules
Day of the Week	*Body Area or Rest Period*
Sample Four-day Week	
Day 1	Chest, triceps, and shoulders
Day 2	Back, biceps, abdominals, and lower body
Day 3	Rest
Day 4	Chest, triceps, and shoulders
Day 5	Rest
Day 6	Back, biceps, abdominals, and lower body
Day 7	Rest
Sample Five-day Week	
Day 1	Chest and triceps
Day 2	Back and biceps

Day of the Week	Body Area or Rest Period
Day 3	Shoulders, lower body, and abdominals
Day 4	Rest
Day 5	Chest, triceps, and shoulders
Day 6	Back, biceps, lower body, and abdominals
Day 7	Rest

Table 21-5 suggests exercises to include for each of the four main push/pull split combinations. You can mix and match these combinations to fit the workouts that we describe for the weekly schedules in Table 21-4.

Table 21-5	Sample Exercises for Push/Pull Split Routines
Body Parts	**Exercises**
Back and biceps	
Back	Assisted pull-up, lat pulldown, seated cable row, dumbbell pullover, one-arm row, back extension
Biceps	Barbell biceps curl, concentration curl, arm curl machine
Chest and triceps	
Chest	Bench press, incline chest fly, vertical chest press machine, cable crossover, push-up
Triceps	Triceps pushdown, triceps kickback, triceps dip machine
Shoulders	
Shoulders	Dumbbell shoulder press, cable lateral raise, front raise, back delt fly, internal/external rotation
Lower body and abdominals	
Legs	Lunge, leg press machine, leg extension machine, leg curl machine, inner/outer thigh machine, standing calf raise
Abdominals	Rolling like a ball, reverse crunch, abdominal crunch with a twist

Vary Your Daily Workout

Now we're going to narrow the focus even further. After you decide that you're going to work, say, your chest, triceps, and shoulders on Monday, you need to decide the order in which to do the exercises. In Chapter 2, we explain that you should work your large muscles before your smaller ones within each zone of your body. However, you still have plenty of options. Certain exercise sequences can save you time by reducing the amount of rest you need between sets; other sequences take longer but give your muscles a tougher challenge. Use the suggestions in the following sections to vary the order of your exercises.

Super sets

Doing a *super set* simply means performing two different exercises without resting between the sets. There are two types of super sets, each with a different purpose:

- ✔ **Same-muscle super sets:** You do consecutive sets of different exercises that work the same muscle group. For example, go immediately from the dumbbell chest press to the chest fly, rest for a minute, and then do the press plus fly sequence again. This type of super set challenges the muscle in question. Just when your pecs think that they've completed a job well done — Bam! You blindside them with another exercise right away.

  You can do super sets with just about any two exercises. Keep in mind that you'll probably use less weight than usual on the second exercise because your muscles are already fairly tired. You may want to enlist a spotter if you're doing super sets that involve lifting a weight directly over your face or head.

  Table 21-6 shows some super set combinations. You can string them all together to form a whole super set workout. Or you can insert any number of these combinations into your workout.

- ✔ **Different-muscle super sets:** With this type of super set, you do back-to-back exercises that work different muscles. For example, go from a front thigh exercise directly to a rear thigh exercise. This type of super set is a great way to speed up your routine because it cuts back on the rest you need to take during a routine. Your front thighs rest while you perform the rear thigh exercise, and vice versa. Table 21-7 shows a sample different-muscle super set routine.

Table 21-6	Sample Same-muscle Super Set Routine
Body Parts	*Exercise Combinations*
Butt and Legs	Squat + lunge
Back	Lat pulldown + machine row
Chest	Bench press + Push-up
Shoulders	Dumbbell shoulder press + lateral raise
Biceps	Barbell biceps curl + dumbbell biceps curl
Triceps	French press + bench dip
Abdominals	Basic abdominal crunch + abdominal crunch with a twist

Table 21-7	Sample Different-muscle Super Set Routine
Body Parts	*Exercise Combinations*
Butt and legs + chest	Leg press + vertical chest press machine
Back + quadriceps	Dumbbell pullover + leg extension machine
Shoulders + hamstrings	Shoulder press + leg curl machine
Biceps + legs	Barbell biceps curl + calf raise
Triceps + abdominals	Triceps pushdown + basic abdominal crunch
Wrists + lower back	Wrist curl + back extension

Giant sets

Giant sets take the super set idea one step farther: Instead of doing two consecutive sets of different exercises without rest, you string *three* exercises together. For example, for a killer abdominal workout, you could link together three different abdominal exercises, rest, and then repeat the sequence. Or, to save time in your workout, you could move from a back exercise to a chest exercise to a butt exercise. Table 21-8 shows some of our favorite giant sets that you can work into your routines.

Table 21-8	Suggested Giant Exercise Sets
Body Parts	*Exercise Combinations*
Abdominals	Basic abdominal crunch + reverse crunch + abdominal crunch with a twist
Butt and legs	Leg press machine + leg extension machine + leg curl machine
Back	Lat pulldown + cable row + seated back machine
Chest	Dumbbell chest press + chest fly + cable crossover
Shoulders	Shoulder press + front raise + lateral raise

Circuits

A *circuit* is a routine in which you do one set each of several exercises, taking little or no rest between sets. Then you repeat the whole shebang as many times as you want. The typical circuit uses weight machines because they save you time. (In Chapter 18, we list exercises for a typical weight machine circuit.) However, you can create your own circuit by using free weights or a free weight/machine combination. Here are some basic rules to keep in mind when designing your circuit workout:

✔ Try to alternate upper, lower, and middle body (abdominal and lower back) muscles so that no single muscle group gets tired too quickly. However, you also can do opposing muscle groups in the same region of the body, such as chest and back or quadriceps and hamstrings.

✔ Switch between lying, standing, and seated exercises very carefully. Moving from one posture to another too quickly can cause sudden changes in blood pressure, which can cause you to feel dizzy or pass out.

✔ Even though you're moving quickly between exercises, don't speed up the repetitions within a set. Good form still applies.

✔ Expect to use about 20 percent less weight than usual for each exercise because you're moving so fast. Sure, your front thighs are resting while you work your rear thighs, but your whole body, including your heart and lungs, is still working at a pretty quick pace.

✔ Keep your concentration and focus on each exercise. It's easy to adapt to doing a circuit that you become familiar with and give less effort. Remind yourself each time to approach your circuit with energy.

✔ Try not to do circuits more than once a week. Circuit training is a good way to pull yourself up out of rut, but you won't gain as much strength from working out this way.

Advanced Training Techniques

After you choose which exercises to do and what order to do them in, you still have a few decisions to make. Suppose that you're going to perform three sets on the leg extension machine. Are you going to perform the same number of repetitions for each set? Or do you want to decrease the number of repetitions from one set to the next so that you can lift more weight?

Pyramids

If you have the time or inclination to perform at least five sets of an exercise, consider a pyramid. You start with a light weight and then gradually work your way up to the heaviest weight you can lift for one or two repetitions. Or you could do a modified pyramid. Instead of piling on the weight until you can do only one repetition, stop at the point where five or six reps is tough. This is a better approach for beginners and for people who don't have a buddy to spot them while lifting heavy weights.

You can also do a descending pyramid, starting with the heaviest weight you think you can lift once, and working down until you're lifting a weight that allows you to perform 12 to 15 reps. However, don't do your heaviest set without first doing at least one warm-up set.

A third option is to combine a regular pyramid with a descending pyramid. In other words, you could start with ten reps and a light weight, work your way up to a heavy weight and one to three reps, and then work your way back down to a light weight and ten reps again. This technique brings new meaning to the word *fatigue*. Expect to lift a lot less weight on the way down than you do on the way up. For example, if you can bench-press 80 pounds ten times on the way up, you may be able to bench press 80 pounds only six times on the way down. For the ten-rep set, you may be lifting only 50 pounds.

Breakdowns

Breakdown training is just another way of tiring out the muscle. You do multiple sets of an exercise without resting between sets; meanwhile, you decrease the weight for each set. Suppose that you're doing the lateral raise. First line up four to six sets of dumbbells near you, from heaviest to lightest. After a light warm-up set, do ten repetitions with the heavy set, put the weights down, do eight reps with the next lightest dumbbells, put those down, and so on (until you either run out of gas or run out of dumbbells). Breakdowns also are fun to do with machines because, instead of putting down and picking up weights, all you have to do is move the pin.

Another option is to do modified breakdowns by using just two different weights. For example, first choose a weight that enables you to do ten repetitions, and then immediately put it down and pick up a lighter weight, squeezing out as many repetitions as possible until failure, usually about four or five.

Negatives

Negatives is an advanced technique that can cause extreme muscle soreness, so beginners shouldn't try it. Someone helps you lift a weight, and then you're on your own for the lowering, or *negative,* phase of the lift. The negative phase is also referred to as the *eccentric* phase, pronounced EE-sentric, as opposed to ECK-sentric. The positive, or lifting, phase is called the *concentric* phase.

Your muscles generally can handle more weight when you lower a weight than when you lift it, so this technique gives you a chance to max out on the negative phase. This is a good technique to try on the bench press and many lower body machines such as the leg extension and leg curl because it's easy for your buddy to help you lift up a handle or a machine's lever. Negative sets done with machines are safer than free weight negative sets because you're not in danger of dropping a dumbbell on your dental work if your arms or shoulders suddenly give out.

Chapter 22

Workouts for Special Needs

. . . .

In This Chapter

▶ Weight training tips for kids and teens

▶ Training considerations before and after baby comes

▶ Modifying workouts for people who are larger sized

▶ Building and maintaining strong bones

▶ Lifting considerations for the older adult

. . . .

*W*ith today's high-tech lifestyle, weight training offers many benefits if done consistently over the span of a lifetime. Why? Because the conveniences of modern living eliminate almost all the natural activity that would normally challenge us physically as we go through our day.

In this chapter, you discover how to modify basic training for different stages in life. As we know all too well, life is filled with ups and downs and twists and turns. Here, you understand how to keep on training or start a training program regardless of your current age or circumstance. Whether you're designing a program for yourself, supervising your kids, or giving suggestions to your older parents, the information in this chapter offers valuable insight into important considerations to keep weight training safe, effective, and fun. For specific medical conditions, always be sure to check first with your healthcare provider.

Training Tips for Kids and Teens

Shirley's college freshman roommate Carol called her one day and asked if she wouldn't mind coming over and helping out her two sons, Bob and Bill, with a weight training program. At the time, they were 8 and 10 and very much interested in sports and getting stronger. Like many responsible parents, Carol wanted to encourage her kids' interest in training, but she wanted to make sure that they didn't hurt themselves or affect the natural progress of their growth. And, because kids will be kids, she wanted to be sure that they understood how to do everything safely and properly from the outset. Of course, Shirley was thrilled to help and had a fantastic time enjoying their youthful energy, fresh questions, and creative interpretations.

Benefiting from youth resistance training

Today's youth definitely benefit from training their muscles. Kids are subject to the same conditions as adults — a life filled with computers, cars, and inactive forms of recreation and entertainment. Leading researchers that specialize in youth fitness have found that children as young as 6 years old benefit from training. The key factor is the maturity of the child and whether he pays attention and follows directions. As Carol suspected, youth training has its risks of injury, but the benefits outweigh the risks as long as the activities are supervised and kept safe. The following list is some of the benefits kids gain from strength training:

- ✔ Stronger muscles
- ✔ More muscle endurance
- ✔ Increased confidence and self-esteem
- ✔ Improved coordination and balance
- ✔ Better body composition (more lean muscle mass and less body fat)
- ✔ More energy to participate in other physical activities
- ✔ Lower risk of injury from youth sports
- ✔ Stronger bones for improved bone density over a lifetime
- ✔ Better sports performance
- ✔ Starting a good habit of regular exercise for a healthy lifestyle
- ✔ More social skills and lessons gained from interaction and cooperation by finding out how to work with others while training

Knowing what is age appropriate

Children aren't mini-adults. They're growing. Inappropriate training damages growth cartilage with serious consequences. Kids don't need to use a lot of fancy equipment. Body weight provides the challenge for many child appropriate exercises. You need to show children that weights aren't toys.

Workout safety guidelines for kids

The following are a few of the important safety guidelines for you and your kids to follow:

- ✔ Get approval from your child's healthcare provider first.
- ✔ Train under supervision of a qualified professional.
- ✔ Don't train more than two days a week.
- ✔ Keep sessions short and include a warm-up and stretching.
- ✔ Do from eight to ten strength exercises per session.
- ✔ Do 13 to 15 reps per set; one set per exercise.
- ✔ No weight added until 15 reps can be done easily.
- ✔ If weight is added, add in small 1- to 3-pound increments.
- ✔ Never lift a maximum or near-maximum weight load.
- ✔ Keep training fun and noncompetitive.
- ✔ Always choose a conservative approach.
- ✔ Balance conditioning muscles with aerobic activities.
- ✔ Make sure to eat properly and get plenty of sleep.
- ✔ Don't overtrain.

Safety guidelines for teens

Children and adolescents shouldn't do powerlifting or bodybuilding or repetitive use of maximal weight loads in strength training programs until they've reached a level of developmental maturity. This level is described as "Tanner stage 5" in medical circles and means that they've passed the period of maximal speed in the growth of their height. The reason for concern about the dangers of serious weight training is that when teens are growing the epiphyses, a part of bone, is especially vulnerable to injury. As an average, both boys and girls reach this stage of development by age 15. However, individuals differ widely. This is why any more rigorous training should never be undertaken without full consideration by your child's healthcare provider and a sports medicine physician.

All the kids' guidelines apply to teens with the added caveat that more rigorous training shouldn't be undertaken until the teen has reached physical maturity. At that point, a teen can start training as an adult at a moderate level.

Keep in mind that kids are subject to tremendous amounts of body image pressure both from the media and from their peers. Listen carefully to how your child describes how she feels about training. Pay attention to personal comments about appearance. If your child shows any sign of exercise or eating disordered behavior, consult a professional right away.

Trying a sample kid or teen routine

The following routine is a sample of a total body conditioning routine that uses body weight for resistance. The risk of injury is very low and the potential conditioning benefits are great. See Table 22-1 for a sample youth routine.

Table 22-1	Sample Youth Routine
Body Part	*Exercises*
Total body warm-up	Marching, jogging, jumping rope, jacks, skips, arm circles, and so on
Upper body	
Back	All fours spinal stabilization
Chest	Modified push-up
Lower body	
Butt and legs	Squat, lunge
Abdominals	Plank, basic abdominal crunch, bicycle

Lifting Weights Before and After Baby

Thankfully, we live in a modern era where research now supports that it's okay for a woman to be active while she is pregnant. Being physically fit helps you through your pregnancy and speeds your recovery after you have a baby. Pregnancy, however, isn't a time to increase your training program. What you should strive for is to maintain a healthy moderate level of activity. Always check with your healthcare provider before you start an exercise program when you're pregnant and continue to evaluate the safety and appropriateness of your training as your pregnancy progresses and after you give birth.

Benefiting from prenatal and postpartum resistance training

Every woman's pregnancy is unique. While all pregnancies follow the same general pattern, each mother carves her own experience. Weight training is beneficial because it helps relieve the stress of pregnancy, targets supportive muscles while the body is undergoing significant change, and helps prepare the body for birth. The following is a list of some of the benefits pregnant and postpartum women gain from strength training.

✔ Maintain muscle strength and endurance.

✔ Improve circulation and provide relief from swelling.

✔ Increase feelings of well-being and self-esteem.

✔ Improve coordination and balance, especially when the center of gravity is changing frequently.

✔ Relief from back pain.

✔ Prevent or relieve urinary incontinence.

✔ More energy for daily activities.

✔ Help keep digestion regular.

✔ Improve quality of sleep.

✔ Relieve muscle cramps.

✔ Heighten body awareness during a time of rapid change.

✔ Speed recovery after birth.

Several studies show that women who exercise compared to women who don't exercise during their pregnancy have less problematic deliveries and more rapid recoveries after labor.

Modifying exercise routines for safety

The American College of Obstetrics and Gynecology provides guidelines for exercise during pregnancy. Multiple studies have been conducted that show that exercise during pregnancy doesn't increase risk of miscarriage or birth abnormalities. Any type of extreme training isn't recommended. And, sports that involve a high risk of falling such as downhill skiing or adventure racing aren't recommended. The following are a few of the important safety guidelines for prenatal and postpartum women:

✔ Get approval from your healthcare provider first.

✔ Follow a balanced program of weight training, aerobic activity, and stretching.

✔ Don't overstretch.

✔ Avoid breath holding.

✔ Always remember to breathe.

✔ Avoid exercise to exhaustion.

✔ Avoid standing for long periods of time.

✔ After the first trimester, avoid lying on your back for more than a minute or at all, depending on whether you feel faint.

✔ Eat appropriately and drink plenty of fluids (6-8 ounces of water for every 15 minutes of activity).

✔ Wear loose, comfortable clothing, a supportive bra, and maternal support belt as needed.

✔ Exercise at a moderate intensity, without excess fatigue.

✔ Never lift a maximum or near-maximum weight load.

✔ Avoid quick changes in body position.

✔ Always choose a conservative approach.

✔ Include aerobic activities in your overall training program.

✔ Don't start training after delivery until at least six weeks have passed and your healthcare provider has approved you for exercise.

✔ Don't overtrain.

Trying a sample routine

Because body positioning becomes more of a challenge as pregnancy progresses, the band and ball are useful tools for the pregnant exerciser. Table 22-2 shows a sample ball and band routine.

Table 22-2	Sample Prenatal Ball and Band Routine
Body Part	*Exercises*
Total body warm-up	Low impact rhythmic activities such as walking or marching
Lower body	
Butt and legs	Wall squats, ball march

Body Part	Exercises
Upper body	
Back	Pelvic tilt, band lat pulldown
Chest	Wall push-up
Shoulders	Band internal and external rotation, band one-arm shoulder press
Biceps	Band biceps curl
Triceps	Band triceps extension
Abdominals	Ball abdominal crunch
Core	All fours spinal stabilization

Training Big, Beautiful Bodies

Shirley trained members of a gym in Redwood City, California, named, Women of Substance®, with the motto, "A woman is much more than the measure of her numbers." Lisa Tealer and Dana Shuster cofounded this gym that was based on size acceptance. Shirley enjoyed training at this facility that celebrated size diversity and prided itself on being a "safe" place for women of all shapes and sizes to exercise.

Understanding why all shapes and sizes benefit from stronger muscles

All people, regardless of size, benefit from improving their muscular strength and endurance. Strong muscles make everyday living easier and more enjoyable, give you more energy, and prevent injuries. While media images of celebrities and models may give us the impression that most people are thin, the truth is that the average American is a person who is larger sized.

An untrained person with large body mass often has joint issues that include back and knee pain. The potential for risk may be high if movements aren't performed correctly.

Larger-sized people enjoy all the same benefits from weight training that smaller people do. Bodybuilders are of course larger-sized people. They're comfortable in the weight room. What this section addresses are the concerns of someone who is larger sized and who wants to get or stay in shape to improve health or fitness. The following is a list of some of the benefits to be gained from resistance training.

- Build muscle strength and endurance.
- Reduce aches and pains, especially back pain.
- Increase feelings of well-being and self-esteem.
- Improve body awareness and understanding of how muscles should feel when they work.
- Reduce or prevent injuries.
- Increase lean muscle mass and improve body composition.
- More energy for daily activities.
- Possibility of reduced blood pressure.
- Improve quality of sleep.
- Improve blood glucose utilization.
- Improve balance and coordination.

Considering safety guidelines and other tips

The following are a few of the important safety guidelines for larger-sized people:

- Get approval from your healthcare provider first.
- Follow a balanced program of weight training, aerobic activity, and stretching.
- Research gyms to find a place with equipment that supports large-bodied people such as bodybuilding men.
- For standing exercises, use a wall for support until it's no longer needed.
- If it is too tiring to stand, do seated exercise alternatives on a sturdy bench.
- Pay particular attention to form and body positioning.
- Don't change body positions quickly.
- Always move in a slow controlled manner — don't swing weights.

✔ Eat appropriately and drink plenty of fluids.

✔ Wear comfortable, supportive clothing made from fabrics that breathe. Avoid excess fabric because chafing occurs under the arms or between legs.

✔ Exercise at a moderate intensity.

✔ If you're uncomfortable on your knees, try to do exercises lying face down instead of kneeling. Alternatively, try putting extra cushioning under your knees to see if it becomes uncomfortable. If an exercise hurts, don't do it.

✔ Make sure that benches are wide, sturdy, and stable before using them to train.

✔ Make sure that you know how to get up off the floor.

If you're concerned about how to get up from or down to the floor to do exercises on your back, abdomen, or side, follow these simple steps.

1. **To get down to the floor:** Begin with a wide stance and put your hands on your thighs. Squat, and while bending your knees, lower one knee to the floor, extend one hand out for support, and lower your hips to the side on the floor.

2. **To get up from the floor:** With your hands on the floor, assume a wide stance with both knees and your toes on the floor and heels up. Walk your hands in, push off with your hands, and roll your weight into your heels. Continue to walk your hands up to your thighs and push up to a standing position.

Keep in mind that your training is an opportunity to enhance your life and make you feel better. Genetics play a strong role in the ultimate size and shape that all of us attain naturally through training. Celebrate the joy of living in a strong and sound body and of being your personal best. Train for you and not as a result of pressure from anyone else or from society to be anything other than the strong person that you are.

Trying a sample routine

Here's a sample routine for a larger-sized person. Exercise standards are the same for any adult training program. Suggested exercises include seated versions and use of the wall to provide more support if needed. Be sure to include stretching in your programs.

Table 22-3	Sample Routine for a Larger-sized Person
Body Part	*Exercises*
Total body warm-up	Low-impact rhythmic activities such as walking or marching
Lower body	
Butt and legs	Squat, side-lying leg lift, side-lying inner thigh lift
Upper body	
Back	Dumbbell pullover, back extension
Chest	Wall push-up
Shoulders	Dumbbell shoulder press, back delt fly, internal and external rotation
Biceps	Concentration curl
Triceps	Triceps kickback
Abdominals	Basic abdominal crunch, oblique crunch
Core	Plank, side plank

Building and Keeping Strong Bones

In Chapter 2, we discuss weight-training principles. An important concept covered in that chapter is specificity of training. Our bodies are remarkably resilient and adapt primarily in response to the specific challenges that we give ourselves. That is why knowing why you want to train is important.

Training to strengthen your bones is a specific goal. As a result of numerous studies scientists have conducted, the American College of Sports Medicine (ACSM) has issued a position stand on Bone Health with recommendations for exercises that preserve bone. While exercise is critically important, nutritional factors, such as the importance of calcium in the diet, is also essential to maintain bone density. To find out more about osteoporosis specifically, see *Osteoporosis For Dummies* (Wiley).

For adult men and women to preserve bone, do a combination of weight bearing aerobic activities such as stair climbing, walking and jogging, or jumping activities and weight training. Up to age 30, we want to work on building up our bone density. After the age of 40, the goal is to retain as much bone density by stopping or slowing the rate of bone loss.

As Chapter 18 shows, training at an intensity of sixty percent of your 1-rep maximum is a 16 to 20 reps to fatigue, so any amount of weight training that you do benefits your bones, and the more you progress to higher levels of intensity (heavier weights and fewer reps) the greater the benefits that you'll receive.

Eighty-five percent intensity is six to seven reps to fatigue, which is a challenging load. As you progress, follow the general rule of thumb of increasing sets before you increase weight. If you've mastered three sets to fatigue; then start to increase weight.

Lifting into the Golden Years

Weight training is definitely appropriate for grandpas and grandmas. In fact, it's among the best things that you can do for your health and well-being. Having strong muscles allows us to live independently. Being able to dress oneself, go to the toilet alone, and feel comfortable going to the store to run errands are a part of enjoying a feeling of personal freedom. Training as an older adult can set you free.

In one research study, older adults who lived in a nursing home were put on a weight training program twice weekly. Remarkably, even participants over the age of 90 improved their strength and mobility. One resident became so much stronger that he left the facility. Others were able to dress by themselves for the first time in ages.

Reaping rewards from training as an older adult

Many of the things we formerly associated with aging, we now know are simply a result of disuse. Here are some of the many benefits of regular weight training for older adults.

- ✔ Increase muscular strength and endurance.
- ✔ Keep functional independence to enjoy a full and active life.
- ✔ Improve confidence and self-esteem.
- ✔ Maintain strong bones and prevent osteoporosis.
- ✔ Keep balance and reduce the risk of falls and the fear of falling.
- ✔ Improve digestion and relieve constipation.
- ✔ Improve glucose utilization to avoid onset of diabetes.

- ✔ Reduce discomfort from arthritis.
- ✔ Help prevent low back pain.
- ✔ Help maintain healthy blood pressure levels.

Observing safety guidelines and training tips

While training provides a host of benefits, a more conservative approach is recommended for older adults, who are considered to be those over the age of 50. If you've trained regularly over the course of a lifetime, you may be chronologically 50, but have the biological health of someone who is more like a 40-year-old. Make your personal adjustments accordingly. Keep in mind that, even for the frail elderly, such as the 90-year-old in the nursing home, the risk of being inactive is worse than the risk of injury from training. Here are important safety guidelines for weight training and older adults:

- ✔ Get the approval of your healthcare provider first.
- ✔ Train a minimum of two days per week.
- ✔ Do one set of eight to ten exercises that challenge all the major muscle groups.
- ✔ Do 10 to 15 repetitions per set.
- ✔ Progress conservatively.
- ✔ Include a slightly longer warm-up, up to 10 minutes, and gentle stretches.
- ✔ Do each exercise in a slow and controlled manner.
- ✔ Move through your active range of motion.
- ✔ Incorporate balance exercises.
- ✔ Don't do any exercise that causes pain.

Chapter 23

Adding Yoga and Pilates for Flexible Strength and Coordination

*Y*oga and Pilates, activities touted to increase strength and flexibility, are the two fastest growing programs in fitness facilities among all age groups. How are these activities different from and similar to weight training? What are the benefits of incorporating all three modes of exercise into your fitness program? How many days a week should you do each one? Will you go broke doing all these activities? Will your body collapse from exhaustion? This chapter answers all these questions and more.

Examining Yoga and Pilates

Each mode of exercise is explored in detail later in the chapter, but here's the difference between the two activities in a nutshell. Both of these exercises are mind-body disciplines. Yoga is rooted in ancient East Indian cultural traditions. In contrast, Pilates is a modern exercise practice with influence from yoga, as well as Chinese acrobatics, gymnastics, and boxing.

Harmonizing with yoga

The physical practice of yoga, known as *hatha yoga*, developed in India more than 5,000 years ago and consists of a series of poses, known as *asanas*, that you hold anywhere from a few seconds to several minutes. Yoga moves

- ✔ Require a blend of strength, flexibility, and body awareness
- ✔ Promote union of body, mind, and spirit
- ✔ Prepare the body for the discipline of meditation and other spiritual yoga practices

Most hatha yoga styles include the same basic poses but differ in terms of how quickly you move, how long you hold each pose, how much breathing is emphasized, and how much of a spiritual aspect is involved. While in the Indian tradition, all physical yoga is hatha yoga, in America, different styles of hatha yoga have been given new names such as power, flow, or hot yoga.

Other yoga styles are named after the individual people who spread the exercise in America. For example, Iyengar yoga, named after B.K.S. Iyengar, is the most widely practiced style of hatha yoga in America and offers more modifications for beginners and uses multiple props. Other styles, such as Bikram yoga, are for people who can already fold themselves into shapes that resemble pretzels in a very hot room.

Moving with Pilates

Pilates (pih-LAH-teez) is an exercise form named after Joseph Pilates, the former boxing and self-defense trainer who developed the Pilates technique in Germany at the turn of the 20th century. Many Pilates moves were inspired by yoga, although some were inspired by gymnastics, Chinese acrobatics, and boxing. Pilates mat classes involve a series of specialized calisthenics exercises; rather than hold the positions, as in certain styles of yoga, you're constantly moving, as in a flow or *vinyasa* yoga style, which consists of a series of moves performed continuously as in the Sun Salutation.

Private and small-group lessons are taught on medieval-looking machines with names such as the Trapeze Table and the Reformer. The Trapeze Table looks like a four-poster bed that's been rigged for torture, with its array of springs, straps, poles, and bars. The Reformer looks like a cot rigged up with assorted springs, straps, and pads and was, in fact, inspired by modifications made to cots by Joseph Pilates to provide rehabilitation exercise to people who were still in hospital beds.

Benefiting from Yoga and Pilates

Some yoga and Pilates practitioners claim that yoga and Pilates are superior to weight training because these disciplines make you stronger without creating bulky muscles. It's true that yoga and Pilates build strength without bulk — but, in reality, so can strength training with free weights or machines. The only way to end up with barrel-sized biceps is to train for it by lifting super-heavy weights and performing a minimal number of repetitions. Genetics also plays a role in how your muscles develop. So, choosing yoga or Pilates simply because you're trying to develop strength without bulk is buying into a fitness myth. However, there are plenty of other excellent reasons to take up these alternative modes of exercise. Following is a rundown.

Engaging your whole body with yoga and Pilates

Weight training tends to emphasize individual body parts; you think about working your chest muscles or your shoulders or your hamstrings. Magazines promote "The Ultimate Ab Workout" or "Eight Moves for a Better Butt." With most weight training exercises — especially with those performed on machines — you work one or two muscle groups without involving any others.

Yoga and Pilates take a different approach and require you to engage virtually your whole body at once. For instance, when performing a thigh exercise, you don't simply straighten and bend your leg, as you would in a traditional weight training exercise for your quads. Instead, you must

- ✔ Engage your butt muscles in order to sit evenly
- ✔ Use your abs and lower back to avoid wiggling back and forth
- ✔ Work your upper body muscles to keep your back and neck in alignment

This approach is similar to the approach in core stabilization exercises discussed in Chapter 17, but yoga and Pilates are more than core conditioning.

The benefit of working so many muscle groups simultaneously is that this is the way you're likely to use them in everyday life. It may not seem that lying on your stomach and arching your chest off the floor is a position you often assume during your life. But if you think about it, the way you use your lower back in an exercise like this is pretty similar to the way your lower back muscles spring into action whenever you have to screw in a light bulb that's just within your reach or when you put something back up on a high shelf.

Yoga and Pilates place particular emphasis on your "core" muscles:

- Abdominals
- Lower back
- Spinal muscles

These muscles add important value to training with yoga or Pilates because the target areas don't get much action in a weight machine workout. When all those small, internal muscles are optimally strong, they also lend support, stability, and added strength to your weight room activities. You may find that you can up your poundage in the weight room if you include regular yoga or Pilates sessions in your repertoire.

Increasing your flexibility with yoga and Pilates

Weight training has an undeserved reputation for making your muscles tight; in reality, lifting weights can actually increase your flexibility somewhat if you go through the entire range of motion. However, strength training — even under the best of circumstances — isn't going to make a big difference in how freely your muscles and joints move. (That's why we strongly recommend stretching on a regular basis. See Chapter 8.)

Yoga and Pilates can noticeably improve your flexibility (see Figure 23-1). Shirley has trained many individuals who are able to touch their toes for the first time in their lives after doing Pilates and yoga exercises. You may never be able to fold yourself into a human half-sandwich, but if you put time and effort into these pursuits, you'll surprise yourself by how pliable your body becomes.

Improving your balance, coordination, and concentration with yoga and Pilates

Some weight training moves, such as the squat and the lunge (and other advanced moves not included in this book), do require a fair amount of balance and coordination. But for the most part, strength training simply gives you strength. Lying facedown on a hamstring machine and kicking your legs up doesn't exactly train you to float down a flight of stairs without having to look at your feet.

Figure 23-1:
The Active Cat is an excellent yoga posture for back health.

But yoga and Pilates moves tend to be more complicated. Consider a Pilates move called the teaser.

- ✔ Lie on your back with your arms overhead and your legs straight and off the ground at a 45-degree angle.

- ✔ Lift your upper body and torso off the floor and try to reach your fingers to your toes.

This move requires more balance, strength, and flexibility than you could possibly imagine. When you first try this move, you usually tip over sideways. The teaser can take several years just to start to perform this move with grace and fluidity. These disciplines require a lot of concentration and body awareness.

Can Yoga and Pilates Replace Weight Training?

Probably not. One of the best reasons to lift weights is to maintain and build bone density so you'll have enough bone in reserve to prevent osteoporosis later in life. Currently, no studies show whether yoga and Pilates strengthen bones. For the most part, because you're only using your own body weight and gravity for resistance, you don't work against as much resistance during a yoga or Pilates routine as you do during a challenging weight workout. But this presumes a higher level of fitness. If you're new to exercise, body weight alone may be very challenging. Shirley writes a monthly Mind-Body Exercise News column for IDEA Fitness Journal, is a certified yoga and Pilates instructor, and is the IDEA Mind-Body Spokesperson. She reviews studies regularly. Evidence from numerous yoga studies shows that yoga builds muscle and Pilates studies show that Pilates exercises effectively condition core muscles.

While yoga and Pilates can build muscle, unless you add extra weight, yoga and Pilates exercises can't provide as much resistance as a solid weight training program. It's important to build muscle for the same reason it's crucial to build bone: to bank it for the future when, inevitably, you'll have less of it.

For these reasons, yoga and Pilates are complimentary to — not replacements for — weight training.

Fitting Yoga and Pilates into Your Fitness Program

First, accept that you can't do everything in life! You can't be a full-time investment banker *and* a professional TV critic *and* a world-class pole-vaulter. There just isn't enough time in the day. By the same token, unless you're a fitness professional, you can't devote yourself to weight training, yoga, and Pilates — especially when you're also (we hope) doing cardiovascular exercise. With that said, incorporate either yoga or Pilates in your workout program. Which one? Try out both and see which one you like best.

Deciding between yoga and Pilates may take a while because so many different styles of yoga and different Pilates contraptions exist and because various instructors may conduct the same class differently. From our experience, Pilates mat classes tend to be similar nationwide, but the quality of instruction may vary widely. Yoga classes vary more because there are different styles of hatha yoga. During this tryout period, here are some suggestions:

> ✔ Drop to two weight-training sessions a week and take a third day to try an alternative exercise.
>
> ✔ Take a two-week break from weight training (don't worry; your muscles won't disintegrate) and try a number of different yoga and Pilates classes and/or instructors.

After your tryout period, decide on a weight-training alternative: private Pilates lessons, a power yoga class at your gym, or a Sivananda yoga (defined below) class at a studio. This isn't a lifetime commitment, of course. But it's a good idea to choose one route and stick with it for at least a couple months. This gives you enough time to see whether you enjoy this type of workout and are getting benefits.

As for your weekly schedule: Lift weights twice a week and integrate yoga or Pilates twice a week. Doing any of these activities just once a week typically isn't enough for a beginner to see results and get the hang of proper technique. Studies, however, show that participants benefit from yoga training as little as one hour once a week. So try to fit it in twice a week, but if one is all that you can do, it's better than nothing.

Diving into Yoga

Yoga classes have become amazingly popular as people search for ways to complement the pounding and pumping they do in the gym. But this doesn't mean that yoga is easy. Yoga can be extremely demanding, both in terms of flexibility and strength. Even if you can bench-press a heavy load in the gym, you may find yourself lacking the strength to hold a yoga pose for a minute (see Figure 23-2). A good rule to follow in yoga, Pilates, and in weight training: Don't try to keep up with anyone else. Go at your own pace.

Different styles of yoga

You can choose from many different types or styles of yoga. If you try out yoga at a health club or fitness facility, the best way to select a class is by choosing one that is at your appropriate level such as beginner, gentle or restorative, intermediate or advanced. Even if you are an experienced athlete, if you have never done yoga before, you should start in a class for beginners.

> ✔ **Sivananda yoga:** Allows for a broad range of abilities from beginner to more advanced. The moves are fairly straightforward; for instance, you may practice something as simple as sitting up straight or standing with good posture. Sivananda may be a good place for beginners to start.

Figure 23-2:
The Warrior
is a classic
yoga
posture.

- ✔ **Ashtanga:** A style of hatha yoga known in America. Also called power yoga. Ashtanga is more physically demanding in terms of flexibility, strength, and stamina. You move from one posture to another without a break, and you jump from one position to another. For beginners, this may be more discouraging than invigorating.

- ✔ **Kundalini:** Kundalini yoga is a style of hatha yoga that focuses on awakening and directing the subtle energy that is stored at the base of spine. You practice breathing exercises such as "breath of fire" and single nostril breathing, in addition meditation. This is an intense style of practice that would not be appropriate for beginners.

- ✔ **Ananda:** Ananda yoga emphasizes a traditional approach to hatha yoga, keeping in mind that the purpose of physical postures is to prepare the body and mind for the rigors of meditation. Ananda yoga is features the use of affirmations with each posture. The style is more flowing, soft, and gentle and is appropriate for beginners. It can be made more difficult for more experienced practitioners.

Most gyms and workout studios don't advertise the style of yoga practiced, and the gym staff probably won't know much about what's being taught. Your best bet is to ask the instructor what her style and teaching philosophy is. Look for a class with the word *beginner* or *novice* in the title. If you accidentally wander into a more advanced class, you may wind up feeling like one of those tangled necklaces that mysteriously appears in your jewelry box.

For more of an in-depth look at yoga, check out *Yoga For Dummies* (Wiley).

Finding a qualified yoga instructor

Instructors can't obtain a national yoga certification, so we can't list certain credentials to look for in a teacher. The Yoga Alliance recommends that qualified instructors have a minimum of 200 to 500 hours of training. Instructors who've met this standard can register with the Yoga Alliance. Because registration is voluntary, instructors who aren't registered may be highly qualified. Here are some tips for choosing a yoga instructor:

- ✔ Rely on your own judgment.

- ✔ Ask for recommendations from your friends.

- ✔ Ask the instructor what type of teacher's training she's had and how many years of experience she has.

- ✔ Look for yoga instructors who wander around the room correcting class members' techniques and offering modifications for less flexible people.

Getting the Lowdown on Pilates

Like yoga, Pilates emphasizes correct form rather than brute strength. Many of the moves look easy but are deceptively tough (see Figure 23-3). Most Pilates moves emphasize the principle of opposition: You strengthen one muscle, while you stretch the one on the opposite side of the joint. For instance, the mat class move known as *the hundred*, involves pumping your arms up and down as you lie on your back with your legs lifted off the floor straight out in front of you. The purpose of the hundred is to strengthen your abs and front of thighs as you stretch out your lower back, back of thighs, and arms.

We also love that, like weight training and yoga, Pilates is progressive. Although you can't add an extra 5-pound weight plate every time an exercise becomes easy, whenever you master a move, another slightly different, slightly harder version of the move is there to take its place. It can take months to master the basics and years to become an expert.

Figure 23-3:
The Downward Facing Leg Pull is part of a Pilates mat class.

Pilates classes and private instructors aren't tough to find in most cities. Similar to yoga, there's no national certification. The Pilates Method Alliance has created a certification examination offered first in 2005, but many instructors may be highly qualified and experienced who haven't taken this particular examination. In order to find a good Pilates instructor,

✔ Get recommendations from people you trust.

✔ Ask the instructor a lot of questions about her training, certification, and experience.

Be aware: Pilates is expensive. Private lessons run from $50 to $200 a session. More and more studios and health clubs offer small group classes on the equipment for lower prices. Mat classes are a relative bargain at $12 to $25 per session, but that's still more than many monthly gym memberships. Some gyms offer Pilates classes to members at no additional charge and offer private instruction at a discount. Shop around. If Pilates interests you, read *Pilates For Dummies* (Wiley) for a detailed account of the exercises and benefits for your body.

Part V
The Part of Tens

The 5th Wave   By Rich Tennant

"Okay, I know I need to start working out. Now, can I please have my soap-on-a-rope back?"

In this part . . .

We perpetuate the notion that all of the important information in the universe fits neatly in groups of ten. (Although we never really got the hang of the metric system, we do like the concept of tens.) We describe ten great (G-rated) exercises that you can do with a $3 piece of latex rubber and show you ten ways to have a ball. Then, we close with ten thoughts on supplements, diets, and healthy eating.

Chapter 24

Ten (Okay, Eleven) G-Rated Things You Can Do with Latex Rubber

In This Chapter

▶ Traveling with your exercise bands
▶ Using rubber safely
▶ Sharing band exercises

*W*hen it comes to firming up your muscles, a strip of latex rubber or tubing is a lot more useful than you may expect. Bands are flat strips of rubber. Tubing is round and hollow and comes to exercise by way of the operating room, where it was originally used as surgical tubing. Bands and tubing can't provide as much resistance as free weights or machines, but you can develop a surprising amount of strength and muscle tone. In this chapter, we present ten or so band exercises and offer tips for using bands safely. The photos accompanying the exercises show bands, but tubing can just as easily be used instead of the bands to supply the required resistance.

Before You Start, Get a Big Rubber Band!

Bands are particularly helpful if you want to keep up your strength work when you travel. You can't very well lug around a complete set of chrome dumbbells in your suitcase. (And we hate to imagine how an airport metal detector would react.)

Bring along your training tools: Band, tube, and stretch strap. Even if you're booked into a hotel that has a gym, you'll be happy to have carry-on "weights" and something to help you stretch. Shirley trains executives who are always on the road. Even in top luxury hotels, fitness centers aren't always well equipped. Each of her training clients travels with a band, tube, and stretch strap in their suitcase. This way, they can easily keep up their programs and stay in shape, no matter what time zone or situation.

Make sure that you use a band designed for exercising. Exercise bands cost next to nothing. You can purchase a set of three bands for less than $10 or one exercise tube for approximately $15, depending on the level of resistance (heavier resistance bands or tubes are more expensive), from manufacturers such as SPRI® or Thera-Band®, or from catalogs such as *Fitness Wholesale*®, (call 800-537-5512) or go online to www.fwonline.com, and *The Complete Guide to Exercise Videos,* available from Collage Video Specialties (call 800-433-6769). Purchase latex-free bands or tubing if you have allergies.

Buy tubing with cords or plastic or padded handles attached if you want to splurge. The handles make holding an end in one or both hands much easier. Tubing with handles may come in handy in such exercises as the band biceps curl, described later in this chapter. The handles aren't practical for exercises (such as the band butt blaster) that require tying your band in a circle; however, manufacturers do make figure-eight style and circular tubing that work well for these exercises. Because bands are inexpensive, we recommend investing in several. In general, the shorter and/or the thicker the band, the harder it is to pull and the more resistance it provides. Bands come in several different shapes:

- ✓ Circular
- ✓ Figure eight
- ✓ Flat and wide
- ✓ Tubes (resembling surgical tubes)

Wear weight-training gloves when you use exercise bands to increase comfort for your hands.

Preparing for Your Band Workout

Experiment with different shapes, sizes, and thicknesses to determine which band you like best for each exercise. Shirley recommends buying bands at least four to five feet in length to increase your exercise options. You can always choke up on the band to make the resistance harder. Have all your bands within reach as you begin your workout so you don't waste time hunting under the couch for the right one. It's a good idea to keep all of your exercise equipment in one place, such as a basket in the corner of the room.

You're almost ready for your band workout. First, here are some tips for working out with bands:

- ✔ Make sure that the band is securely in place before each set.

  Liz was demonstrating the band row exercise to a class when the band slipped off her feet and popped in her face. Ouch! Without missing a beat, she informed the class that this was how *not* to use a band and went on to warn them about the dangers of misusing a band. She would've gotten away with it, too, if the band hadn't slipped off and popped her in the face again 20 minutes later while she was demonstrating another exercise.

- ✔ If an exercise calls for you to hold the end in each hand (and your band doesn't have handles), loop the ends *loosely* around the palms of your hands. Leave a little slack so as you pull on the band the rubber doesn't tighten up around your hand and cut off the circulation to your fingers.

- ✔ If an exercise calls for you to stand on the band with your feet together, place both feet on the center of the band and then step one foot out to the side so that you have about six inches of band between your feet. This stance prevents the band from sliding out from under you.

Bands are meant to be stretched and used for exercises. That doesn't mean that they last forever. Occasionally, your bands need replacing. Follow these suggestions for maintaining bands and knowing when to chuck the old ones and buy new:

- ✔ Frequently check for holes and tears by holding your band up to a light. If you find even the slightest tear, replace the band immediately, because it can break at any moment and may snap back at you.

- ✔ Long-term care: If you use the flat bands frequently and on sweaty skin, periodically rinse them in clean water, towel or drip dry, and store in a zip-lock bag with a little baby powder. Just shake off the powder before your next use.

Integrate your favorite band exercises into your regular weight training routine. If you plan to use a band when you travel, practice these exercises beforehand so that you don't waste time trying to figure out what to do. As with all other resistance exercises, do 8 to 15 repetitions per set and do at least one set per muscle group. (We tell you which muscle group each band exercise strengthens.) When you can perform 15 repetitions easily, make the exercise tougher by using a shorter or thicker band.

Band Squat

The band squat adds resistance to the squat in lieu of free weights. This exercise strengthens your butt, quadriceps, and hamstrings. Use caution if you're prone to lower back, hip, or knee pain.

Getting set: Hold the end of a band in each hand and stand on top of the center of the band so that your feet are hip-width apart and your hands are at your sides. Stand tall with your abdominals pulled in and shoulders square. See photo A in Figure 24-1.

The exercise: Sit back and down, as if you're sitting on a chair. Bend your knees and lower yourself as far as you can without leaning your upper body more than a few inches forward. Never go lower than the point at which your thighs are parallel to the floor, and don't allow your knees to move out in front of your toes. After you feel your upper body fold forward over your thighs, stand back up, pushing through your heels and taking care not to lock your knees. Throughout the exercise, keep your shoulders relaxed, head up, and your eyes focused directly in front of you. See photo B in Figure 24-1.

Figure 24-1: Never go lower than the point at which your thighs are parallel to the floor.

Band Butt Blaster

The band butt blaster does a better job of working your butt than many of the butt machines you find in gyms. Use caution if you have lower back problems.

Getting set: Tie a foot-long band in a circle and place it around both feet at the instep. Next, kneel on your elbows and knees. Flex your left foot. Pull your abdominals in. See photo A of Figure 24-2.

The exercise: Keeping your knee bent, lift your right leg and raise your knee to hip height. Slowly lower your leg back down, taking care not to let the band go slack. Your knee should almost, but not quite, touch the floor between repetitions. Do the same number of repetitions with each leg. See photo B of Figure 24-2.

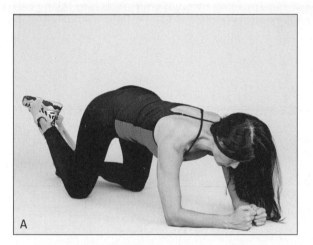

Figure 24-2:
Your knee should almost, but not quite, touch the floor between repetitions.

Band Outer Thigh Lift

The band outer thigh lift is a challenging exercise that specifically targets your outer thigh muscles.

POSTURE PATROL

Make sure that you keep your abdominals pulled in to protect your lower back.

Getting set: Tie an exercise band (between one- and two-feet long) in a circle. Lie on the floor on your left side with your legs a few inches in front of you, knees slightly bent, and head resting on your outstretched arm. Place the band around your thighs, just above your knees. Bend your right arm and place your palm on the floor in front of your chest for support. Align your right hip directly over your left hip and pull your abdominals in so your back isn't arched. See photo A of Figure 24-3.

The exercise: Keeping your knee slightly bent, raise your right leg until your foot reaches shoulder height. Hold the position for a moment, and then slowly lower your leg back down, keeping tension on the band the entire time. Switch sides, and do the same number of repetitions with your left leg. See photo B of Figure 24-3.

Figure 24-3:
Pull your abdominals in so that your back isn't arched.

Band Calf Press

The band calf press targets your calf muscles. As a bonus, it also strengthens your shins, upper back, and biceps, especially if you keep tension on the band as your toes move both toward you and away from you.

Getting set: Holding one end of a flat band in each hand at waist level, sit on the floor with your legs straight out in front of you and wrap the band around the ball of your right foot. Bend your right knee slightly and lift it up in the air. Sit up straight and bend your left knee if you want to. Just don't round your back. See photo A of Figure 24-4.

The exercise: Point your toe as you pull back on the band. Hold this position a moment and, while maintaining your pull on the band, flatten your foot and pull your toes back as far as you can. Complete the set and then do the exercise with your left foot. See photo B of Figure 24-4.

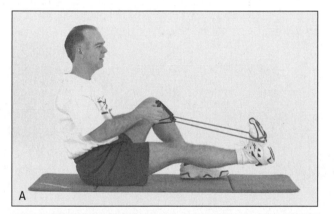

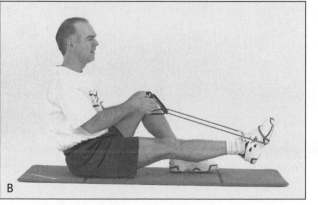

Figure 24-4: While maintaining your pull on the band, flatten your foot and pull your toes back as far as you can.

Band Lat Pulldown

The band lat pulldown mimics the lat pulldown you do on a machine. Like the machine version, the band lat pulldown works your upper back muscles with some emphasis on your shoulders and biceps.

Be especially careful to follow the form guidelines if you're prone to neck discomfort.

Getting set: Sit in a chair or stand with your feet hip-width apart and hold an end of the exercise band in each hand. Raise your left arm over your head with your left palm facing in and your right palm facing forward just above shoulder level. Your elbows should be slightly bent. Stand tall with your abdominals pulled in and your knees relaxed. See photo A of Figure 24-5.

The exercise: Keep your left arm still. Bend your right elbow down and out to the side, as if you're shooting an arrow straight up into the air. Keeping your wrist straight, pull the band until your right hand is to the side of your right shoulder, the band is tight, and your right elbow points down. Slowly straighten your arm. Switch sides, alternating arms as you complete the set. See photo B of Figure 24-5.

Figure 24-5: With your left arm still, bend your right elbow down and out to the side, as if you're shooting an arrow straight up into the air.

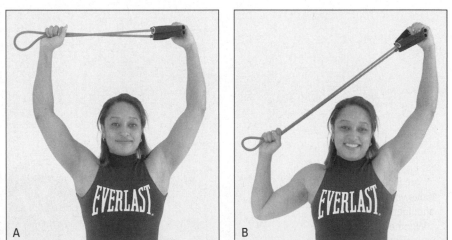

Band Push-up

The band push-up makes the push-up more challenging because in addition to lifting your bodyweight you are pushing up against a resistance band. This exercise strengthens your chest, shoulders, triceps, and abdominals.

If you have lower back, neck, or elbow problems, you may want to skip this push-up variation.

Getting set: For this exercise, use a band that's at least three-feet long. Wrap the band around your upper back and hold an end in each hand. Lie face down on the floor with your elbows bent and your palms on the floor in front of your shoulders. Bend your knees and cross your ankles. Tilt your forehead toward the floor and pull your abdominals in so your back doesn't sag. See photo A of Figure 24-6.

The Exercise: Straighten your arms and press your body up. (Adjust the band so it's taut when your arms are straight.) Slowly bend your elbows and lower yourself down until your elbows are just above your shoulders. Your chest may touch the floor, depending on the length of your arms and the size of your chest. See photo B of Figure 24-6.

Figure 24-6: Lower yourself down until your elbows are just above your shoulders. Whether your chest touches the floor depends on your arm and length and chest size.

Band One-arm Shoulder Press

The band one-arm shoulder press strengthens your entire shoulder muscle, with additional emphasis on your triceps.

Pay special attention to your form if you have a history of lower back or neck problems.

Getting set: Stand on top of one end of the band near the handle so that your feet are hip-width apart. Hold the other handle in your right hand and place your left hand on your hip, right palm facing forward. Raise your right hand to shoulder height so that your elbow is bent, your upper arm is parallel to the floor, and your palm is facing forward. Keep your head centered between your shoulders, pull your abdominals in, and relax your knees. See photo A of Figure 24-7.

The exercise: Straighten your arm overhead and then slowly bend your arm until your elbow is slightly below shoulder height, but no lower. After you've completed a set with your right arm, do an equal number of reps with your left. See photo B of Figure 24-7.

Figure 24-7:
Bend your arms until your elbows are slightly below shoulder height but no lower.

Band External Rotation

The external rotation strengthens the rotator cuff muscles.

Getting set: Tie a band around a stable object. Hold one end of the band in your hand on the side that is opposite to the side where the band is tied with your palm facing in. Bend your elbow 90 degrees. See photo A in Figure 24-8.

The exercise: Keeping your elbow in place, move your hand a few inches away from you to increase tension in the band and then slowly move it back to the starting position. See photo B in Figure 24-8.

Band Internal Rotation

The internal rotation exercise strengthens the rotator cuff muscles and helps to prevent shoulder injuries.

Getting set: Turn around and hold the band in your other hand on the same side where the band is tied. Hold your arm as in the external rotation. Pull your arm toward you to create more tension. See photo C in Figure 24-8.

The exercise: Pull your arm toward you to create more tension. Move your arm out again. See photo D in Figure 24-8.

Figure 24-8: Keep your elbow in place during both of these exercises.

Band Double Biceps Curl

The band double biceps curl, an excellent imitation of the barbell biceps curl, targets your biceps.

Use caution if you're prone to elbow injuries.

Getting set: With an end of the band in each hand, stand on top of the center of your exercise band so your feet are hip-width apart. Straighten your arms down at your sides, palm down. Stand tall with your abdominals pulled in and your knees relaxed. See photo A of Figure 24-9.

The exercise: Bend your elbows and curl both arms up until your hands are in front of your shoulders. Don't permit your elbows to travel forward as you curl. The band should be taut at the top of the movement. Slowly straighten your arms completely. See photo B of Figure 24-9.

Figure 24-9:
Don't let your elbows travel forward as you curl.

A

B

Band Triceps Extension

As you might guess, the band triceps extension strengthens your triceps muscle. It's important to train your triceps because there are very few every-day life tasks that challenge these muscles.

Go easy on this exercise if you experience elbow discomfort.

Getting set: While holding onto one end of the band with your left hand, stand with your feet as wide as your hips and place your left palm over the front of your right shoulder. Hold the other end of the band in your right hand with your palm facing inward. Bend your right elbow so that it's at waist level and pointing behind you. You can lean slightly forward from your hips if you find that position comfortable, but always keep your abdominals in and your knees relaxed. See photo A of Figure 24-10.

The exercise: Keeping your elbow stationary, straighten your right arm out behind you so the band gets tighter as you go, but don't allow your elbow to lock. Then bend your elbow so your hand travels back to your waist. Reposition the band to work your left triceps. See photo B of Figure 24-10.

Figure 24-10:
Keeping your elbow stationary, straighten your right arm out behind you so that the band gets tighter as you go.

Chapter 25

Ten Ways to Have a Ball (Almost Literally)

*U*sing the exercise ball to work out is one of the most fun ways to tone your body. Because of their roundness, balls are unstable. Every move has the added challenge of balance making your core stabilizers work. You can even substitute the ball for the bench in some of your weight training exercises and add dumbbells. In this chapter, you gather some tips for using balls safely and discover ten basic ball exercises.

Picking Out the Right Ball

To get an effective ball workout, you must use a quality ball that is the correct size for your body. From her work with private training clients, Shirley believes that size is the most common mistake people make. Exercisers simply think that bigger is better and cheaper is more economical. To get a workout that produces results, the size and quality of your ball does matter. More information is available in *Exercise Balls For Dummies* (Wiley), but this chapter covers the basics for you.

When you sit on your ball, your knees should be at a right angle, like the corner of a square. For people who are shorter than 4 feet 8 inches, ball size should be 45 cm. For people who are 4 feet 8 inches to 5 feet 3 inches, ball size should be 55 cm. For people who are 5 feet 3 inches to 6 feet, ball size should be 65 cm. For people who are taller than 6 feet, ball size should be 75 cm. The softer the ball, the easier it is to balance. Therefore, if you're a beginner, you may want to buy a slightly larger ball and underinflate it so it will be softer, more comfortable, and easier to balance. For a more challenging workout, fully inflate your ball so that it rolls easily and is more difficult to balance. Make sure that you use a ball designed for exercising. You can purchase a ball from manufacturers such as SPRI®, Thera-Band®, FitBALL®, and Resist-a-Ball®. These manufacturers also sell videos and DVDs with workout routines led by certified fitness professionals.

Look for the following features when you're shopping for your ball:

- **Weight-tested:** Manufacturers create balls that can hold up to 1,000 pounds. While the largest weight-tested ball may not be necessary for your needs, check a ball's specifications before you purchase it. Make sure that your exercise ball has been weight tested to hold at least 600 pounds or more.

- **Burst-resistant:** Balls are now made of tougher materials that are more puncture resistant. Because the worst ball injuries generally occur from falls to the ground if a ball bursts, get the strongest ball possible to prevent this from happenings. In addition, the more puncture resistant your ball, the longer it is likely to last in case it accidentally rolls over or into any sharp objects.

- **Slow-deflation:** A ball that deflates slowly if punctured reduces the risk of injury. Deflation rate is important because injuries can occur if a ball bursts and deflates suddenly, causing you to fall to the ground. Injury risk increases if you're holding dumbbells because of the added weight and strain on your arms. If you're holding onto a weight, you don't have the use of your hands to catch yourself. A slow-deflation ball is worth the extra $5 to $10 dollars more it may cost.

Using Exercise Balls Safely

Balls require little maintenance aside from occasional cleaning and inflation. Consider the following list when maintaining and using your exercise ball:

- **Storage:** Your biggest challenge is deciding how to store your ball. If you don't have space, deflate and inflate your exercise ball in between uses. If you need to do this, buy an electric pump. The pump saves you time and relieves stress.

  Some balls have *udders* to prevent them from rolling around, like udders on a cow. This can be handy for storing it in a corner of your family room as the udders can be used to prop up the ball. Other balls come with plastic circular stands — preventing your ball from rolling. Make sure that you don't store any exercise balls near a heat source, as it can cause the ball to expand or soften and weaken the ball's surface.

- **Cleaning:** Clean your ball with a soft cloth or sponge and clean hot water or mild soapy water if needed. Chemical cleaners may break down and damage the ball's surface. Always use your ball on a clean dry floor.

This precaution goes a long way toward keeping your ball clean and avoiding punctures.

- ✔ **Pumps:** Many balls sold today come with manual pumps — usually hand or foot pumps. If you're maintaining one ball and only inflating it occasionally, a manual pump should work well for you. However, if you're frequently going to inflate and deflate your ball, purchase an electric pump.

- ✔ **Practice space:** Make sure that your practice space is large enough to work with a ball. The exercise area should be longer and wider than your height. Make sure that furniture with sharp edges has been cleared from the space. Remember that your balance is challenged when you work with the ball, so you may not control your movements perfectly. Keep your workout space free and clear.

Use your ball exercises as part of your weekly strength training routine or rotate ball exercises in and out of your regular workouts. The variety challenges your muscles in different ways and also keeps your workouts fresh and fun. As with all other resistance exercises, perform between 8 and 15 repetitions per set and at least one set per muscle group, unless indicated otherwise in the specific exercise. (We tell you which muscle group each ball exercise strengthens.) When you can perform 15 repetitions easily, make the exercise tougher by decreasing the base of support (by picking up one foot or by bringing legs closer together) or by adding weight.

Ball Crunch

The ball crunch strengthens the abs by requiring you to keep your balance and reducing movement except for the crunch. If you're stronger, take advantage of the greater range of motion possible by being on a rounded surface instead of flat on the floor.

Getting set: Sit on top of the center of your ball with your feet flat on the floor and placed as wide as you need to keep your balance. The closer together that you place your legs, the more difficult the exercise. Place your hands behind your head so your thumbs are behind your ears. Don't lace your fingers together.

Hold your elbows out to the sides and round them slightly in. Tilt your chin slightly and lengthen the back of your neck. Pull your abdominals inward as you walk your feet slightly forward and lean back on to the ball so your entire back, from your tailbone to your shoulders, is resting on the ball. Your head and arms will be suspended above the ball. See photo A of Figure 25-1.

The exercise: Curl up and forward so your shoulder blades lift up off the ball. Move slowly and carefully to help maintain your balance and reduce any movement other than the crunch. Hold for a moment at the top of the movement, and then lower slowly back down. See photo B of Figure 25-1.

Figure 25-1:
Move
slowly to
maintain
balance.

Ball March

The ball march works your butt, the back of your thighs, and your core stabilizers. It's very challenging, so be patient as you increase your core strength.

Use caution if you have lower back problems.

Getting set: Sit on top of the center of your ball with your feet flat on the floor and hip-width apart. Place your hands behind your head so your thumbs are behind your ears. Don't lace your fingers together.

Hold your elbows out to the sides and round them slightly in. Tilt your chin slightly and lengthen the back of your neck. Pull your abdominals inward as you walk your feet slightly forward and lean back on to the ball so your back is resting on the ball. The farther out that you walk your feet away from the ball, the harder the exercise. Your head and arms will be suspended above the ball. Look down your torso. See photo A of Figure 25-2.

The exercise: Keeping your abs and buttocks muscles tight and your body parallel to the ground, alternately lift your right and left foot up and down as if you're marching in place. Work up to at least ten repetitions with each leg, concentrating on keeping your torso parallel to the ground. See photo B of Figure 25-2.

Figure 25-2: Concentrate on keeping your hips up.

Ball Oblique Crunch

The ball oblique crunch targets all of your abdominals, especially the obliques that wrap around your waist.

Getting set: Sit on top of the center of your ball with your feet flat on the floor and placed as wide as you need to keep your balance. The closer together that you place your legs, the more difficult the exercise. Place your hands behind your head so your thumbs are behind your ears. Don't lace your fingers together.

Hold your elbows out to the sides and round them slightly in. Tilt your chin slightly and lengthen the back of your neck. Pull your abdominals inward as you walk your feet slightly forward and lean back on to the ball so your entire back, from your tailbone to your shoulders, is resting on the ball. Your head and arms will be suspended above the ball. Refer to photo A of figures 25-1 and 25-2.

The exercise: Curl up and rotate your right shoulder toward your left hip so your right shoulder blade lifts up off the ball. Keep your hips stable on the ball. Move slowly and carefully to help maintain your balance and reduce any movement other than the crunch. Hold for a moment at the top of the movement, and then lower slowly back down. Repeat on the left side.

Ball Extension

The ball extension strengthens the muscles that support your back along your spine, your lower back, and your buttocks. This is a great conditioning exercise if you have a healthy back as it strengthens the muscle that support your spinal column and the muscles of the lower back.

If you experience any pain or have lower back problems don't do this exercise.

Getting set: Kneel behind your ball and lay your belly on it. Roll your body as you walk your feet back and straighten your legs (the ball should support your lower torso). Place your arms either at your sides, behind your head, or extended outward in a Y-position, depending on your strength and ability to stabilize your shoulders and avoid hunching. Use the arm position that enables you to keep your shoulders down and stable as you strengthen your back muscles. Lengthen the back of your neck and align your ears over your shoulders. See photo A of Figure 25-3.

The exercise: Pull your abdominals inward and tighten your buttocks as you lift your chest upward. Keep your shoulders down and neck straight. Avoid dropping your head. Hold for a second before lowering and repeating. See photo B of Figure 25-3.

Figure 25-3:
Keep your
shoulders
down and
your
abs and
buttocks
tight.

Ball Plank

The ball plank is a fantastic core exercise. It challenges your shoulder stabilizers, your abs and back, and your buttocks muscles.

Be sure to pull your pelvic floor up and your abs in as you exhale.

Getting set: Kneel behind your ball and lay your belly on it. Roll your body as you walk your feet back and straighten your legs (the ball should support your lower torso). Lengthen the back of your neck and keep your ears level with your shoulders. Refer to photo A of Figure 25-3.

The exercise: Pull your abdominals inward and tighten your buttocks as you walk your hands forward. Stop at a point that is challenging with your hands directly beneath your shoulders. You feel that your muscles are working, but you are still able to maintain correct form. The further your shoulders are away from the ball, the harder the exercise. Keep your shoulders down and neck straight. Avoid dropping your head. Work up to a 30-second hold. Alternatively, hold for a few seconds, walk your hands back in and repeat three to five times.

Ball Push-up

The ball push-up adds variety to your push-up routine. This exercise strengthens your chest, shoulders, triceps, and abdominals and tones your buttocks.

If you have lower back, neck, elbow, or wrist problems, you may want to skip this push-up variation.

Getting set: For this exercise, set up as if you're going to do a ball plank (described above). Kneel behind your ball and lay your belly on it. Roll your body as you walk your feet back and straighten your legs (the ball should support your lower torso). Lengthen the back of your neck and align your ears over your shoulders.

Pull your abdominals inward and tighten your buttocks as you walk your hands forward. Stop at a point where you can still maintain proper form but you feel that your muscles are working hard to keep your body stable, with your hands directly beneath your shoulders. The farther your shoulders are away from the ball, the harder the exercise. See photo A of Figure 25-4.

The exercise: Slowly bend your elbows and lower yourself down. Hold for a few seconds. Straighten your elbows as you push yourself up to repeat. See photo B of Figure 25-4.

Figure 25-4:
Pull your abdominals inward and keep your buttocks tight to support your torso.

Ball Leg Lift

The ball leg lift is a great buttocks strengthener, because you need to use your gluteal muscles to lift your legs. Keep your abdominals pulled inward to support your lower back.

Getting set: Kneel behind your ball and lay your belly on it. Roll your body as you walk your feet back and straighten your legs (the ball should support your lower torso). Lengthen the back of your neck and align your ears over your shoulders. Place your hands directly under your shoulders. Keep your shoulders down and tighten your buttocks. See photo A of Figure 25-5.

The exercise: Alternately, raise and lower your right and left leg up to hip height and down to the ground. See photo B of Figure 25-5. Hold for a few seconds before you lower slowly back down. As you get stronger, progress to lifting both legs at the same time. See photo C of Figure 25-5.

Figure 25-5:
Keep your
shoulders
down and
tighten your
buttocks.

Ball Bridge

The ball bridge strengthens the muscles of the buttocks and the back of the thighs while it works your core stabilizers. This is one of Shirley's favorite ball exercises on the planet.

Getting set: Lie face up on the floor and place your feet on top of the ball. Rest your arms at your sides, palms facing up. This position helps to open up your chest and shoulders and prevents you from using your arms to push yourself up. Relax your shoulders and lengthen the back of your neck. See photo A in Figure 25-6.

The exercise: Tighten your buttocks and your hamstrings and push yourself up through your heels. Squeeze your buttocks and back of thighs as you hold for a few seconds and then lower slowly back down. Keep pulling your abdominals inward to support your lower back. See photo B of Figure 25-6.

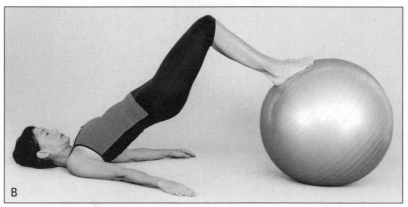

Figure 25-6: Squeeze the muscles of your buttocks and back of thighs at the top of the movement.

Ball Side-Lying Outer Thigh Lift

The ball side-lying outer thigh lift strengthens your outer thighs and challenges your core stabilizers, because you need to hold your body still as you lift your leg.

Keep your abdominals pulled inward to support your lower back.

Getting set: Kneel next to your ball and lay your hip and waist on it. Rest the ball directly under your arm and bend your top elbow as if you're hugging the ball. Place your top arm either on the ball or behind your head. Keep your inside knee bent with your foot flat for support. Straighten your top leg. See photo A of Figure 25-7.

Pull your abdominals inward and tighten your buttocks to support your lower back. Keep your torso perpendicular to the ground.

The exercise: Raise your top leg until your feet is at hip height. Hold for a few seconds and then lower slowly back down. After you've completed a set on one side, switch and do an equal number of reps for your other leg. See photo B of Figure 25-7.

Figure 25-7: Lift your foot up to hip height.

Ball Side-Lying Double Leg Lift

The ball side-lying double leg lift improves your inner and outer thighs and your buttocks, and challenges your core stabilizers, because you need to stabilize your upper body and hips as you lift the ball.

If you have lower back problems, don't do this exercise if you experience any pain or discomfort.

Getting set: Lie on your side — torso perpendicular to the ground — and place the ball in between your ankles. Relax your upper body with one arm under your head. Place your top arm in front of your torso with your palm down like a kickstand. See photo A of Figure 25-8.

Pull your abdominals inward and tighten your buttocks to support your lower back. Make sure that your lower ribs don't flare out.

The exercise: Tighten your inner thigh muscles and squeeze the ball. Lift the ball a few inches off the ground and hold for a few seconds before lowering slowly to the ground. After you've completed a set on one side, switch and do an equal number of reps for your other leg. See photo B of Figure 25-8.

Figure 25-8:
Keep your abdominals pulled inward to avoid arching your back.

Chapter 26

Ten Thoughts on Supplements, Diets, and Healthy Eating

*I*n this chapter, you get the lowdown on some of today's popular nutritional supplements and diets, along with some sensible tips for healthy eating. No matter what substances you ingest or diets you follow, remember this: If you use your body as a research lab, you run the risk of the experiment going awry. You may end up with unwanted hair, liver damage, or even, in extreme cases, a new address six feet underground. Some of the side effects and after-effects may not be immediate. Ten years from now, the supplements you've sworn by may turn out to be the pills about which scientists say, "We hope you never took *that*."

Understanding Why Supplement and Diet Ads Are Confusing

We read a newspaper article in which teenagers were asked why they smoke. "If cigarettes were really so bad for you," one kid said, "they wouldn't be legal." Many dieters and weight lifters resort to the same rationalization when they buy dietary supplements of suspicious value. If these pills were harmful, these people figure, the government would've pulled them off the market.

Not necessarily. The U.S. Food and Drug Administration (FDA) has limited power to regulate dietary supplements. Manufacturers don't have to prove that a supplement is safe; the responsibility is on the FDA to prove that a product is dangerous before it's yanked from the shelves. As a result, bogus or potentially dangerous supplements sell for years before the FDA gathers enough complaints to launch an investigation. Furthermore, the Federal Trade Commission (FTC), which is in charge of enforcing truth-in-advertising laws, can't sue every manufacturer of bogus supplements. So when you see a pill bottle that says, "Reduces body fat and increases lean muscle!" don't assume that the claim is true. Simply step back and think about it: If this supplement could "cure" obesity, which is one of America's leading health issues, don't you think the medical community would be all over it? If it sounds too good to be true, it usually is.

So if you can't trust advertising and you can't be sure that the government has identified all unsafe or useless dietary supplements, where should you get your nutritional advice? Most certainly don't gather advice from the most muscular lifter in the weight room or from the leanest member of your body sculpting class. Instead, seek advice from reputable sources, such as registered dietitians and the FDA. (Even though the agency can't yank every bogus supplement, the FDA does try to warn the public when products are being investigated.) The following sections look at some of the popular supplements promoted in health clubs.

Overdoing Supplements

A few years back, Doris Shafran, Liz's mother-in-law, became very ill. She felt continually nauseous, her skin flushed, and she lost weight rapidly. When Doris began having fainting spells, she was admitted to the hospital. Test after test showed nothing out of the ordinary; her doctors were baffled. Finally, a sharp resident discovered that for more than 11 years, Doris had been taking niacin — an over-the-counter vitamin supplement shown to lower blood cholesterol levels. But the niacin had built up to such toxic levels in Doris's body that it caused all the aforementioned symptoms, plus some serious impairment of her liver. She stopped taking the niacin supplement and recovered completely.

Mind you, niacin has a scientifically proven track record of reducing blood cholesterol levels, and doctors often recommend it to their patients. If you can get in this much trouble with a supplement that's well researched and may have the approval of your physician, imagine the potential dangers of taking a substance that scientists know virtually nothing about. Why are many people popping the latest "miracle supplement" like breath mints or blindly following the newest diet in an effort to achieve the following?

- ✔ (a) Burn body fat
- ✔ (b) Gain muscle
- ✔ (c) Increase energy
- ✔ (d) Get stronger
- ✔ (e) All the above

If you find that your answer to the question lies above, continue reading this chapter to educate yourself on the latest crazes and find out what may be best for you. Remember — always consult a dietician or your physician for health advice.

Uncovering the Fat-burner Chitin

Recent easy weight-loss-solution salespeople have found not one but two weight-loss supplements they claim to believe in. Their "Exercise in a Bottle" infomercial also features a pitch for Fat Trapper, a pill that contains chitin.

- ✔ **What it is:** Chitin is a substance found in the exoskeletons of shrimp, crab, and other shellfish.

- ✔ **The claims:** The Fat Trapper "literally traps fat before it gets into your system." In other words, chitin attaches to fat in the stomach and prevents its absorption in the digestive tract. To demonstrate the effectiveness of this pill, bacon grease is poured into a glass of water and then the Fat Trapper is added. When globs of fat form and fall to the bottom, Fat Trapper declares its ability to absorb up to 120 grams of fat.

  Several Web sites promoting chitin, and a similar compound called chitosan, make incredible weight-loss claims. One site boasts about a Finnish study in which subjects lost 8 percent of their body weight in 4 weeks.

- ✔ **The reality:** The bacon grease demonstration is impressive — until you remember that oil and water separate naturally anyway! In reality, the few studies that have been done on chitin and related substances show that they absorb only three to five fat grams — the equivalent to a pat of butter. (And these studies were performed on rats.) The only research we found conducted on human beings and published in a legitimate scientific journal stated that, after four weeks, subjects who took chitosan supplements didn't lose any more weight than subjects who took a phony pill. Furthermore, the research speculates that long-term use of the supplements may lead to nutritional deficiencies because chitin may prevent the body from absorbing fat-soluble substances such as vitamin D, vitamin E, and essential fatty acids.

Understanding a Muscle-builder: Creatine

When creatine first became popular, this strength-building supplement was primarily marketed in powder and pill form. Now creatine has become so popular that it's found in energy bars and even smoothies.

> ✔ **What it is:** Creatine is a nitrogen-containing substance produced naturally in your body and found in meat, poultry, and fish. Creatine is a building block for several amino acids, which are themselves the building blocks for protein.
>
> ✔ **The claims:** Creatine gives you more energy during high-intensity exercises so you can work out longer and harder, therefore building more strength and muscle mass. (One of the more cleverly titled brands is called Kick Some Mass.)
>
> ✔ **The reality:** This stuff actually seems to have some value — under certain circumstances. Several, but not all, creatine studies suggest that the substance helps weight lifters and sprinters build muscle and gain strength. Creatine may also help tennis players, football players, and others who play sports that require short bursts of energy (generally less than 30 seconds).

But creatine works only if you stick to a serious weight lifting program. If you take creatine every day but don't work out, you'll become as muscular as if you were drinking lemonade every day. Also, if you don't have the genetic predisposition toward building huge muscles, you can suck down a truckload of creatine and lift weights six hours per day, and you still won't be Mr. Olympia. Also, individual responses to creatine supplementation vary greatly.

Unraveling the High-protein Craze

Several best-selling diet books and some inaccurate reporting in major newspapers strengthen the popularity of high-protein diets. Advocates claim that high-carbohydrate diets — the type of diet promoted by the majority of the medical community — have made us fatter as a nation now than at any other point in history. ("Pasta Makes You Fat" blared a *New York Times* headline that was later retracted.)

High-protein diet gurus tell us that eating high-carbohydrate foods (like pasta, bagels, fruit) makes us fat and causes *insulin resistance* — a condition that blocks the delivery of glucose and keeps insulin floating around in the blood. This is simply not true. Here's the real deal on how your body uses carbohydrates:

1. You eat carbohydrates.

2. Your body breaks the carbs down into *glucose*, a form of sugar that fuels energy.

3. Glucose floods the bloodstream and triggers your pancreas to release the hormone insulin.

4. Insulin is like a key that opens the door of the muscle cell walls to draw glucose from the blood into the muscle tissue.

5. Muscles use the glucose as energy.

6. Whatever the muscles don't use (for example if you're not active), is stored for future use as fat.

However, according to high-protein proponents, a diet high in carbohydrates triggers insulin resistance. This excess insulin, diet books say, leads to weight gain in two ways:

✔ By causing people to crave more carbohydrates (and therefore overeating)

✔ By triggering the body to store excess calories as fat

Now, this theory of "insulin resistance" has a few problems. For one thing, research hasn't proven that high-carbohydrate diets cause people to overeat. True, eating sugary foods can cause people to crave more sugary foods, and some people are more prone to cravings than others. However, you can't lump all carbohydrates into the same category, as many diet books do. Potatoes, whole-wheat breads, and apples, which are considered complex carbohydrates, don't trigger the same type of sugar rush as doughnuts, which are made up of simple carbohydrates. Some research suggests that corn syrup, which is present in many processed or "boxed" foods is metabolized differently in the body than plain sugar and may lead to insulin problems. This research is not definitive, but if you are concerned, you can avoid products sweetened with corn syrup. If you're sensitive to simple carbohydrates, cut back on sugary and highly processed foods, and you may respond well to a diet that's relatively high in protein, but spaghetti isn't off limits (try whole-grain pasta). Aim for a mix of complex carbohydrates, proteins, and fats at each meal. The ideal ratio of protein to the other nutrients differs for each person.

Blaming insulin for weight problems

Also realize that *any* excess calories you eat — whether from carbohydrates, protein, or fat — stores as fat; it's not necessarily insulin's fault. You can't cast insulin as the evil creator of body fat. Insulin resistance has serious health consequences, such as diabetes and high blood pressure, but it hasn't been proven to *cause* weight gain (and insulin resistance isn't as common as some high-protein diet gurus would have you believe). On the contrary, many experts believe that being overweight is what appears to cause insulin resistance. When insulin-resistant people lose weight and exercise, the condition often disappears.

Reducing saturated fat

One major problem with many of the so-called high-protein diets is that many are too high in fat, particularly saturated fat (the artery-clogging kind), and low in fiber. Dr. Atkins, father of the whole protein diet craze, even recommended bacon, sausage, and pastrami as "risk reducing" foods! This diet is so wacky that Dr. Atkins recommended limiting your intake of most types of fruits and vegetables. (Atkins was once booed at a government-sponsored diet debate when he said he wouldn't spend any money to research his questionable theories.)

Depriving your body of calories

So why do some people lose weight (at least temporarily) on these diets? Lack of calories. And, another process called ketosis. When the body is overloaded with proteins, the kidneys work overtime to flush out the system and you excrete a lot of water. This is not true weight loss because it is not fat. It is simply rapid dehydration and the water needs to be replaced to maintain good health. Ketosis is also why people on high-protein diets tend to have bad breath. None of the diet craze books tell you that the eating plans are also low in calories — some plans call for less than 1,000 calories per day. If you eat fewer calories than you burn, you're going to lose weight no matter what type of food the calories come from.

You are extremely likely to gain the weight back. Very low-calorie diets slow your metabolism and make you feel deprived. And in fact, upping your protein intake, particularly if you've been eating low protein for a while, may initially help you quickly satisfy your hunger.

We have nothing against protein. In fact, protein helps make a meal more satisfying, so you're not tempted to overeat. And some people do need more protein and less carbohydrate than others. But don't rely on one of these high-protein diets as a magic bullet for weight loss.

Building Muscle with Protein

Ironically, while many people turn to protein to lose weight, another segment of the population turns to protein for the opposite reason: to gain weight. Bodybuilders, football players, and skinny guys who want to go up a few shirt sizes guzzle high-protein shakes, pop protein pills, and mix up amino acid concoctions. "Get Big Now!" boasts an ad for a chocolate-flavored powder that contains 42 grams of protein per serving.

Do these guys have the right idea? Not really. Serious athletes do need slightly more protein than the average person. They need more carbohydrates and fat, too. However, most Americans eat twice the amount of protein they need, so the chances of a weight lifter not getting enough protein are slim. In fact, if you eat too many calories, your body stores these calories as fat, even if many of the calories came from "Ripped Fuel Thermogenic Protein Drink."

Although mountains of research debunk the idea that high-protein diets build muscle, this theory is alive and well in most gyms.

Finding Healthy Energy Bars

Just a few years ago, the only people who gobbled down energy bars were hardcore athletes who bought them in gyms or health food stores. Now PowerBars are as mainstream as Hershey bars. You can find them — along with Clif Bars, Steel Bars, Met-RX bars and countless others — at the convenience store checkout counter. At one recent trade show, we counted 27 different energy bar companies marketing at least 8 varieties each! You may wonder: Are energy bars just high-priced candy bars, or do they have any nutritional value? And do they all taste like moldy chalk dust? You may also wonder which nutrient mix is best.

Here's the lowdown on energy bars.

> ✔ **Energy bars aren't meal replacements.** Energy bars can be a nutritional source of supplemental energy, but they're certainly no substitute for a well-balanced meal.
>
> One trade show marketer told Liz that his company's bar was the perfect food, better than anything nature has ever come up with. He made this claim despite the fact that the bar tasted like wet shoe leather and contained zero grams of fiber.

✔ **The main benefit of energy bars is convenience.** Keep a bar in your gym bag or the glove compartment of your car, and it won't turn into some biological experiment.

Be sure to drink 12 to 16 ounces of water whenever you eat a bar. Otherwise, the bar may sit like a rock in your stomach and cause nausea. The carbohydrate has to be diluted so it digests and absorbs easier into the bloodstream.

✔ **Use bars to fuel up before a workout or to refuel right afterward.** Some bars contain almost entirely carbohydrates. Others are high in protein and low in carbs. Still other bars have an equal balance of carbs, protein, and fat.

- **High carb bar:** Your best bar is high in carbohydrates because carbs are used the quickest in your body. (These bars usually contain 40 to 45 grams of carbs, about 70 to 80 percent of their total calories.)

- **High protein bar:** High-protein bars are popular among weight lifters, but after a workout, your muscles need a combination of protein and carbohydrate for muscular repair and refueling to optimize recovery for the next workout.

- **Balanced bar:** Bars containing 40 percent carbohydrate, 30 percent protein, and 30 percent fat may taste better than the high-carb bars because of the added fat, but the extra fat also takes longer to digest. (And some still taste like spackle.)

Balanced bars may be most helpful for long aerobic workouts, such as a three-hour bike ride, because they keep you satisfied longer than a high-carb bar. Just know that they provide energy less efficiently than carbohydrate-dense bars.

Shirley's friend, Christopher Gardner, PhD, is director of Nutritional Studies at the Stanford Prevention Research Center at Stanford University. In his opinion, energy bars are just fancy candy bars. His advice is to eat them if you enjoy them, but don't consider that you're doing something good for your body. The best foods, in his opinion, are minimally processed, whole foods, which are chock-full of antioxidants, vitamins, minerals, and fiber that all contribute toward good health.

Eating Chocolate for a Healthy Snack

Eating chocolate after a meal may reduce the risk of heart disease.

Chocolate: Fruit or vegetable?

Cocoa comes from cacao trees. These trees produce pods and inside the pods are seeds. These seeds are called cocoa beans and are technically seeds from the fruit of the cacao tree. So, to be technically precise, we could consider chocolate to be derived from a fruit. Research shows that these cacao seeds are rich in a phytochemical (a chemical from a plant) known as flavonoids. Flavonoids are antioxidants that help to keep your blood flowing smoothly by helping to prevent the oxidation of low-density lipoproteins (LDL), "bad" cholesterol. In other words, it helps to prevent the "bad" cholesterol to form into artery-clogging plaque. The action of the flavonoids in the bloodstream occurs shortly after eating.

Not all chocolate provides this benefit. For chocolate to enhance your health, it must contain a minimum of 60 percent cocoa. This high concentration is typically found in the darker forms of cocoa. Read the label. White chocolate contains no healthy value. While it's important to remember that no *one* food is a magical cure-all, it's good to know that something as pleasurable as a bite of deep, dark chocolate after a meal actually contributes to better heart health. And, moderation is key.

Check Bissinger's Handcrafted Chocolatier to find all natural, high antioxidant chocolates made with no artificial flavors, preservatives, or trans-fats. Find Bissinger's line of "Spa Chocolate" on the Internet at www.bissingers.com or by calling 800-325-8881.

Enjoying a Variety of Whole Foods

We are what we eat in the sense that our bodies rebuild themselves with the nutrients that we ingest. The best sources of nutrients are minimally processed whole foods — whole grains, vegetables, fruits, and other plant-based foods. To illustrate the importance of plant foods in your diet, consider this:

- ✔ If you never ate meat again in your life and instead ate only a balanced vegetarian diet, you would still be healthy and stay alive.

- ✔ If you never ate a plant-based food again, you would soon die of lack of essential nutrients you need to survive.

People can't survive without eating plants. This isn't a testimonial for vegetarianism. This fact highlights the importance of consuming lots of plant-based foods and varying your diet.

Choosing Organic and Free-Range Products

Meats have a role in a healthy diet. Simply reduce the percentage of meat and enjoy it more as a side dish, rather than the main event. The best meats for your health are those produced on organic farms. Large-scale agribusiness producers follow practices that undermine the health value of meat. For example, producers give animals large amounts of hormones to accelerate animal growth so the producers can hurry the animals to slaughter. Animals eat foods containing animal by-products, the parts of the animal that can't be sold for meats, to minimize waste turning otherwise vegetarian animals into cannibals.

In contrast, organic farmers allow animals to eat natural foods. Animals roam freely and get to enjoy exercise and fresh air.

As a result, choosing to consume organic and free-range products has definite health benefits:

- ✔ Meats are lower in levels of saturated or unhealthy fats.
- ✔ Meats are higher in health-enhancing fats.
- ✔ Chickens produce eggs that have lower levels of cholesterol.

Organic farmers also use sustainable methods of farming that don't deplete, strip, and destroy the land, but instead support the land for continued healthful uses. Make sure when you read labels that a food is "certified organic" and not simply labeled as healthy or natural, as those terms do not have standardized definitions.

The recommendation to eat as many organic whole grains, fruits, vegetables and plant-based foods isn't meant to be a strict and impossible standard. No one eats a perfect diet. You need to enjoy your life and eating fast-food pizza from time to time may be a part of that pleasure. The recommendation promotes your health and well-being through nutrition and eating a well-balanced fresh, whole foods diet that is rich in plant-based foods. Rely on fast foods and other packaged and processed items as exceptions that are consumed in small quantities and don't provide the bulk of your diet. For further information on balancing your nutrition, check out *Nutrition For Dummies* (Wiley).

Index

BUSINESS, CAREERS & PERSONAL FINANCE

0-7645-5307-0

0-7645-5331-3 *†

Also available:

- ✔ Accounting For Dummies †
  0-7645-5314-3
- ✔ Business Plans Kit For Dummies †
  0-7645-5365-8
- ✔ Cover Letters For Dummies
  0-7645-5224-4
- ✔ Frugal Living For Dummies
  0-7645-5403-4
- ✔ Leadership For Dummies
  0-7645-5176-0
- ✔ Managing For Dummies
  0-7645-1771-6

- ✔ Marketing For Dummies
  0-7645-5600-2
- ✔ Personal Finance For Dummies *
  0-7645-2590-5
- ✔ Project Management For Dummies
  0-7645-5283-X
- ✔ Resumes For Dummies †
  0-7645-5471-9
- ✔ Selling For Dummies
  0-7645-5363-1
- ✔ Small Business Kit For Dummies *†
  0-7645-5093-4

HOME & BUSINESS COMPUTER BASICS

0-7645-4074-2

0-7645-3758-X

Also available:

- ✔ ACT! 6 For Dummies
  0-7645-2645-6
- ✔ iLife '04 All-in-One Desk Reference
  For Dummies
  0-7645-7347-0
- ✔ iPAQ For Dummies
  0-7645-6769-1
- ✔ Mac OS X Panther Timesaving
  Techniques For Dummies
  0-7645-5812-9
- ✔ Macs For Dummies
  0-7645-5656-8

- ✔ Microsoft Money 2004 For Dummies
  0-7645-4195-1
- ✔ Office 2003 All-in-One Desk Reference
  For Dummies
  0-7645-3883-7
- ✔ Outlook 2003 For Dummies
  0-7645-3759-8
- ✔ PCs For Dummies
  0-7645-4074-2
- ✔ TiVo For Dummies
  0-7645-6923-6
- ✔ Upgrading and Fixing PCs For Dummies
  0-7645-1665-5
- ✔ Windows XP Timesaving Techniques
  For Dummies
  0-7645-3748-2

FOOD, HOME, GARDEN, HOBBIES, MUSIC & PETS

0-7645-5295-3

0-7645-5232-5

Also available:

- ✔ Bass Guitar For Dummies
  0-7645-2487-9
- ✔ Diabetes Cookbook For Dummies
  0-7645-5230-9
- ✔ Gardening For Dummies *
  0-7645-5130-2
- ✔ Guitar For Dummies
  0-7645-5106-X
- ✔ Holiday Decorating For Dummies
  0-7645-2570-0
- ✔ Home Improvement All-in-One
  For Dummies
  0-7645-5680-0

- ✔ Knitting For Dummies
  0-7645-5395-X
- ✔ Piano For Dummies
  0-7645-5105-1
- ✔ Puppies For Dummies
  0-7645-5255-4
- ✔ Scrapbooking For Dummies
  0-7645-7208-3
- ✔ Senior Dogs For Dummies
  0-7645-5818-8
- ✔ Singing For Dummies
  0-7645-2475-5
- ✔ 30-Minute Meals For Dummies
  0-7645-2589-1

INTERNET & DIGITAL MEDIA

0-7645-1664-7

0-7645-6924-4

Also available:

- ✔ 2005 Online Shopping Directory
  For Dummies
  0-7645-7495-7
- ✔ CD & DVD Recording For Dummies
  0-7645-5956-7
- ✔ eBay For Dummies
  0-7645-5654-1
- ✔ Fighting Spam For Dummies
  0-7645-5965-6
- ✔ Genealogy Online For Dummies
  0-7645-5964-8
- ✔ Google For Dummies
  0-7645-4420-9

- ✔ Home Recording For Musicians
  For Dummies
  0-7645-1634-5
- ✔ The Internet For Dummies
  0-7645-4173-0
- ✔ iPod & iTunes For Dummies
  0-7645-7772-7
- ✔ Preventing Identity Theft For Dummies
  0-7645-7336-5
- ✔ Pro Tools All-in-One Desk Reference
  For Dummies
  0-7645-5714-9
- ✔ Roxio Easy Media Creator For Dummies
  0-7645-7131-1

* Separate Canadian edition also available
† Separate U.K. edition also available

Available wherever books are sold. For more information or to order direct: U.S. customers visit www.dummies.com or call 1-877-762-2974.
U.K. customers visit www.wileyeurope.com or call 0800 243407. Canadian customers visit www.wiley.ca or call 1-800-567-4797.

WILEY

SPORTS, FITNESS, PARENTING, RELIGION & SPIRITUALITY

0-7645-5146-9

0-7645-5418-2

Also available:
- Adoption For Dummies
  0-7645-5488-3
- Basketball For Dummies
  0-7645-5248-1
- The Bible For Dummies
  0-7645-5296-1
- Buddhism For Dummies
  0-7645-5359-3
- Catholicism For Dummies
  0-7645-5391-7
- Hockey For Dummies
  0-7645-5228-7

- Judaism For Dummies
  0-7645-5299-6
- Martial Arts For Dummies
  0-7645-5358-5
- Pilates For Dummies
  0-7645-5397-6
- Religion For Dummies
  0-7645-5264-3
- Teaching Kids to Read For Dummies
  0-7645-4043-2
- Weight Training For Dummies
  0-7645-5168-X
- Yoga For Dummies
  0-7645-5117-5

TRAVEL

0-7645-5438-7

0-7645-5453-0

Also available:
- Alaska For Dummies
  0-7645-1761-9
- Arizona For Dummies
  0-7645-6938-4
- Cancún and the Yucatán For Dummies
  0-7645-2437-2
- Cruise Vacations For Dummies
  0-7645-6941-4
- Europe For Dummies
  0-7645-5456-5
- Ireland For Dummies
  0-7645-5455-7

- Las Vegas For Dummies
  0-7645-5448-4
- London For Dummies
  0-7645-4277-X
- New York City For Dummies
  0-7645-6945-7
- Paris For Dummies
  0-7645-5494-8
- RV Vacations For Dummies
  0-7645-5443-3
- Walt Disney World & Orlando For Dummies
  0-7645-6943-0

GRAPHICS, DESIGN & WEB DEVELOPMENT

0-7645-4345-8

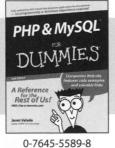

0-7645-5589-8

Also available:
- Adobe Acrobat 6 PDF For Dummies
  0-7645-3760-1
- Building a Web Site For Dummies
  0-7645-7144-3
- Dreamweaver MX 2004 For Dummies
  0-7645-4342-3
- FrontPage 2003 For Dummies
  0-7645-3882-9
- HTML 4 For Dummies
  0-7645-1995-6
- Illustrator cs For Dummies
  0-7645-4084-X

- Macromedia Flash MX 2004 For Dummies
  0-7645-4358-X
- Photoshop 7 All-in-One Desk
  Reference For Dummies
  0-7645-1667-1
- Photoshop cs Timesaving Techniques
  For Dummies
  0-7645-6782-9
- PHP 5 For Dummies
  0-7645-4166-8
- PowerPoint 2003 For Dummies
  0-7645-3908-6
- QuarkXPress 6 For Dummies
  0-7645-2593-X

NETWORKING, SECURITY, PROGRAMMING & DATABASES

0-7645-6852-3

0-7645-5784-X

Also available:
- A+ Certification For Dummies
  0-7645-4187-0
- Access 2003 All-in-One Desk
  Reference For Dummies
  0-7645-3988-4
- Beginning Programming For Dummies
  0-7645-4997-9
- C For Dummies
  0-7645-7068-4
- Firewalls For Dummies
  0-7645-4048-3
- Home Networking For Dummies
  0-7645-42796

- Network Security For Dummies
  0-7645-1679-5
- Networking For Dummies
  0-7645-1677-9
- TCP/IP For Dummies
  0-7645-1760-0
- VBA For Dummies
  0-7645-3989-2
- Wireless All In-One Desk Reference
  For Dummies
  0-7645-7496-5
- Wireless Home Networking For Dummies
  0-7645-3910-8